you

JOSEPH FRANK
University of Massachusetts

HARCOURT BRACE JOVANOVICH, INC.
New York · Chicago · San Francisco · Atlanta

© 1972 by Harcourt Brace Jovanovich, Inc.

All rights reserved.
No part of this publication may be reproduced or transmitted in any form or by any means, electronic or mechanical, including photocopy, recording, or any information storage and retrieval system, without permission in writing from the publisher.

ISBN: 0-15-598420-9
Library of Congress Catalog Card Number: 76-185805

Printed in the United States of America

ACKNOWLEDGMENTS

For their amiable and affirmative assistance I wish to thank Frank Clark, Charles Eidsvik, Florence Frank, Walker Gibson, Dorothy Lucas, Richard Noland, and Arnold Well, all of the University of Massachusetts at Amherst; J. Robert Bashore, Jr., of Bowling Green State University; and Eben Ludlow, Marilyn Cooper, Geri Davis, Yvonne Steiner, Kenzi Sugihara, and Peter Kaldheim at Harcourt Brace Jovanovich. They have all helped me to make this a serious but not a solemn book.

TEXT
THE CITY QUESTION. Reprinted from *Street Poems* by Robert Froman, by permission of The McCall Publishing Company. Copyright © 1971 by Robert Froman. JAMES AGEE. From *Let Us Now Praise Famous Men* by James Agee and Walker Evans. Reprinted by permission of the publishers, Houghton Mifflin Company. MALCOLM X. From *The Last Year of Malcolm X* by George Breitman. Reprinted by permission of Pathfinder Press. Copyright © 1965 by Merit Publishers and Betty Shabazz. THE WINDHOVER. From *The Poems of Gerard Manley Hopkins,* published by Oxford University Press. TW. Copyright, 1950, by E. E. Cummings. Reprinted from his volume *Poems 1923–1954* by permission of Harcourt Brace Jovanovich, Inc. JOHN CAGE. Copyright © 1952 by John Cage. Reprinted from *A Year from Monday,* by John Cage, by permission of Wesleyan University Press. WILLIAM BURROUGHS. From *Naked Lunch*. Reprinted by permission of Grove Press. Copyright © 1959 by William Burroughs. THE GARBAGE WARS. From *The Garbage Wars* by Donald Finkel. Copyright © 1969, 1970 by Donald Finkel. Reprinted by permission of Atheneum Publishers. Appeared originally in the *New Mexico Quarterly*. MILK TOAST. Reprinted with the permission of The Macmillan Company from *The Art of Eating* by M. F. K. Fisher. Copyright © 1954 by M. F. K. Fisher. AT LUNCH. By Russell Baker. Copyright © 1971 by The New York Times Company. Reprinted by permission. ROBERT COLES. From *Still Hungry in America* by Robert Coles and Al Clayton. Copyright © 1969 by Robert Coles. By

(continued on page 280)

preface to the student

You is intended to prod, not massage, to provide internal challenges, not external models. As the title suggests, the book attempts to get each of you to look into yourself. Socrates said that the unexamined life is not worth living; certainly it is not worth writing about.

You is based on two assumptions: that each of you potentially has something to say, and that you can say it in many ways, using many different voices. No one is incapable of learning to write, and there is no necessarily correct style or prescribed voice. The book is thus intended to give you confidence that you have something to say, and that that something can be both valid and unique. To accomplish this, every selection, every question, every picture, tries to get you to think, talk, and write about the subject you know best: yourself.

You is also concerned with perception, for how and what you perceive determines who you are. The first part of the book deals with how you see, hear, smell, taste, and touch; the second part with how you perceive yourself, as an individual, in relation to society, and in relation to the universe. You might consider this arrangement as being from the simple to the complex, but any assignment can be either simple or complex depending on how you respond to it. Perhaps after you have used the book you will be able to write with more assurance and effectiveness. Perhaps, too, you will become better acquainted with someone with whom you will have to spend the rest of your life: you.

J. F.

contents

PREFACE iii

introduction 4

    PHOTOGRAPHS from *L'Avventura* by Michelangelo Antonioni
    COLOR PLATE: *Vega Pal V* by Victor Vasarely

you and your senses 14

    EYE: SEEING 18

        COLOR PLATE: Red hydroid
        CARTOON by Charles Addams
        Nude Descending a Staircase, #2, by Marcel Duchamp
        "The City Question" by Robert Froman
        FROM *Let Us Now Praise Famous Men,* text by James Agee and
            photographs by Walker Evans

    EAR: HEARING 38

        SPEECHES by Winston Churchill, George Wallace, Malcolm X,
           Spiro Agnew, and Gloria Steinem

"The Windhover" by Gerard Manley Hopkins
"tw" by e. e. cummings
FROM *A Year from Monday* by John Cage

NOSE: SMELLING   50

COLOR PLATE: flower and garbage
ADVERTISEMENT for Fresh deodorant
FROM *Naked Lunch* by William Burroughs
"The Garbage Wars" by Donald Finkel

MOUTH: TASTING   58

"Milk Toast" by M. F. K. Fisher
"At Lunch" by Russell Baker
COLOR PLATE: food
FROM *Still Hungry in America* by Robert Coles
A Modest Proposal by Jonathan Swift
CARTOON by Charles Addams
FROM *The Golden Bough* by James Frazer

SKIN: TOUCHING   78

COLOR PLATE: ADVERTISEMENT for Madame Rochas bath products
ADVERTISEMENT for Pub cologne
"How Grandgousier Learned of Gargantua's Marvelous Mind Through the Latter's Invention of a Rump-Wiper" by François Rabelais
FROM *Brave New World* by Aldous Huxley
FROM *Expanded Cinema,* text by Gene Youngblood and photographs by Ferdinand Boesch
FROM *A Moment of Time* by Richard Hughes

YOUR SENSE OF YOU   94

YOU AND YOUR SELF   98

COLOR PLATE: *Between Heaven and Hell No. II* by Arlene Sklar-Weinstein
FROM *The Teachings of Don Juan* by Carlos Castañeda

LETTER by Sigmund Freud
Self-Portrait by Antonio Frasconi
"Fern Hill" by Dylan Thomas
FROM *The Children of Sanchez* by Oscar Lewis
FROM *1984* by George Orwell
"The Unknown Citizen" by W. H. Auden

YOU AND OTHERS 138

FROM *The Way to Rainy Mountain* by N. Scott Momaday
"Towards a Walk in the Sun" by K. William Kgositsile
Prologue to *Invisible Man* by Ralph Ellison
"My Kinsman, Major Molineux" by Nathaniel Hawthorne
"Dovisch in the Wilderness" by Herbert Wilner
"The Lottery" by Shirley Jackson
"Han's Crime" by Naoya Shiga
MEDITATION by John Donne
"Man and Animal: The City and the Hive" by Susanne K. Langer

YOU AND THE UNIVERSE 234

The Ten Commandments
CARTOON by Donald Reilly
"Dover Beach" by Matthew Arnold
"Night-Sea Journey" by John Barth
FROM *Hamlet* by William Shakespeare
"The Myth of Sisyphus" by Albert Camus
"Eclipse" by John Updike
COLOR PLATE: *Mystery and Melancholy of a Street* by Giorgio de Chirico
Revelation 21:1–4
COLOR PLATE: earth

conclusion 260

"Meeting People in Daily Life and in Prose" by Walker Gibson
"Reading the First-Person-Singular" by Walker Gibson

you

You are what you perceive and how you perceive it. You create your own world. As an experiment, look at the following four pictures from the final scene of Michelangelo Antonioni's movie *L'Avventura*. What does the woman in these pictures perceive? What does the man perceive? What does the cameraman perceive? What story do you perceive? Compare your reactions with those of someone else. Are your perceptions—and your worlds—the same?

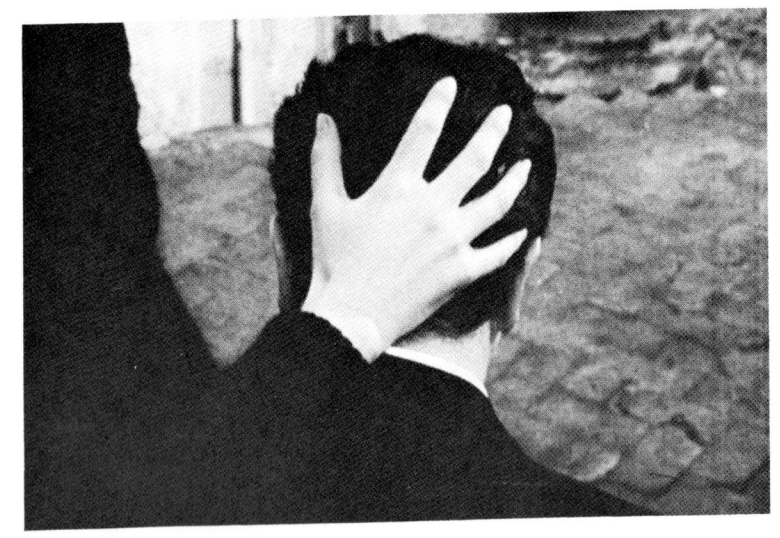

The relative and personal nature of perception is corroborated by the "uncertainty principle" which underlies modern physics. When physicists attempt to observe the smallest units of matter, the mere act of observation affects what they see. Scientists can precisely observe the location of a particle *or* its velocity; they cannot precisely do both at the same time. Nor can they precisely predict where any given particle will be, because the accuracy of the measurements of position and velocity are in inverse proportion to each other. Contemporary physics, at its most basic level, is thus a science of probabilities, not of certainties.

Try another experiment. Stand at least six feet away from a person and describe him or her. Then try it from six inches away. At six inches do you yourself become part of what you perceive? Have you noticed that the closer you get to something—a particle in a physics experiment or a person on a couch—the more you become the context that determines its behavior and meaning? In scientific terms, your involvement in the process of observing affects the neutrality of the outcome.

Psychologists use the term *perception* to refer to those processes by which we become aware of the world around us. Our senses tell us that there are things "out there" in the physical world, such as trees, garbage, people. But our "perceptual" world—the world of seen, heard, smelled, tasted, and touched objects within which we live—is not an accurate representation of the actual physical world. Our eyes, for instance, are blind to all but a very narrow band of electromagnetic radiation; our ears are deaf to sounds of extremely high or low pitch. We cannot see X-rays, radio waves, gamma rays, infrared or ultraviolet light; and we cannot detect high-pitched sounds that our dogs and cats hear with no effort. Presumably there was never enough evolutionary pressure on the human race requiring us to develop such abilities.

Not only are we blind and deaf to certain aspects of our environment but we also misperceive or misjudge other aspects, either accidentally or on purpose. When we watch a "moving" object on a TV or movie screen, we get the impression of a single object moving, but what we are actually being presented with is a series of pictures, none containing any motion and each slightly different from the previous one.

Think of a representational landscape painting. Hills seem to recede into the distance, clouds hover over an apparently faraway horizon—but what we really see are streaks of color on a flat canvas. We know we are looking at a flat surface and yet we respond to its three-dimensional quality.

What we actually perceive depends on what information reaches us through our sense organs and on how our brains use this information. But both the reception and the use of this information are affected by what we remember about previous perceptions. The brain receives current sensory information. Then, using a complex set of operations and drawing on what it "knows" about what is usually true, it tries to construct a stable percept. Thus our mental representation of an external object depends not only on that object but on our past perceptions of the external world.

For example, look at the two patterns at left. They may not make much sense unless you recognize them as representing familiar objects. Maybe they are incomplete pictures of an alarm clock and an elephant. Look at them again. Now can you see them as just a random collection of blobs and lines?

The energy reaching your eyes from such patterns is much the same whether or not you recognize the patterns; yet the nature of your perception is very different. The brain at first did not have enough unconfusing information to form a stable percept and had to make either a probable hypothesis or wait for more information.

Most of the time we are able to form accurate, stable percepts, but occasionally we are faced with one of the following situations.

(a) The middle prong appears in two places at the same time. Because of conflicting information it is impossible to form a stable percept.

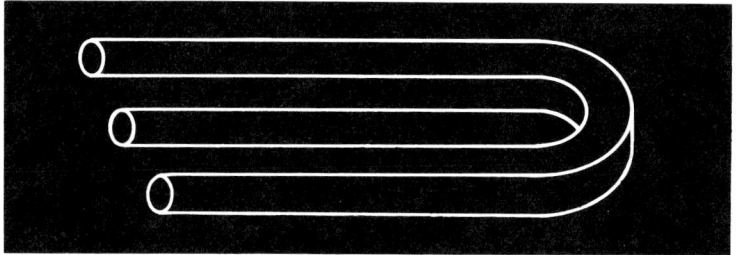

(b) This is seen, alternatively, as a pair of faces looking at each other and as a vase. Thus it is possible to form either of two stable percepts, but difficult to maintain either of them.

(c) The upper bar appears longer than the lower, though they are the same length. It is therefore possible to form a stable percept, but it is clearly inaccurate.

Do you see this painting as a flat pattern on a page or as a three-dimensional object? What does it do to you?

Victor Vasarely, *Vega Pal V,* 1971

 If we wish to describe something that occurred in the past, our description will depend not only on how we perceived it then but also on the way in which we remember that perception. Look at the pattern at left. Then cover the pattern with your hand and try to describe it.

Unless you recognized the object, you may have had difficulty giving it a meaningful description. But when you are told that the pattern represents a musical instrument (or even further, that it represents a violin), you can probably form a stable percept and remember it. You still may not be able to recall and describe the various strokes making up the pattern, but you will probably be able to recall and describe its general meaning, its violin-ness.

Obviously the way we describe a situation depends on our perception of it, but can this statement be reversed? To what extent does our perception of an object or pattern depend on the language we use to describe it, either to ourselves or to others? Perception has been defined by some psychologists as a process of putting things into namable categories. Thus, at least in part, our perceptions depend on the categories we have available. Even if this is not always true at the actual moment of perception, still the way in which we recall something does depend on our ability to place it in a category, to encode it verbally—to put it into words.

Obviously, too, words are symbols, not things. You cannot climb up or picnic under *tree,* though by using appropriate words you can describe swaying on a branch or lunching in the woods. Also, words are not fixed; they are constantly changing. As one historian of language has pointed out: a few centuries ago when you lifted up a hood you saw a monk; now you see a carburetor. And each of us uses words differently, depending on our audience. Your locker-room vocabulary is probably different from the words you use in the classroom. Or, to put it from the point of view of your audience: ''stuff it'' means one thing to a taxidermist, another to a cop.

The symbolic and changing nature of language is what gives it life. For most of us Latin is a dead language. English—no matter in what form or dialect—is alive, and you can speak it with many voices. Think of how many ways you can secretly whisper of love, how many ways you can publicly shout of hate; how many ways you can talk to yourself of fear or hope, how many ways you can apologize or brag to others; how many ways you can speak for yourself, how many ways you can say what others want you to say.

Also remember that words are tricky. How often have you fooled yourself by inwardly saying, I had to do it, without defining what you meant by "had to"? But the fact that you have survived as a functioning human being shows that you have been able to fit your language to your own needs and to adjust it to the expectations of others.

When we speak to someone we supplement our words with gestures—a raised eyebrow, a curled lip, a clenched fist—and we help convey what we mean by the tone of voice we use. For instance, say "you're great" with an affectionate gesture and a sincere tone, then with an angry gesture and a sneering tone. But when we cannot talk to someone in person, we have to rely on written words to communicate our perceptions, our meanings, our world.

Learning to write is always a process of trial and error. There are no magic models to imitate, no necessarily right answers to aim at. For each of us lives in his own perceptual world, a world not exactly like that of anybody else. When you describe any part of it, your description is necessarily unique because what you perceive and the words you use to categorize and record that perception, either for yourself or for others, are your possession, your contribution:

you.

joy
are your senses

you and your senses

You are now asked to investigate how you see, hear, smell, taste, and touch. Besides giving these five senses and your sensory imagination exercise, you are also invited to develop your voice. You can respond in a variety of ways to what follows, and each response may require a slightly different voice. You possess many voices, and if you have confidence in yourself, you can strengthen them. After all, what you have to say and how you say it are what make you both a participating member of the human race and a unique individual.

EYE

What do you see when you first wake up in the morning? Is it what you expect to see—the familiar clock and window and wall? Shut your eyes for a moment: can you still see the clock, the window, the wall?

When you wake up in a strange place, do you see things differently because they are *not* what you expected to see? Do you look more carefully at what you see than when you wake up in familiar surroundings?

In the following pages you are asked to try some experiments with seeing. Most of them invite you to wake up in a strange place, to see the world around you in a fresh way. This book consists only of flat printed pages; you have to supply the third dimension of depth. You can also supply—in fact, you cannot help supplying—whatever other dimensions in space and time your own experience has given you.

When you look at a picture your first response is usually to try to determine what the picture represents or what it means. In the box at left draw the simplest picture you can that suggests *tree*.

If you lived in Greece thirty-five hundred years ago, this is how you would have "written" one kind of *tree,* and the few people who could have read your tablet would have recognized *fig tree*.

Pictographs are a primitive form of writing. Here is another example, even more remote from our modern alphabet, though it is less than one hundred years old.

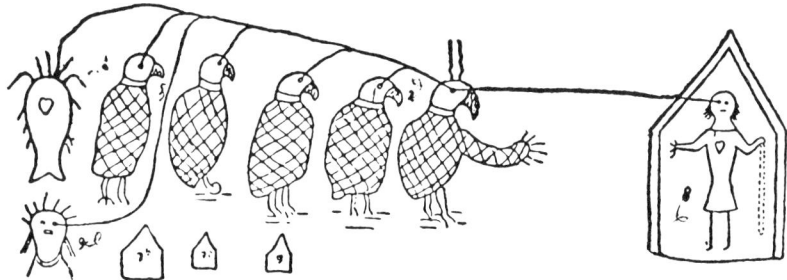

This message of friendship was sent from an American Indian chief to the president of the United States—the figure in the White House. The chief, identified by the lines rising from his head, who is sending the message, and the four warriors behind him, belong to the eagle totem; the fifth warrior is of the catfish totem. The figure at lower left is evidently also a powerful chief. The lines joining the eyes indicate harmony, and the three houses indicate the willingness of the Indians to adopt white men's customs.

Nonverbal "writing" is not entirely a thing of the past. These signs are used to direct people who speak many different languages. Design a similar sign that indicates

       this way to men's room   **first aid**
       no parking   **interpreter available**

21

Write a sentence using only pictures, and ask someone to "read" it. How does writing with pictures change the way you see the objects and ideas you are trying to express?

Which of these three pictures do you most quickly recognize as a picture of a tree? Which seems most real? Describe what you see when you look at each picture. Then describe what you see when you look at the Greek pictograph representing a fig tree. What different sorts of information do you get from the pictograph and each of the three pictures?

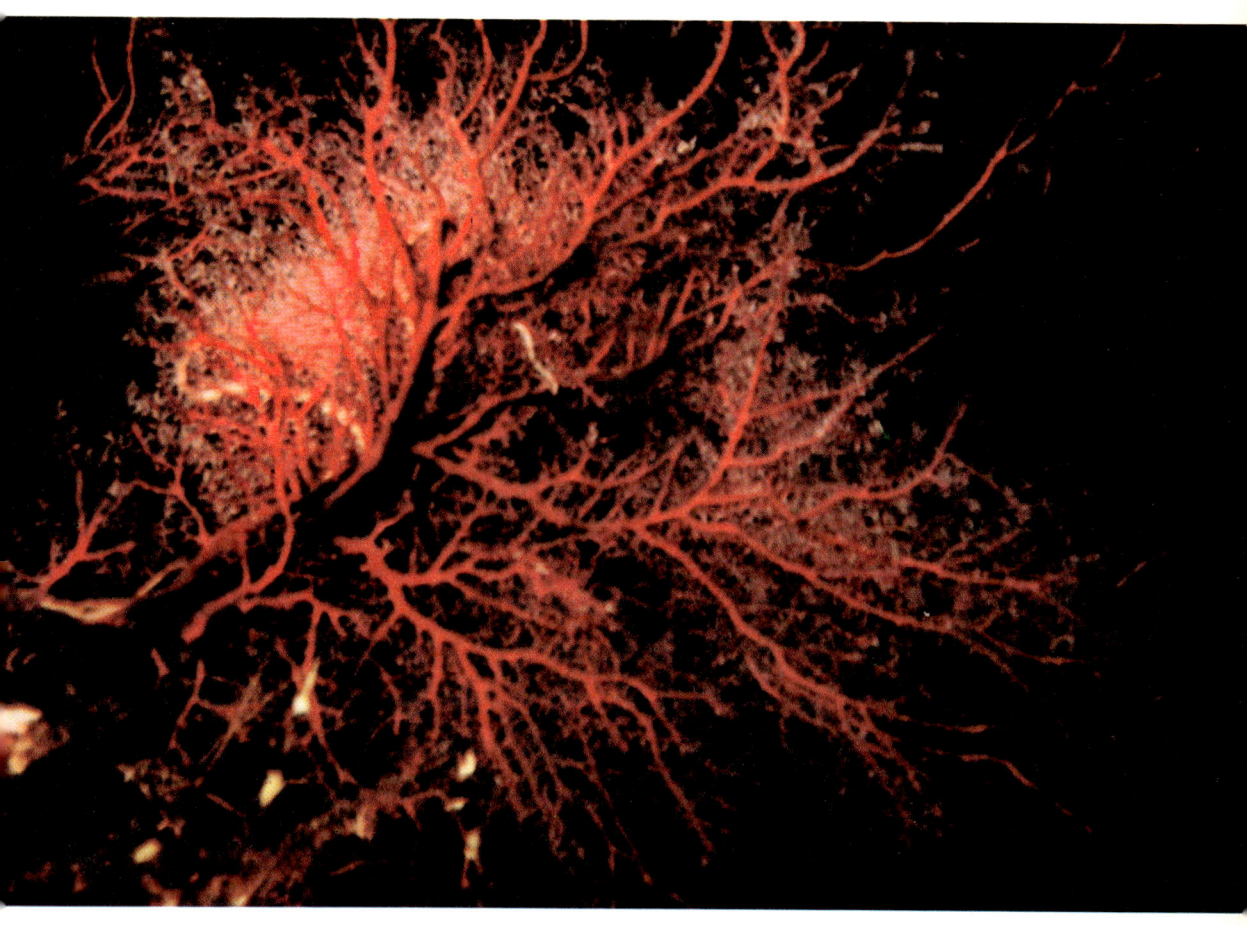

When you look at this photograph you may feel you are in an unfamiliar place. Where is it? What sort of trees are you looking at?

The picture on the preceding page is an underwater photograph of soft coral. Now that you know what it is, do the "trees" look different? Describe what it would feel like to climb one of them. What is strange about "climbing" under water?

Now look at something very familiar: look at yourself in the mirror. What do you see? What do you look for? What is good about your face? What is bad about it? How would you recognize yourself if you saw yourself in a crowd?

If you wanted a photograph that did most justice to you, would you want it in color or in black and white? How close should the camera be? Would you like a profile shot or a full-face portrait? What caption other than your name would you give the picture?

What caption would you give these pictures? Has this woman had a sad or a happy life? What else do you know about her? Look at just the third picture: does what you see there fit in with what you said about her?

In theory at least, the caption—the words—will supplement the picture and the picture will supplement the words. Write a single short caption that could be used for *both* the pictures on this page. Then expand your caption into a paragraph explaining why these two pictures are alike in what they say and how they say it.

These next two pictures may seem very different from each other. But try to write a single short caption that could apply to both. What is each picture saying about life? How are their messages the same? How are they different?

27

Pictures in combination, like words in combination, can tell a story. These three photographs are arranged in two different sequences. Write a story based on the first arrangement, then rewrite it, based on the second sequence of pictures.

So far you have been looking at representational photographs and pictures. But there are more abstract ways of seeing. This cartoon tells a fantastic story. What is that story? Why do you find the cartoon funny? Would it still be funny if there were no observer in the picture?

Drawing by Chas. Addams;
Copr. © 1940, 1968, The New Yorker Magazine, Inc.

Marcel Duchamp, *Nude Descending a Staircase, #2,* 1912

What title would you give this painting? Do you think the title the artist gave it is appropriate?

Is there any way in which the painting is more real than this photograph? Look at the painting again: do you see it differently? Supply a title for both the painting and the photograph that is not *Nude Descending a Staircase.*

Here is the tired lady, at the bottom of the stairs, as "drawn" by a computer.

32

What is strange about this picture? How would you feel about being scanned by a computer?

Now reverse the process and go from words to pictures. Here are six statements: what picture do you see in your mind as you read each of them?

Wait for me.   **Stop crowding me.**
I want to go home.   **Ouch!**
I love you.   **Bullshit.**

Choose the one for which you saw the clearest picture and try to find an illustration in a current magazine or newspaper that resembles what you saw. What movie or TV program have you seen recently that one of these six statements could be an appropriate title for? Rough out directions for a short film that would be appropriate for one of them.

The sense of change and motion in a film affects how and what you perceive. Even if you are not now in a position to make a movie of your own, you can still approximate the effect. Punch a small hole in a sheet of paper and look through the hole; then move the sheet of paper quickly toward and away from your eye. Describe what you saw as objectively as you can, including how it moved and changed.

Here is a picture drawn with words. How does the shape of the poem affect its meaning? What would you lose if it were printed as prose?

THE CITY QUESTION
Robert Froman

                                Wino? Junkie?
                sidewalk.   Hurt?
        on   Sick?
    face
                                   Knife
 on   in
Man   pocket?

                                Danger?

                              Medicine
                           in
                   die May   pocket?
            without
         it?

         Forget
         him?

        Leave

        him

       to

       the

       cops?

     Or try to help?

Write a poem that has a shape appropriate to its subject: for instance, a pistol, a skyscraper, a pyramid.

One of the finest books to combine words and pictures is *Let Us Now Praise Famous Men* (1939). Walker Evans did the photography, James Agee the text. The sentence that follows summarizes what the pictures and words, dealing with three poverty-stricken farm families in the South, tried to accomplish.

For in the immediate world, everything is to be discerned, for him who can discern it, and centrally and simply, without either dissection into science, or digestion into art, but with the whole of consciousness, seeking to perceive it as it stands: so that the aspect of a street in sunlight can roar in the heart of itself as a symphony, perhaps as no symphony can: and all of consciousness is shifted from the imagined, the revisive, to the effort to perceive simply the cruel radiance of what is.

Look at the photographs on the next pages and read the sentence again. What do you think Agee means by "the cruel radiance of what is"? Take a scene familiar to you and, attempting to see it as you think Agee and Evans would, describe it.

35

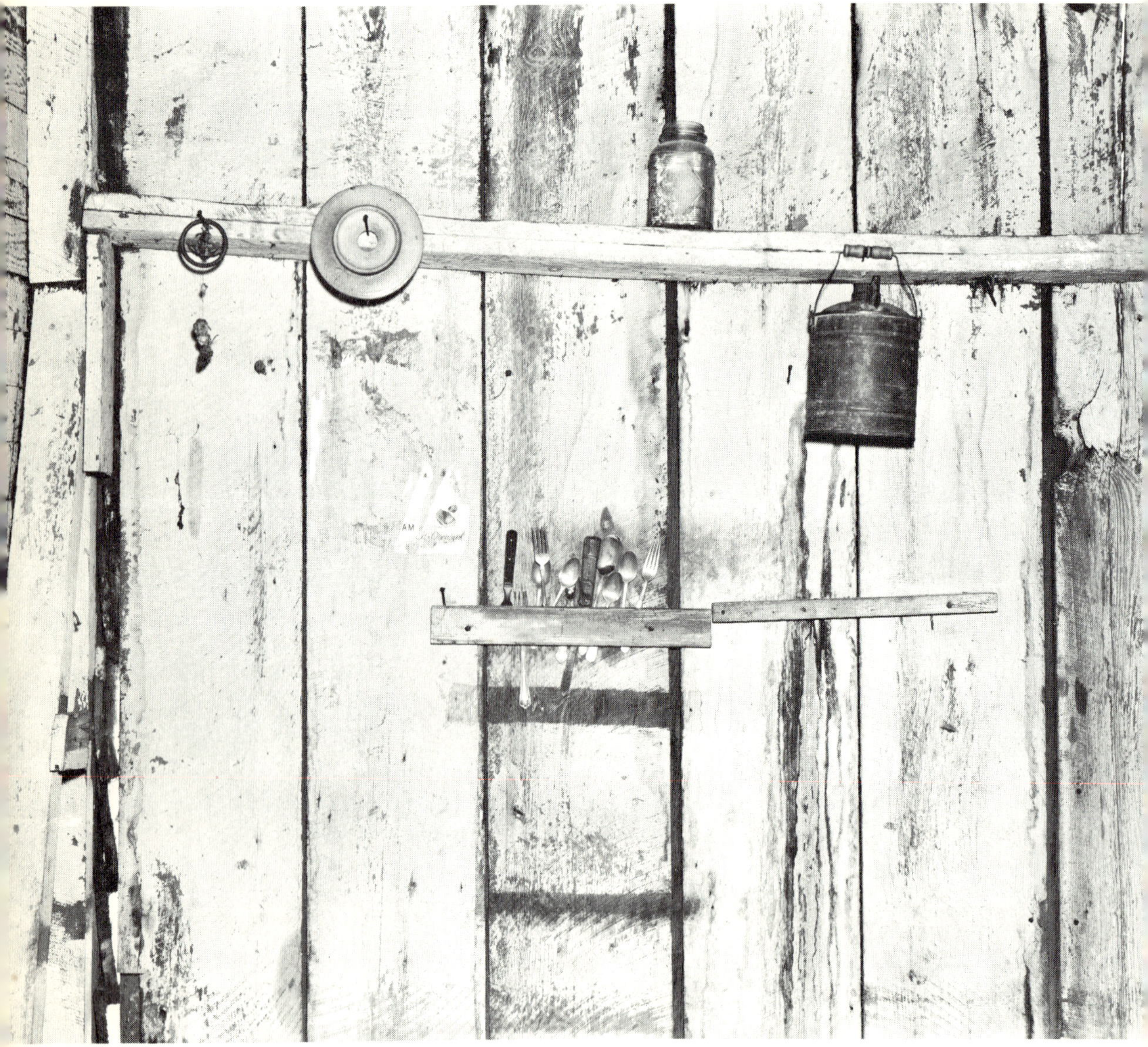

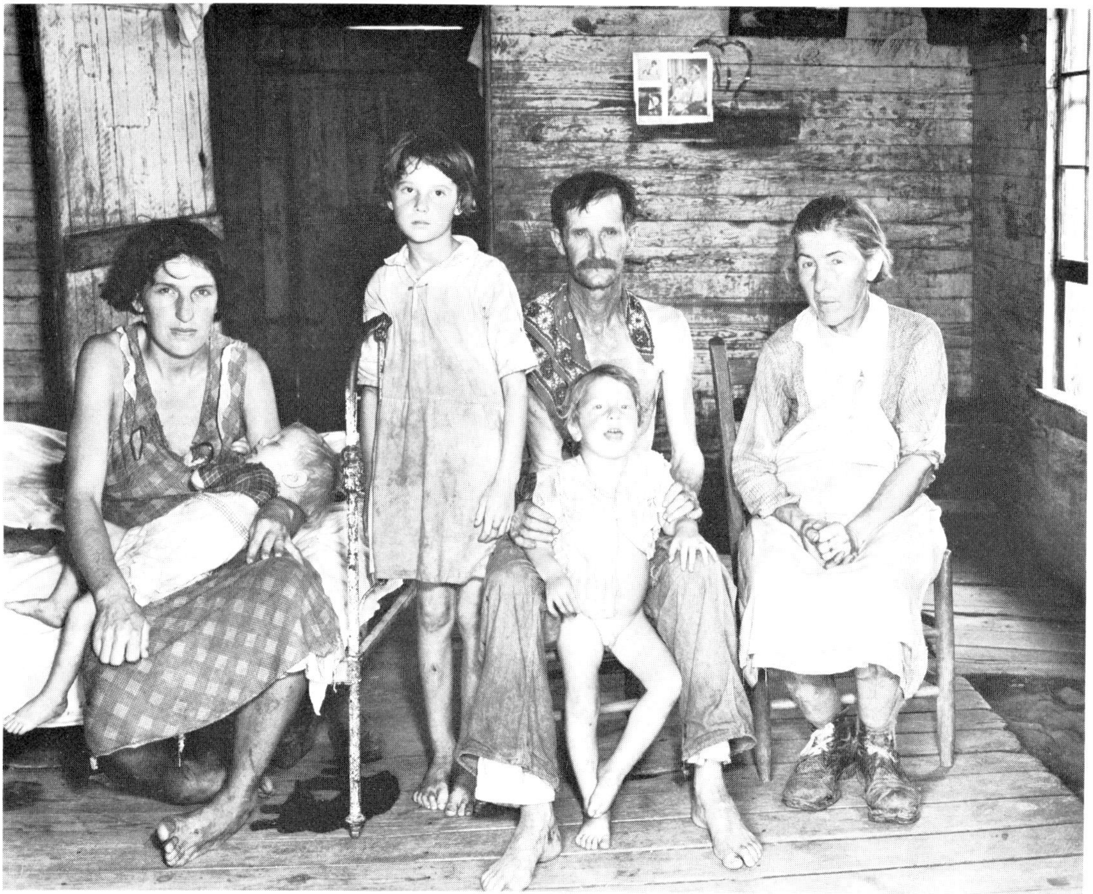

EAR

HEARING

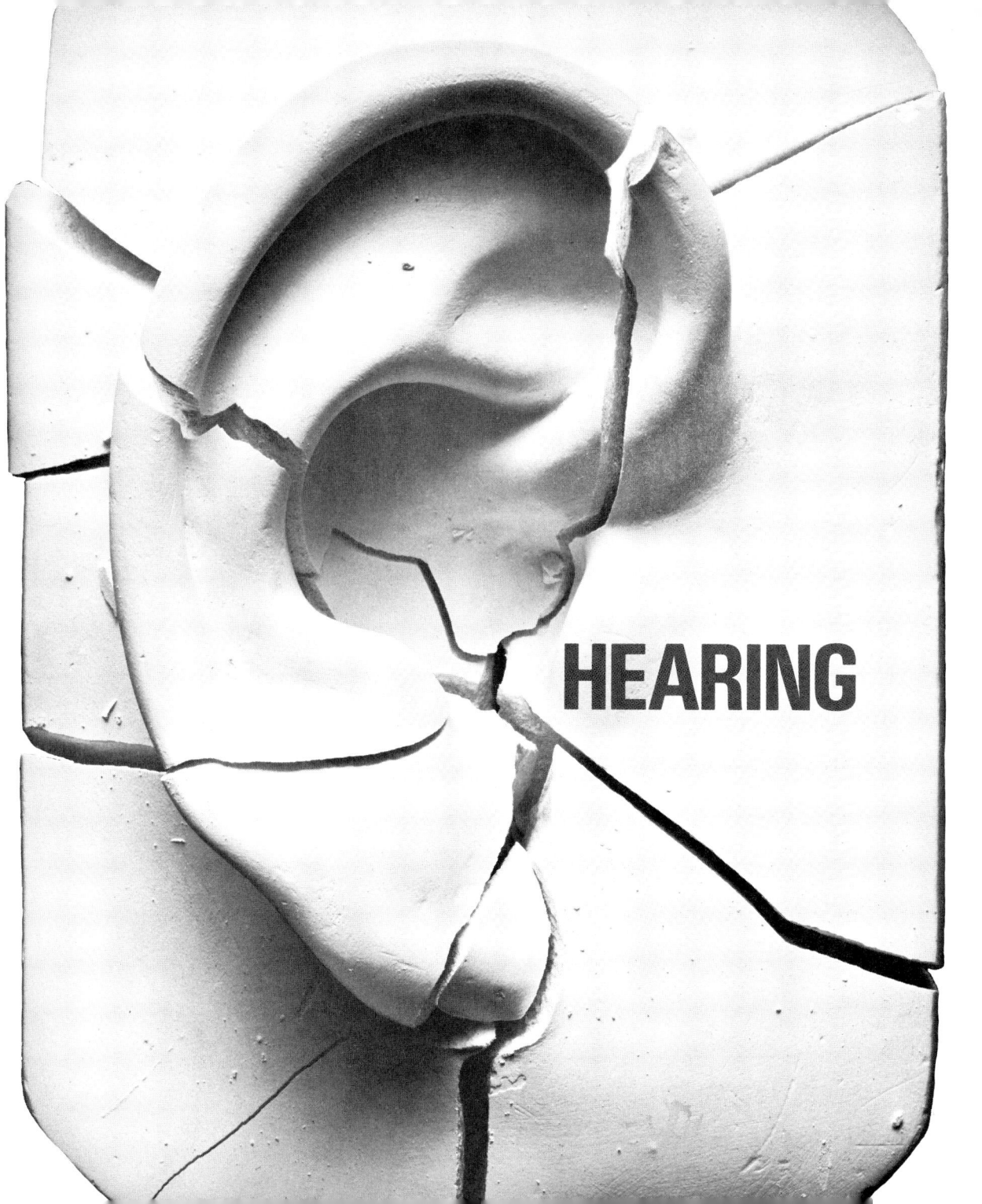

In investigating how and what you see, you had to use your imagination to supply depth to the two-dimensional pages and to look behind the words and pictures. In exploring how and what you hear, you will have to use your imagination again—this time to supply the sound effects. And what you hear often determines what you see. Next time you go to the movies, notice the extent to which the sound track determines what part of the screen your eye concentrates on.

When you read slowly, you apparently hear a lot of the words, even if you are not consciously aware of hearing them. (When you read more quickly, this inner voice tends to disappear.) Read the following words slowly to yourself and, as you do, try to be aware of what you are hearing.

Boom Boom Boom

Oh, say can you see

Lucy in the sky with diamonds

Did you hear the words in your own voice or in someone else's? Did you also hear thunder or cannons or music—a brass band, for instance, or a rock group?

Whose voice or voices do you hear in these two rhymes?

**Roses are red, violets are blue,
Sugar is sweet, and so are you.**

**Ha! ha! ha! He! he! he!
You've got a face like a chimpanzee!**

Describe the first voice you remember hearing. What did it say? How did it sound?

Now try to hear five nonprivate voices.

Winston Churchill speaking to Parliament early in the Second World War:

To form an administration of this scale and complexity is a serious undertaking in itself, but it must be remembered that we are in the preliminary stage of one of the greatest battles in history, that we are in action at many points in Norway and in Holland, that we have to be prepared in the Mediterranean, that the air battle is continuous and that many preparations have to be made here at home. In this crisis I hope I may be pardoned if I do not address the House at any length today. I hope that any of my friends and colleagues, or former colleagues, who are affected by the political reconstruction, will make all allowance for any lack of ceremony with which it has been necessary to act. I would say to the House, as I said to those who have joined this Government: "I have nothing to offer but blood, toil, tears and sweat."

We have before us an ordeal of the most grievous kind. We have before us many, many long months of struggle and of suffering. You ask what is our policy? I will say: It is to wage war, by sea, land and air, with all our might and with all the strength that God can give us; to wage war against a monstrous tyranny, never surpassed in the dark, lamentable catalogue of human crime. That is our policy. You ask, What is our aim? I can answer in one word: Victory—victory at all costs, victory in spite of all terror, victory, however long and hard the road may be; for without victory, there is no survival. Let that be realized; no survival for the British Empire; no survival for all that the British Empire has stood for, no survival for the urge and impulse of the ages, that mankind will move forward towards its goal. But I take up my task with buoyancy and hope. I feel sure that our cause will not be suffered to fail among men. At this time I feel entitled to claim the aid of all, and I say, "Come, then, let us go forward together with our united strength."

George Wallace giving his Inaugural Address as Governor of Alabama in 1963:

It is very appropriate . . . that from this Cradle of the Confederacy, this very heart of the great Anglo-Saxon Southland, that today we sound the drum for freedom as have our generations of forebearers before us time and again down through history. Let us rise to the call of the freedom-loving blood that is in us and send our answer to the tyranny that clanks its chains upon the South. In the name of the greatest people that have ever trod this earth, I draw the line in the dust and toss the gauntlet before the feet of tyranny . . . and I say . . . segregation now . . . segregation tomorrow . . . segregation forever.

Malcolm X speaking in behalf of black radicalism in 1964:

You get freedom by letting your enemy know that you'll do anything to get your freedom; then you'll get it. When you get that kind of attitude, they'll label you as a "crazy Negro," or they'll call you a "crazy nigger"—they don't say Negro. Or they'll call you an extremist or a subversive, or seditious, or a red or a radical. But when you stay radical long enough, and get enough people to be like you, you'll get your freedom.

Spiro Agnew on the campaign trail in 1970:

The great question for all of us this fall is becoming clearer and clearer. Will America be led by a President elected by a majority of the American people, or will we be intimidated and blackmailed into following the path dictated by a disruptive radical and militant minority of the pampered prodigies of the radical liberals in the United States Senate? . . . We have more than our share of the nattering nabobs of negativism.

Gloria Steinem speaking at the June Commencement of Smith College in 1971:

The politics of motherhood. We have seen that the state regards us as a means of production. Isn't it interesting that motherhood becomes sacred, that the Madonna image is prevalent, whenever the state needs workers and the state needs soldiers? Motherhood is not an instinct. If it were, we would not need to be told to do it. It would be like taking one's hand from the fire. Sex in human beings has never been as directly related to conception as it is in animals. Human beings are the only animal that can experience orgasm at times when they cannot conceive. So perhaps God, perhaps She, had something else in mind for us.

Describe what you think each of these five voices sounded like. What gestures do you imagine each speaker using? How do you think the audience reacted? In terms of each speaker's purpose, which of these five do you think was the most effective? Which was the least effective?

Poetry, much more than prose, is addressed to the ear. Read this poem aloud with as much expression as you think suitable.

> **Hickory, dickory, dock!**
> **The mouse ran up the clock.**
> **The clock struck one,**
> **And down he run.**
> **Hickory, dickory, dock!**

Why is this poem easy to remember? Why is its rhythm appropriate? In what ways, if any, are the first and last lines effective?

This poem is ostensibly about a bird, the windhover, but the subtitle suggests other meanings. Read the poem aloud, paying close attention to the sound and movement of the words. Does the poem suggest the flight of a bird? Why is the poem effective? Would a prose account of a religious experience have the same impact? Write a poem that suggests a speeding car or a soaring airplane or a galloping horse.

Gerard Manley Hopkins

THE WINDHOVER

TO CHRIST OUR LORD

I caught this morning morning's minion, king-
   dom of daylight's dauphin, dapple-dawn-drawn Falcon, in
     his riding
  Of the rolling level underneath him steady air, and striding
High there, how he rung upon the rein of a wimpling wing
In his ecstasy! then off, off forth on swing,
  As a skate's heel sweeps smooth on a bow-bend: the hurl
     and gliding
Rebuffed the big wind. My heart in hiding
Stirred for a bird,—the achieve of, the mastery of the thing!

Brute beauty and valour and act, oh, air, pride, plume, here
  Buckle! AND the fire that breaks from thee then, a billion
Times told lovelier, more dangerous, O my chevalier!

   No wonder of it: shéer plód makes plough down sillion
Shine, and blue-bleak embers, ah my dear,
  Fall, gall themselves, and gash gold-vermilion.

And read this poem by e. e. cummings aloud.

tw

o o
ld

o

nce upo

n
a(
n

o mo

re
)time
me

n
sit(l
oo
k)dre

am

Does the way the poem sounds help clarify its meaning? If not, what changes would you make so that sound and sense do come together?

The problem of sound and meaning is a complex one. As in seeing, we tend to hear what we expect to hear, what our memories and conditioning tell us to hear. For instance, what sort of musical background would you expect in a movie about young love, or about car racing, or in a western? We can even supply sounds we know are missing. The following ''word'' is actually a sentence with all the vowels taken out. What does it say?

Nvrgvsckrnvnbrk.

We also hear and see words within the traditions and limitations of our own language. In English the sound of a bell is usually written as *ding-dong,* in French *tam-tam,* in German *bim-bam-bum.* An American cat apparently says *meow,* a French cat *minou-minou.* Do you think these differences result from differences in what Americans, Frenchmen, and Germans *hear*? Write the noise you think a dog makes. Is *bow-wow* the most accurate rendition?

Many words other than simple sound effects like *bang* are formed by imitating noises—*babble, tintinnabulation,* and *murmur,* for example. Write a description of a scene using the sounds of words to indicate what you hear and what you want the reader to hear.

John Cage has long been a leader in the relatively new field of electronic music. The following excerpt is the beginning of a lecture he gave at the Juilliard School of Music in 1952. Using Cage's instructions in his prefatory remarks, read part of the lecture aloud. Then suggest what kind of music and noises and silences you would have accompany that part. All types of sound effects, in any kind of volume and combination, are allowable—from a noisy riveting gun to a soft violin, from a roaring racing car to a subdued acoustic guitar. You can specify as many instruments, tapes, amplifiers, and other equipment as you find appropriate.

In 1952 I was invited to speak at the Juilliard School of Music—not by the Director but by the students. They were having a series of meetings and students from other music schools were also attending. My lecture was in four parts, in all of which I applied processes of collage and fragmentation to texts which I had written earlier. There was in addition some new material. While I was lecturing, David Tudor performed a number of pieces at the piano, compositions by Morton Feldman, Christian Wolff, and myself. To coordinate our program, we used chronometers. I began the first part at 0′ 00″, the second at 12′ 10″, the third at 24′ 20″, the fourth at 36′ 30″. David Tudor's program was made without my knowing anything about it in advance. I had written my text in four columns to facilitate a rhythmic reading and to measure the silences. I read each line across the page from left to right, not down the columns in sequence. I tried to avoid an artificial manner which might have resulted from my being too strictly faithful to the position of the words on the page. I used the rhythmic freedoms one uses in everyday speech.

In the course of a	lecture last winter on	Zen Buddhism,	Dr. Suzuki said
:	"Before studying	Zen,	men are men and
mountains are	mountains	.	While studying Zen
things	be-come confused	:	one doesn't know ex-
actly what is	what and which is	which	.
After studying	Zen,	men are men and	mountains are mountains
."			After the lecture
the question was	asked	:	"Dr. Suzuki
,	what is the	difference between	men are men and
mountains are	mountains	before studying	Zen and
men are men and	mountains are	mountains	after studying Zen
?"		Suzuki answered	:
"Just the same	, only	somewhat as	though you
had your feet	a little off the ground."		
			Now, before studying
music,	men are men	and sounds are sounds.	
music	things aren't clear	.	While studying
			After studying
music	men are men and	sounds are sounds.	That is to say:

```
At the beginning,        one can     hear     a      sound    and     tell       immediately
that   it    isn't    a   human    being    or      something    to look      at
;                        it is high or low            —
                                      has a        certain timbre and          loudness,
lasts   a   certain      length   of    time and   one can hear it.            One then       decides
whether       he       en-joys it     or    not    ,              and        gradually          de-
velops                  a set           of   likes and dislikes              .
                                                    While     studying        music
things         get a little confused              .                          Sounds      are    no
longer just sounds,      but are letters:        A,    B,    C,   D,        E,             F,
G.                       Sharps and flats.       Two of them, four           or even       five
octaves apart            are called    by    the same letter                 .
If a sound     is        unfortunate enough to   not have       a           letter               or
if  it  seems to be      too complex,            it is tossed              out of the system
on the grounds:          it's   a    noise     or unmusical                 .
                         The      privileged    tones    that remain        are arranged          in
modes or scales          or nowadays             rows,             and an abstract
process begins           called composition     .                           That is,              a
composer                 uses the sounds       to express an idea           or                    a
feeling         or       an integration        of these
In the    case of    a   musical idea          , one is told                that         the
sounds    themselves     are  no longer        of consequence               ;
what   'count'           are    their          re-lationships.      And yet       these         re-
lationships              are generally         quite simple                 :
a canon    is    like    children   playing    follow the leader            .
A fugue    is     a      more    complicated   game                         ;              but it can
be broken up             by a single sound     : say,    from     a         fire engine's     siren
,              or        from the horn   of a  boat passing by              .
                         The most   that       can be accomplished         by    no    matter
what     musical         idea         is   to  show how intelligent        the composer         was
who had it               ;        and    the   easiest    way    to        ascertain
what             the     musical    idea       was              is  to  get yourself         in
such   a    state of     confusion             that           you         think   that     a
sound   is    not        something to hear     but       rather            something               to
look at                  .                                         In      the case       of a
musical feeling          ,                     a-gain                      the sounds   are  unim-
portant                  ,     what counts  is expression                  .             But the
most   . that   can be   accomplished          by  the musical             ex-pression of feeling is
to show     how          e-motional      the   composer    was             who had it
.                        If anyone    wants  to get a feeling   of         how emotional         a
composer   proved        himself   to be,    he has to confuse             himself   to the same
```

final extent that the	composer did and	imagine that sounds	are not sounds at all
but are Beethoven and	that men are not	men but are sounds	.
Any child will	tell us	: this is simply not	the case.
A man is	a man and a	sound is a	sound.
To realize this	, one has to	put a stop to	studying music
.	That is to say, one	has to stop all the	thinking that
separates	music from living	.	There is all the
time in the	world for	studying music	, but
for living	there is scarcely	any time at all	. For
living takes	place each	instant and	that instant
is always	changing.	The wisest	thing to do
is to open	one's ears	immediately and	hear a sound
suddenly	be-fore one's	thinking has a	chance to
turn it into	something logical,	abstract, or	symbolical
.	Sounds are sounds	and men	are men,
but now	our feet are a	little off the	ground.

49

Sounds can amplify the meaning of discourse, but can they have precise meaning in themselves? Ask a friend to make a series of noises, using his vocal chords and any available noise-makers. Write the story you hear in these noises.

nose

smelling

Many smells are more pleasant to read about than actually to smell. Imagine the way these things smell: a rose, vinegar, the soap you usually use, the earliest smell you can remember. Describe one or two of these smells, but do your best not to be circular: do not, for instance, use the adjective *vinegary* to describe the smell of vinegar.

Have smells ever been a part of your dreams or nightmares? Why would you guess that smells are infrequent in dreams? What do you mean when you say something or somebody stinks?

Perhaps air pollution has deadened our sense of smell, just as noise pollution has deadened our sense of hearing. What things do you smell without really noticing them? Try some that you do not usually think of in terms of smell. For example, what does money smell like? Do pennies smell differently from quarters? Describe the smell of glass. What does this book smell like?

Describe what you smell when you look at each of these pictures. Are you seeing these smells or smelling them? Would you respond differently if these pictures were in black and white rather than in color? Are there any smells you associate with particular colors?

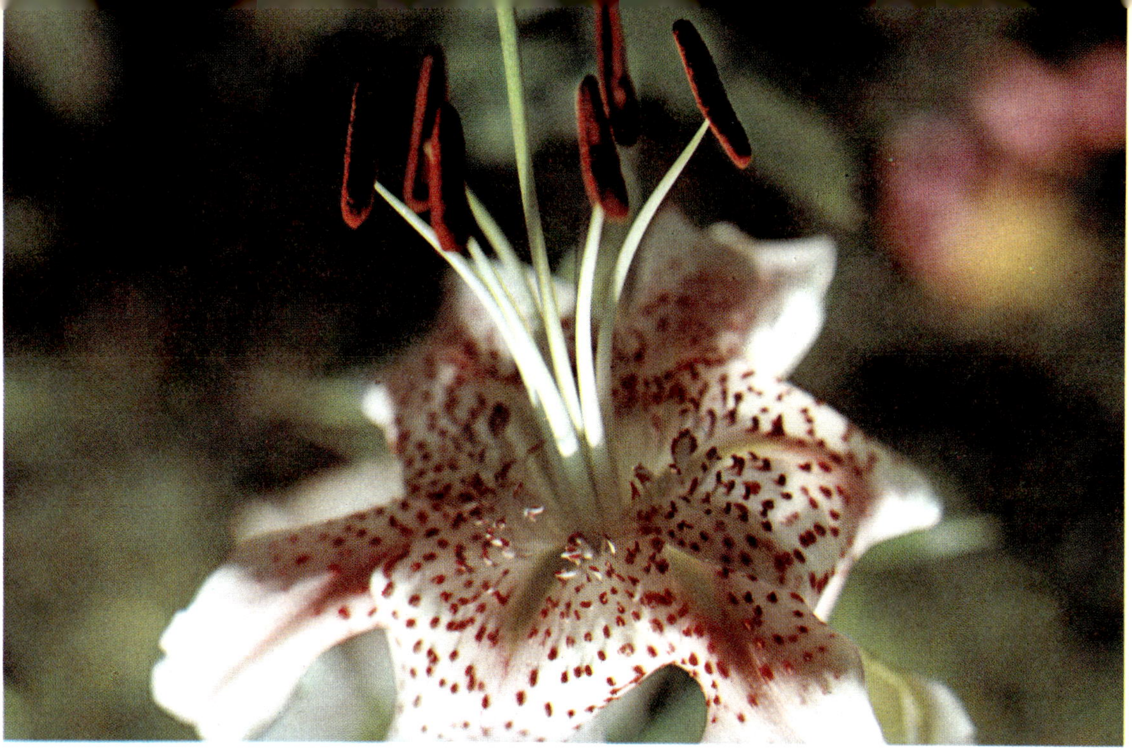

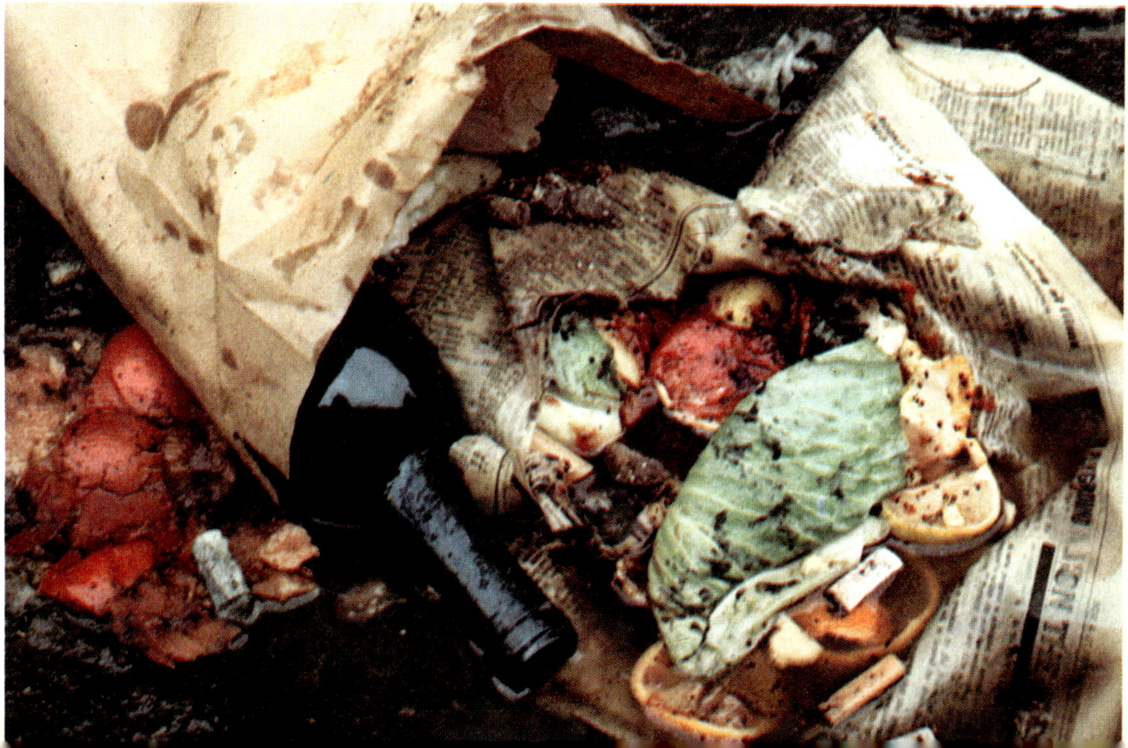

What does this ad want you to smell? Write the copy for a perfume ad that would make you want to buy the perfume. What smells do you associate with love?

Fresh remembers you're a girl, somebody's girl.

This selection from William Burroughs' *Naked Lunch* concludes his vivid account of the life of a junkie.

Yellow smells of skid row sherry and occluding liver drifted out of his clothes when he made the junky gesture throwing the hand out palm up to cope . . .

    smell of chili houses and dank overcoats and atrophied testicles. . . .

He looked at me through the tentative, ectoplasmic flesh of cure . . . thirty pounds materialized in a month when you kick . . . soft pink putty that fades at the first silent touch of junk. . . . I saw it happen . . . ten pounds lost in ten minutes . . . standing there with the syringe in one hand . . . holding his pants up with the other

    sharp reek of diseased metal.

Walking in a rubbish heap to the sky . . . scattered gasoline fires . . . smoke hangs black and solid as excrement in the motionless air . . . smudging the white film of noon heat . . . D.L. walks beside me . . . a reflection of my toothless gums and hairless skull . . . flesh smeared over the rotting phosphorescent bones consumed by slow cold fires. . . . He carries an open can of gasoline and the smell of gasoline envelopes him. . . . Coming over a hill of rusty iron we meet a group of Natives . . . flat two-dimension faces of scavenger fish. . . .

"Throw the gasoline on them and light it. . . .

QUICK . . .

    white flash . . . mangled insect screams . . .

I woke up with the taste of metal in my mouth back from the dead

    trailing the colorless death smell
    afterbirth of a withered grey monkey
    phantom twinges of amputation . . .

"Taxi boys waiting for a pickup," Eduardo said and died of an overdose in Madrid. . . .

    Powder trains burn back through pink convolutions of tumescent flesh . . . set off flash bulbs of orgasm . . . pin-point photos of arrested motion . . . smooth brown side twisted to light a cigarette. . . .

He stood there in a 1920 straw hat somebody gave him . . . soft mendicant words falling like dead birds in the dark street. . . .

"No . . . No more . . . No mas . . ."

A heaving sea of air hammers in the purple brown dusk tainted with rotten metal smell of sewer gas . . . young worker faces vibrating out of focus in yellow halos of carbide lanterns . . . broken pipes exposed. . . .

What do the smells that Burroughs mentions have in common? What overall smell do you think the author wants you to receive? Does he succeed? What smells do you associate with hate?

The Garbage Wars describes the sights and sounds and smells of our cities less directly than the selection from *Naked Lunch,* and places them in a broader historical perspective.

Donald Finkel

THE GARBAGE WARS

The
prison is
the world
of sight,
the light
of the fire
is the
sun.

And he dwelleth in desolate cities, and in houses which no man inhabiteth, which are ready to become heaps.

The city wears about her neck a
garland of dead rats   like an
albatross   where can we stow it?
foul conglomerate   the poor, whom
charity corrupts   brain-damaged
infants marked for the heap by
starvation   the jails filled
to overflowing with the young, the
drunken and the meek   for walking
on the grass   for smoking it
for stealing cars   for lying
in front of them   snipers and
pacifists

    headless dolls, bicycles without wheels, torn cushions vomiting kapok, non-returnable bottles

(from the alleys of history step
the garbage men   an army of dog-catchers
and exterminators   marching on the ghetto
armed with headache balls and sledges)

as an example the General nails
a nation to the stake   sets it
aflame   friend and foe alike
assist via satellite   they get the
message   plain as a head on a pike
dapper little man   glaring through
gunmetal glasses   into the heart of the flame
a silk scarf blooms like a lily at his throat.

The Greeks
set back-
fires to
save their
ships.

They've thrown a wall round the ghetto
withdrawn behind it   the Governor's
doubled the guard   O happy complicity!
on the hill the students have taken
the library   overturn ceremoniously

>
> files for the letters A through E
> one thousand billy-swinging fathers
> burst through the doors   thunder
> of tumbling books   catcalls in the ashes.
>
> *And the fish that was in the river died; and the river stank, and the Egyptians could not drink of the water of the river; and there was blood throughout all the land of Egypt.*

Did Hera-
kleitos
teach a
general
conflagra-
tion?
> And the General   time's ultimate
> garbage man   moves in to clean up
> he rakes the streets with fire
> wipes out the snipers' nests
> (for the purpose at every corner great
> municipal incinerators   and the smoke
> thereof   and the ashes likewise
> consumed   and the residue pressed
> into bricks with which to build
> new incinerators)
>   in the ghetto
> the inmates have set fire to their mattresses
> black clouds of acrimonious smoke
> appall the suburbs
>   the city
> thrashes in her agony   the supermarket
> shrieks through her broken teeth   ten thou-
> sand bedrooms lift their burning eyes to the con-
> stellations for a sign.

What smells does the poem suggest? What do they have in common? What overall smell do you receive? Is this a peculiarly modern smell? When, more than three thousand years ago, the Greeks burned the city of Troy, do you think the sights and sounds and smells were similar to those described in this poem? Illustrate the poem with a few appropriate pictures from current magazines and newspapers.

Write a short account, based mainly on smell, contrasting two distinctly different environments; for example, a ghetto and a suburb, a forest and a beach, a locker room and a classroom.

MOUTH

TASTING

Tasting is inseparable from smelling. The next time you eat, hold your nose and see if you can distinguish the different tastes of the food. Try to imagine the taste of beer, or coffee, or chocolate ice cream without at the same time remembering how they smell. Unless aided by smell, you can discriminate tastes only on the most rudimentary level of sweet, sour, bitter, and salty.

When you smell something, do you also get a sensation of taste? Look again at the picture of garbage on page 53. What taste do you perceive? Does the picture of flowers on the same page evoke any taste? What taste do you associate with love? When you read Burroughs' piece on the dying junkie did you have any sensations of taste? What taste do you associate with hate?

Can words actually make you taste something? Here are two recipes, the first simple and functional, the second humanized and more succulent.

MILK TOAST

Prepare

Hot milk or Thin Cream Sauce

Dip in it

4 to 6 slices toast

Place the toast on plates or a serving dish and pour the rest of the sauce over it. Sprinkle with chopped parsley, ham, or hard-cooked egg.

M. F. K. Fisher

MILK TOAST

for the Ill, Weak, Old, Very Young, or Weary

1 pint milk, part cream if the person
*   is not forbidden that*
4 slices good bread, preferably homemade
sweet butter, if butter is allowed
salt, pepper, if not a child or very ill

Heat the milk gently to the simmering point. Meanwhile have ready 4 freshly toasted slices of bread. Butter them generously. Heat a pretty bowl, deeper than it is wide. Break the hot buttered toast into it, pour the steaming but not boiling milk over it, sprinkle a very little salt and pepper on the top, and serve at once.

It can be seen that compromise lies in every ingredient. The basis for the whole is toasted bread soaked in warm milk. The sweet butter, the seasoning, the cream and the milk—these are sops indeed to the sybarite in even the sickest of us.

  I have used this bland prescription more than once upon myself, recognizing a flicker across my cheekbones, a humming near my elbows and my knees, that meant fatigue had crept too close to the fortress walls. I have found partaking of a warm full bowl of it, in an early bed after a long bath, a very wise medicine—and me but weary, not ill, weak, old, not very young!

  And I remember going one night to a famous restaurant, the quiet, subtly lighted kind like the Chambord, for instance, with a man who was healthier than almost anyone I ever met, because he had just emerged from months of dreadful illness, the quiet, subtly mortal kind. He still moved cautiously and spoke in a somewhat awed voice, and with a courteous but matter-of-fact apology he ordered milk toast for himself, hinting meanwhile at untold gastronomical delights for me.

  I upset him and our waiter, only temporarily however, by asking for milk toast too, not because of my deep dislike of a cluttered table, but because I suddenly wanted the clear, comforting feel of the brew upon my tongue.

While I drank a glass of sherry an increasing flurry surrounded us. It took me some minutes to realize that probably never before in the fifty or so years the restaurant had been there had anyone ordered milk toast—nothing but milk toast. I began to feel as if screens would be whisked up around us, like two unfortunate or indiscreet athletes on a football field. There was a mounting air of tension among the waiters, who increased gradually in our corner of the room from three to about twelve. By the time the silver chafing dishes had been wheeled before us, we had three captains, all plainly nervous, eying the maneuvers from near-by vantage points.

The thing began: butter sizzling here, toast smoking delicately there, rich milk trembling at the bubbling point but no further, a huge silver pepper-mill held ready, salt, *rock*-salt, in a Rumanian grinder, paprika in a tin marked "Buda-Pesth." Helpless, a little hysterical under our super-genteel exteriors, my friend and I waited. The flames flamed. The three captains surged into action. And before we could really follow the intricate and apparently well-rehearsed ballet, two mammoth silver bowls, just like the nursery ones but bigger and more beautiful, steamed before us, and we sat spooning up the most luxurious, most ridiculously and spectacularly delicious milk toast either of us had eaten in our long, full, and at times invalidish lives.

It was a small modern miracle of gastronomy, certainly not worth having illness for, but worth pondering on, in case milk toast might help.

Which of the two recipes tastes better? Describe your favorite food in such a way that the reader will want to eat it.

At Lunch

By RUSSELL BAKER

WASHINGTON, Dec. 2—Al, Nick, Pete and Quentin went to an expensively decorated restaurant for lunch. The food was just as expensive as the decor and almost as tasty.

"The chef here isn't much," Al confided as they sat down, "but they've got the best menu writer on the East Coast. It cost them a fortune to hire him. He'd been in New York writing book-jacket blurbs for Gothic novels."

A waiter took their drink orders, distributed four menus and departed.

After studying his menu a few minutes, Nick said he was thinking of ordering the tender chunklets of milkfed veal, lovingly dipped in the slightest hint of aromatic herb sauce and served in an iron casserole rushed fresh from the famed forges of France.

"That's a little too metallic for my literary taste," Al said. "Personally, I recommend the lumps of luscious backfin crabmeat delicately wrapped in light French crepes to retain the sealed-in flavors and savory juices, baked and covered with sauce Mornay in a delightful sprinkling of parmesan cheese redolent with memories of sunny Naples."

Pete said he was watching his weight, but found it hard to resist the refulgent green lightness of gelatine quivering on an emerald bed of crisp crunchy lettuce born of the mating between sparkling sunshine and cool, clear water in the golden valleys of old California.

Quentin said he didn't see anything on the menu that didn't need editing and thought he'd just have a hamburger, medium rare.

"You can't just ask for a hamburger in a place like this," Al whispered.

"The author would be insulted," said Nick.

"In France, where food really counts for something," said Pete, "men have been shot for less."

"I want a hamburger!" insisted Quentin, who tended to stubbornness. "Medium rare."

"Quent, old boy," said Al, "why not try the Seafood Symphony?"

"Because," said Quentin, consulting the menu, "I don't want succulently clustered clumps of crabmeat, jumbo shrimp, tender lobster meat and fresh salt-water fish sautéed in butter with mushrooms and shallots, blended with thick luscious cream and flavored with shimmeringly shadowed sherry wine to create a symphony in seafood, served in casserole."

The waiter, noting tensions at the table, eased within eavesdropping range.

"Have a Cowpuncher's Dream," urged Nick.

"No steaks," said Quentin.

The waiter, who had overheard, came over. He was miffed.

"Our waiters do not traffic in steak," the waiter said. "Steak is for illiterates."

This put Quentin's back up. "I demand to see the author," he said.

Some time later an overpaid man stuffed with succulent juicy adjectives presented himself. "Hamburger?" he repeated.

"Hamburger," said Quentin. "Medium rare."

The writer wandered to the water cooler, washed his hands, looked up the weather report, made some unnecessary phone calls, looked at his tongue in a mirror for symptoms of fatal disease and, when he had at last exhausted methods of killing time, went to his typewriter.

Returning to Quentin, he asked, "Is the creation you have in mind a magnificently seared thickness of sizzling goodness that has been reduced by grinders of rarest Toledo steel to mouth-watering palate-tantalizers of Kansas City beef beaded with rich ruby globules served on a farm-fresh roll and laced lavishly with great oozing lashings of rarest mustards and onions from faraway Spain?"

"Enough! Enough! Stop!" cried Quentin. "I can't listen to another bite."

The menu writer smiled in triumph and left. The waiter returned. "Are you gentlemen ready to order?" he asked.

"Yes," said Al. "Four coffees."

"And," said Nick, "send our compliments to the author."

Quentin burped with contentment.

What do you think Russell Baker is trying to tell you about "good taste" in our society?

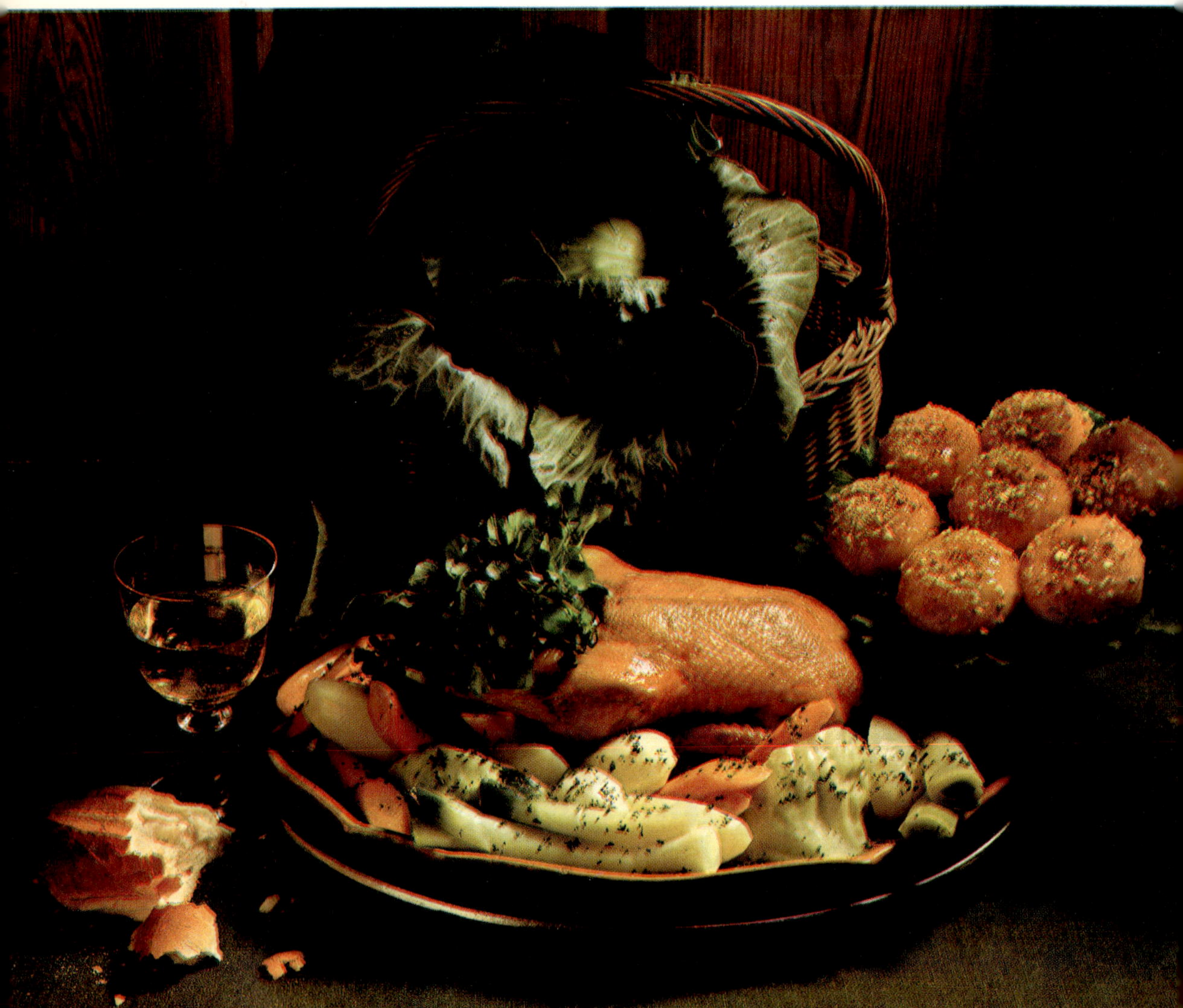

The following interviews are from a book published in 1969 titled *Still Hungry in America,* by Robert Coles. What do these people reveal about the nature of hunger? Does food mean more to them than simply sustenance? Does it mean more to you? Describe the taste of hunger. Would a big meal taste differently if you knew that a hungry child was watching you eat it?

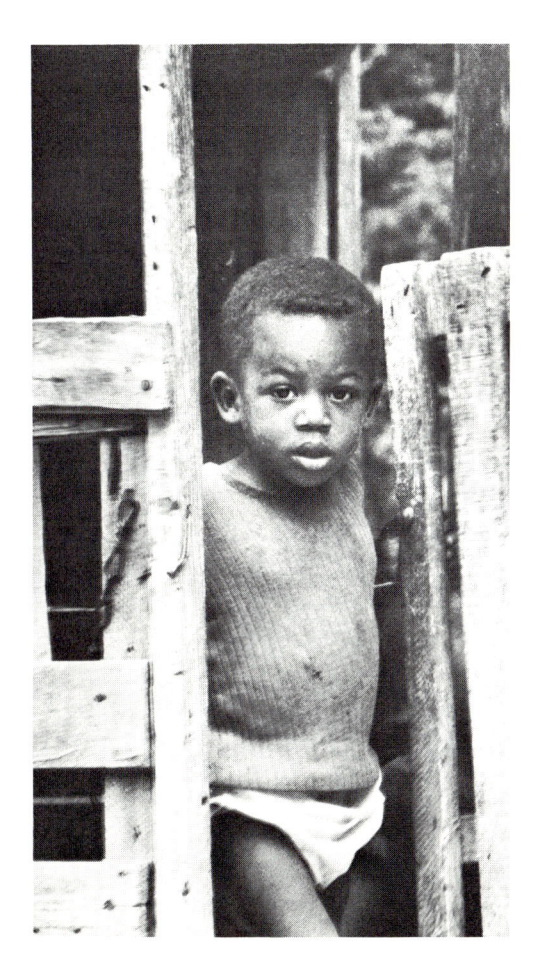

Yes, the nurse told me that milk is best, way better than a Coca-Cola. I said if she thought so, maybe she could come around here with a gallon or two, every day, and then I'd use it for sure. She said we should be smart, and sacrifice, and buy milk when we can, with the money we spend on Cokes. Then what do we do in between, I asked her. What do we do while we're saving up money to buy milk—tell our kids to be patient, and wait until we've got something for them to drink, maybe in another few days? Maybe those coal companies could give each one of us a gallon of milk every week; they'd still be making a fortune on what they take out of this here land. Even if I had the money to get a cow, and get milk from her, I couldn't let her around here to graze. She'd get poisoned by what they've done to our land; it's covered with slime, with the landslides those machines have caused. I hope the people who use our coal know that we don't get a cent out of it and can't afford milk, no, and our county, it's being torn into bits by what they do.

. . .

No, I don't think the Cokes hurt them. I

65

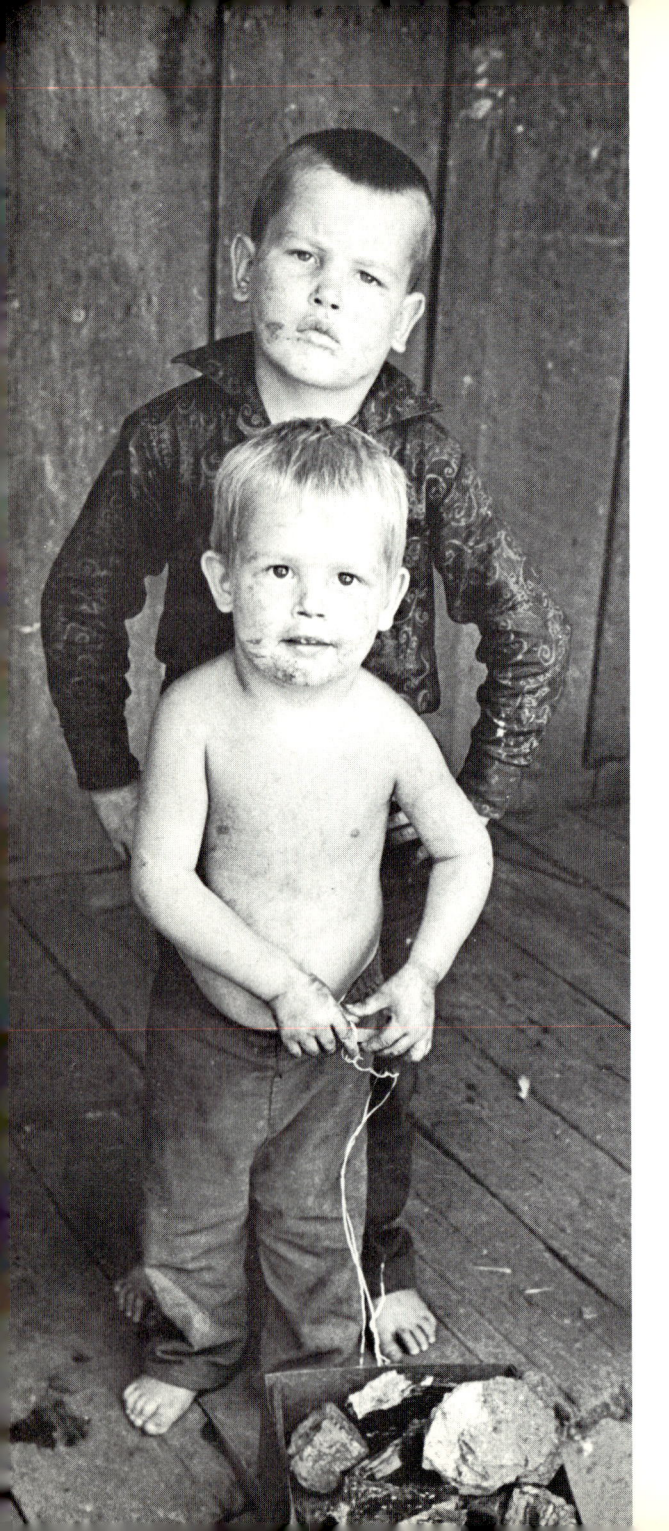

think they feel better with a Coke. They have the bottle to hold, and it keeps them out of mischief, and they're glad to have something of their own, I'll tell you. My little boy, he got himself attached to an orange-pop bottle. It was the first time he ever had orange-pop—no, he's never had orange juice—and he liked it so much that he kept asking me for more, more, more. I said there wasn't any more, not for now. Well, you know, he wasn't really asking, I mean speaking. He was too young. He just grabbed and grabbed, and I thought, oh my, he really does like the orange flavor, and we'll have to try to get some more. My sister is up in Chicago, you know. And she works in a factory there, and she eats real oranges, and she says she can keep a bowl of fruit around, and why don't I come up there. But she wrote it was bitter cold there, and besides she don't be with her kids at all; it's my aunt who's there and takes care of them, so she can work, and they lives all in that two rooms they've got, and nowhere for the kids to go, or anywhere else. So it's bad all over, that's what I believe. The man at the store said that sure you might get better food up there, but with the sun and all down here, you don't need so much. No, I don't believe he was fooling me. He seemed to mean it; though I admit I wondered myself how the kids could get by on the sun and as much food as he'd let me have from his store. So thank God for the commodities the government gives us.

. . .

We'd be gone without government food,

the commodities, you know, and we'd be gone without Cokes, too. I give my kids a Coke and they don't feel hungry no more. And I'm way along—I expect my baby next month, but even so I have to go get that water because we needs a lot and I try to help my husband, and he's tired after a day of cleaning up for the white man. He's one of the janitors in the motel down by the highway, and they pay him real good, twenty dollars by the week, and he can have his lunch. He's sure the fattest one in this family—only he can't get any of the white man's food over to us, that's the trouble. So, when he comes home the first thing we do is go get the water. Oh, it takes it out of you. One day if we ever get enough money, we'd like to move nearer to the town, where they has water inside. That would be something! But I'll tell you, thank God for the Cokes. If we get tired, we can always drink them, and the kids get quieted down real good on them—and they're pure, pure as it's possible to be, so you don't get sick on your stomach from bad water.

. . .

I hear tell that it's bad for our children, what they eat. The teacher, she said we don't do a good job of caring for them, and they shouldn't be having all those "soft drinks," she calls them, and they need more meat and eggs and milk and things like that. We're supposed to go buy them when they snap their fingers and tell us to. And what do we use for money? Maybe they could tell the man at the store to give us back more money,

on the bottles we bring in, and then we could buy the "protein" she keeps telling us about. Sure my kids have bad teeth. So did I and my mother and my daddy and as far back as it goes, probably. But what are we supposed to do? I see the missus and what she eats and her family eats. They don't worry how much this costs and how much that costs. I mean, they do: they talk about whether they can afford some land up there on a lake, for another home, to keep cool and go swimming in the summer. (They already has their air-conditioners, and those machines freeze me to death when I go there in the morning and I'm shaking all night when I get home, but it's good in between.) For us, though, it's different. I have to think every time I buy a loaf of bread. And I can't let my kids tell me they're hungry, they're hungry—because it drives me crazy hearing it, and I tell them to stop, and let me tell you, they know they've got to listen to me—or else. I say we're all hungry. That's the way it's got to be— and maybe one day you'll go out there and make a fortune. I don't know—I say that, too. I admit to them that it don't look like we will. I have to tell them the truth. That's how I talk to them; and they listen.

SPRAY NONFAT DRY MILK
DONATED BY
U. S. DEPARTMENT OF AGRICULTURE
FOR SCHOOL LUNCH
AND OTHER ELIGIBLE PROGRAMS
NOT TO BE SOLD OR EXCHANGED
STORE IN COOL, DRY PLACE
SHERWIN-WILLIAMS PAINTS
12 QUARTS
Enjoy your Home Canning
No. 718
12 QUARTS
Enjoy your Home Canning
No. 718
12 QUARTS
Enjoy your Home Canning
No. 718

Though Jonathan Swift wrote his "Modest Proposal" in 1729, you may find the pictures on the preceding pages relevant to what he had to say. He was outraged by the way England was feeding on Ireland, his homeland, and this is how he expressed his anger.

Jonathan Swift
a modest proposal
for preventing the children of poor people in Ireland from being a burden to their parents or country, and for making them beneficial to the public

It is a melancholy object to those who walk through this great town or travel in the country, when they see the streets, the roads, and cabin doors, crowded with beggars of the female sex, followed by three, four, or six children, all in rags and importuning every passenger for an alms. These mothers, instead of being able to work for their honest livelihood, are forced to employ all their time in strolling to beg sustenance for their helpless infants, who, as they grow up, either turn thieves for want of work, or leave their dear native country to fight for the Pretender in Spain, or sell themselves to the Barbadoes.

I think it is agreed by all parties that this prodigious number of children in the arms, or on the backs, or at the heels of their mothers, and frequently of their fathers, is in the present deplorable state of the kingdom a very great additional grievance; and therefore whoever could find out a fair, cheap, and easy method of making these children sound, useful members of the commonwealth would deserve so well of the public as to have his statue set up for a preserver of the nation.

But my intention is very far from being confined to provide only for the children of professed beggars; it is of a much greater extent, and shall take in the whole number of infants at a certain age who are born of parents in effect as little able to support them as those who demand our charity in the streets.

As to my own part, having turned my thoughts for many years upon this important subject, and maturely weighed the several schemes of other projectors, I have always found them grossly mistaken in their computation. It is true, a child just dropped from its dam may be supported by her milk for a solar year, with little other nourishment; at most not above the value of two shillings, which the mother may certainly get, or the value in scraps, by her lawful occupation of begging; and it is exactly at one year old that I propose to provide for them in such a manner as instead of being a charge upon their parents or the parish, or wanting food and raiment for the rest of their lives, they shall on the contrary contribute to the feeding, and partly to the clothing, of many thousands.

There is likewise another great advantage in my scheme, that it will prevent those voluntary abortions, and that horrid practice of women murdering their bastard children, alas, too frequent among us, sacrificing the poor innocent babes, I doubt, more to avoid the expense than the shame, which would move tears and pity in the most savage and inhuman breast.

The number of souls in this kingdom being usually reckoned one million and a half, of these I calculate there may be about two hundred thousand couples whose wives are breeders; from which number I subtract thirty thousand couples who are able to maintain their own children, although I apprehend there cannot be so many under the present distresses of the kingdom; but this being granted, there will remain an hundred and seventy thousand breeders. I again subtract fifty thousand for those women who miscarry, or whose children die by accident or disease within the year. There only remain an hundred and twenty thousand children of poor parents annually born. The question therefore is, how this number shall be reared and provided for, which, as I have already said, under the present situation of affairs, is utterly impossible by all the methods hitherto proposed. For we can neither employ them in handicraft or agriculture; we neither build houses (I mean in the country) nor cultivate land. They can very seldom pick up a livelihood by stealing till they arrive at six years old, except where they are of towardly parts; although I confess they learn the rudiments much earlier, during which time they can however be looked upon only as probationers, as I have been informed by a principal gentleman in the county of Cavan, who protested to me that he never knew above one or two instances under the age of six, even in a part of the kingdom so renowned for the quickest proficiency in that art.

I am assured by our merchants that a boy or a girl before twelve years old is no salable commodity; and even when they come to this age they will not yield above three pounds, or three pounds and half a crown at most on the Exchange; which cannot turn to account either to the parents or the kingdom, the charge of nutriment and rags having been at least four times that value.

I shall now therefore humbly propose my own thoughts, which I hope will not be liable to the least objection.

I have been assured by a very knowing American of my acquaintance in London, that a young healthy child well nursed is at a year old a most delicious, nourishing, and wholesome food, whether stewed, roasted, baked, or boiled; and I make no doubt that it will equally serve in a fricassee or a ragout.

I do therefore humbly offer it to public consideration that of the hundred and twenty thousand children, already computed, twenty thousand may be reserved for breed, whereof only one fourth part to be males, which is more than we allow to sheep, black cattle, or swine; and my reason is that these children are seldom the fruits of marriage, a circumstance not much regarded by our savages, therefore one male will be sufficient to serve four females. That the remaining hundred thousand may at a year old be offered in sale to the persons of quality and fortune through the kingdom, always advising the mother to let them suck plentifully in the last month, so as to render them plump and fat for a good table. A child will make two dishes at an entertainment for friends; and when the family dines alone, the fore or hind quarter will make a reasonable dish, and seasoned with a little pepper or salt will be very good boiled on the fourth day, especially in winter.

I have reckoned upon a medium that a child just born will weigh twelve pounds, and in a solar year if tolerably nursed increaseth to twenty-eight pounds.

I grant this food will be somewhat dear, and therefore very proper for landlords, who, as they have already devoured most of the parents, seem to have the best title to the children.

Infant's flesh will be in season throughout the

year, but more plentiful in March, and a little before and after. For we are told by a grave author, an eminent French physician, that fish being a prolific diet, there are more children born in Roman Catholic countries about nine months after Lent than at any other season; therefore, reckoning a year after Lent, the markets will be more glutted than usual, because the number of popish infants is at least three to one in this kingdom; and therefore it will have one other collateral advantage, by lessening the number of Papists among us.

I have already computed the charge of nursing a beggar's child (in which list I reckon all cottagers, laborers, and four fifths of the farmers) to be about two shillings per annum, rags included; and I believe no gentleman would repine to give ten shillings for the carcass of a good fat child, which, as I have said, will make four dishes of excellent nutritive meat, when he hath only some particular friend or his own family to dine with him. Thus the squire will learn to be a good landlord, and grow popular among the tenants; the mother will have eight shillings net profit, and be fit for work till she produces another child.

Those who are more thrifty (as I must confess the times require) may flay the carcass; the skin of which artificially dressed will make admirable gloves for ladies, and summer boots for fine gentlemen.

As to our city of Dublin, shambles may be appointed for this purpose in the most convenient parts of it, and butchers we may be assured will not be wanting; although I rather recommend buying the children alive, and dressing them hot from the knife as we do roasting pigs.

A very worthy person, a true lover of his country, and whose virtues I highly esteem, was lately pleased in discoursing on this matter to offer a refinement upon my scheme. He said that many gentlemen of this kingdom, having of late destroyed their deer, he conceived that the want of venison might be well supplied by the bodies of young lads and maidens, not exceeding fourteen years of age nor under twelve, so great a number of both sexes in every county being now ready to starve for want of work and service; and these to be disposed of by their parents, if alive, or otherwise by their nearest relations. But with due deference to so excellent a friend and so deserving a patriot, I cannot be altogether in his sentiments; for as to the males, my American acquaintance assured me from frequent experience that their flesh was generally tough and lean, like that of our schoolboys, by continual exercise, and their taste disagreeable; and to fatten them would not answer the charge. Then as to the females, it would, I think with humble submission, be a loss to the public, because they soon would become breeders themselves: and besides, it is not improbable that some scrupulous people might be apt to censure such a practice (although indeed very unjustly) as a little bordering upon cruelty; which, I confess, hath always been with me the strongest objection against any project, how well soever intended.

But in order to justify my friend, he confessed that this expedient was put into his head by the famous Psalmanazar, a native of the island Formosa, who came from thence to London above twenty years ago, and in conversation told my friend that in his country when any young person happened to be put to death, the executioner sold the carcass to persons of quality as a prime dainty; and that in his time the body of a plump girl of fifteen, who was crucified for an attempt to poison the emperor, was sold to his Imperial Majesty's prime minister of state, and other great mandarins of the court, in joints from the gibbet, at four hundred crowns. Neither indeed can I deny that if the same use were made of several plump young girls in this town, who without one single groat to their fortunes cannot stir abroad without a chair, and appear at the playhouse and assemblies in foreign fineries which they never will pay for, the kingdom would not be the worse.

Some persons of a desponding spirit are in great concern about that vast number of poor people who are aged, diseased, or maimed, and I have been desired to employ my thoughts what course may be taken to ease the nation of so grievous an encumbrance. But I am not in the least pain upon that matter, because it is very well known that they are every day dying and rotting by cold and famine, and filth and vermin, as fast as can be reasonably expected. And as to the younger laborers, they are now in almost as hopeful a condition. They cannot get work, and consequently pine away for want of nourishment to a degree that if at any time they are accidentally hired to common labor, they have not strength to perform it; and thus the country and themselves are happily delivered from the evils to come.

I have too long digressed, and therefore shall return to my subject. I think the advantages by the proposal which I have made are obvious and many, as well as of the highest importance.

For first, as I have already observed, it would greatly lessen the number of Papists, with whom we are yearly overrun, being the principal breeders of the nation as well as our most dangerous enemies; and who stay at home on purpose to deliver the kingdom to the Pretender, hoping to take their advantage by the absence of so many good Protestants, who have chosen rather to leave their country than stay at home and pay tithes against their conscience to an Episcopal curate.

Secondly, the poorer tenants will have something valuable of their own, which by law may be made liable to distress, and help to pay their landlord's rent, their corn and cattle being already seized and money a thing unknown.

Thirdly, whereas the maintenance of an hundred thousand children, from two years old and upwards, cannot be computed at less than ten shillings a piece per annum, the nation's stock will be thereby increased fifty thousand pounds per annum, besides the profit of a new dish introduced to the tables of all gentlemen of fortune in the kingdom who have any refinement in taste. And the money will circulate among ourselves, the goods being entirely of our own growth and manufacture.

Fourthly, the constant breeders, besides the gain of eight shillings sterling per annum by the sale of their children, will be rid of the charge of maintaining them after the first year.

Fifthly, this food would likewise bring great custom to taverns, where the vintners will certainly be so prudent as to procure the best receipts for dressing it to perfection, and consequently have their houses frequented by all the fine gentlemen, who justly value themselves upon their knowledge in good eating; and a skillful cook, who understands how to oblige his guests, will contrive to make it as expensive as they please.

Sixthly, this would be a great inducement to marriage, which all wise nations have either encouraged by rewards or enforced by laws and penalties. It would increase the care and tenderness of mothers toward their children, when they were sure of a settlement for life to the poor babes, provided in some sort by the public, to their annual profit instead of expense. We should see an honest emulation among the married women, which of them could bring the fattest child to the market. Men would become as fond of their wives during the time of their pregnancy as they are now of their mares in foal, their cows in calf, or sows when they are ready to farrow; nor offer to beat or kick them (as is too frequent a practice) for fear of a miscarriage.

Many other advantages might be enumerated. For instance, the addition of some thousand carcasses in our exportation of barreled beef, the propagation of swine's flesh, and improvement in the art of making good bacon, so much wanted among us by the great destruction of pigs, too frequent at our tables, which are no way comparable in taste or magnificence to a well-grown, fat, yearling child, which roasted whole will make a considerable figure at a lord mayor's feast or any other public entertainment. But this and many others I omit, being studious of brevity.

Supposing that one thousand families in this city would be constant customers for infants' flesh, besides others who might have it at merry meetings, particularly weddings and christenings, I compute that Dublin would take off annually about twenty thousand carcasses, and the rest of the kingdom (where probably they will be sold somewhat cheaper) the remaining eighty thousand.

I can think of no one objection that will possibly be raised against this proposal, unless it should be urged that the number of people will be thereby much lessened in the kingdom. This I freely own, and it was indeed one principal design in offering it to the world. I desire the reader will observe, that I calculate my remedy for this one individual kingdom of Ireland and for no other that ever was, is, or I think ever can be upon earth. Therefore let no man talk to me of other expedients: of taxing our absentees at five shillings a pound: of using neither clothes nor household furniture except what is of our own growth and manufacture: of utterly rejecting the materials and instruments that promote foreign luxury: of curing the expensiveness of pride, vanity, idleness, and gaming in our women: of introducing a vein of parsimony, prudence, and temperance: of learning to love our country, in the want of which we differ even from Laplanders and the inhabitants of Topinamboo: of quitting our animosities and factions, nor acting any longer like the Jews, who were murdering one another at the very moment their city was taken: of being a little cautious not to sell our country and conscience for nothing: of teaching landlords to have at least one degree of mercy toward their tenants: lastly, of putting a spirit of honesty, industry, and skill into our shopkeepers; who, if a resolution could now be taken to buy only our native goods, would immediately unite to cheat and exact upon us in the price, the measure, and the goodness, nor could ever yet be brought to make one fair proposal of just dealing, though often and earnestly invited to it.

Therefore I repeat, let no man talk to me of these and the like expedients, till he hath at least some glimpse of hope that there will ever be some hearty and sincere attempt to put them in practice.

But as to myself, having been wearied out for many years with offering vain, idle, visionary thoughts, and at length utterly despairing of success, I fortunately fell upon this proposal, which, as it is wholly new, so it hath something solid and real, of no expense and little trouble, full in our own power, and whereby we can incur no danger in disobliging England. For this kind of commodity will not bear exportation, the flesh being of too tender a consistence to admit a long continuance in salt, although perhaps I could name a country which would be glad to eat up our whole nation without it.

After all, I am not so violently bent upon my own opinion as to reject any offer proposed by wise men, which shall be found equally innocent, cheap, easy, and effectual. But before something of that kind shall be advanced in contradiction to my scheme, and offering a better, I desire the author or authors will be pleased maturely to consider two points. First, as things now stand, how they will be able to find food and raiment for an hundred thousand useless mouths and backs. And secondly, there being a round million of creatures in human figure throughout this kingdom, whose sole subsistence put into a common stock would leave them in debt two millions of pounds sterling, adding those who are beggars by profession to the bulk of farmers, cottagers, and laborers, with their wives and children who are beggars in effect; I desire those politicians who dislike my overture, and may perhaps be so bold to attempt an answer, that they will first ask the parents of these mortals whether they would not at this day think it a great happiness to have been sold for food at a year old in the manner I prescribe, and thereby have avoided such a perpetual scene of misfortunes as they have since gone through by the oppression of landlords, the impossibility of paying rent without money or trade, the want of common sustenance, with neither house nor clothes to cover them from the inclemencies of the weather, and the most inevitable prospect of entailing the like or greater miseries upon their breed forever.

I profess, in the sincerity of my heart, that I have not the least personal interest in endeavoring to promote this necessary work, having no other motive than the public good of my country, by advancing our trade, providing for infants, relieving the poor, and giving some pleasure to the rich. I have no children by which I can propose to get a single penny; the youngest being nine years old, and my wife past childbearing.

Are there any technical flaws in Swift's logic or economics? What is his voice, his tone, in this proposal? Is his proposal in good taste? Is it funny? Is it effective?

How does this Charles Addams cartoon compare to Swift's proposal in meaning? in tone? in effectiveness?

Drawing by Chas. Addams; Copr. © 1939, 1967 The New Yorker Magazine, Inc.

"How do you know you don't like it if you won't even try any?"

Taste cannot be separated from eating. Describe your own eating habits on a normal day. Can you find any meaning in the pattern they follow? Then describe your eating habits on a holiday or a holy day. Why do they follow a different pattern? How do your eating habits differ from those of your grandparents? What is the significance of these differences?

The following selection from James Frazer's *The Golden Bough* discusses an ancient and yet recurrent symbolic pattern in eating.

The practice of killing a god has . . . been traced amongst peoples who have reached the agricultural stage of society. . . . The spirit of the corn, or of other cultivated plants, is commonly represented either in human or in animal form, and . . . in some places a custom has prevailed of killing annually either the human or the animal representative of the god. One reason for thus killing the corn spirit in the person of his representative . . . was to guard him or her (for the corn-spirit is often feminine) from the enfeeblement of old age by transferring the spirit, while still hale and hearty, to the person of a youthful and vigorous successor. Apart from the desirability of renewing his divine energies, the death of the corn-spirit may have been deemed inevitable under the sickles or the knives of the reapers, and his worshippers may accordingly have felt bound to acquiesce in the sad necessity. But, further, we have found a widespread custom of eating the god sacramentally, either in the shape of the man or animal who represents the god, or in the shape of bread made in human or animal form. The reasons for thus partaking of the body of the god are, from the primitive standpoint, simple enough. The savage commonly believes that by eating the flesh of an animal or man he acquires not only the physical, but even the moral and intellectual qualities which were characteristic of that animal or man; so when the creature is deemed divine, our simple savage naturally expects to absorb a portion of its divinity along with its material substance.

What are the implications of the statement, You are what you eat? How can it be supported on an economic basis? a biological basis? a psychological basis? a religious basis?

Meret Oppenheim, *Object,* 1936

Taste is also related to your sense of touch. Would you be willing to drink out of this cup? How would you feel, in both senses of the word, about sipping warm water out of it?

SKIN

TOUCHING

Your sense of touch is just as unique—and just as relative—as your other senses. Try this experiment. Prepare three bowls of water: one hot, one lukewarm, one cold. Put one hand in the cold water, the other in the hot water. Keep them there for a couple of minutes, then put both hands in the lukewarm water. (What do you anticipate you will feel?)

Rub the back of the chair you are sitting on and then rub your cheek. Describe the difference in how they feel and how your fingertips react to the different textures.

Shut your eyes and have someone hand you something to feel. Can you tell what it is?

Describe the feel against your body of your own clothes, from shoes to shirt. What textures do you consider most sensual? What textures make you feel safe? How do your answers differ from those you think your parents might give?

Describe the sensation of lying naked in a bathtub full of Jello.

On what does this ad base its appeal? Are the textures represented in the photograph appropriate to the copy? How did you respond to this ad? How do you respond to the advertisement on page 82? Write some additional copy for the Pub cologne ad that appeals to the sense of touch. How do you account for the differences between the two ads?

What's the difference between an American bath and a French bath?

What's the difference between an American lover and a French lover?

With Rochas, you get stroked along your arms and legs and under your chin and in the crook of your elbow and kissed on the back of your neck and behind your ear where you love it so, with an expert French softness and sweetness you've never felt in the bath before.

Creations for the Bath and After. Cosmetically formulated. The Foam Bath Cream. The Bath Oil. The Soap. The Body Cream with moisturizer. The Spray Deodorant. The Dusting Powder. The Talcum Powder. All are perfumed by a French man's French woman. Madame Rochas.

Parfums Marcel Rochas

**PUB Cologne.
Gutsy as the guy
who wears it.**

Also in the PUB line, After Shave, After Shave Balm, and Deodorant Spray.

What follows is one of the more famous chapters from the still controversial *The Most Horrific Life of the Great Gargantua,* by François Rabelais. The author, a French monk, lived more than four centuries ago, but we still use the word *Rabelaisian* to describe someone who is full of the physical joy of life.

FRANÇOIS RABELAIS

how Grandgousier learned of Gargantua's marvelous mind through the latter's invention of a rump-wiper

About the end of the fifth year, Grandgousier, returning from the conquest of the Canarians, paid his son Gargantua a visit. He was as happy as a father could be at seeing such a child of his; and hugging and kissing him, he proceeded to ask him little childish questions of various sorts. And he also had his share of drinks with the boy and the nurses, questioning the latter very carefully, among other things, as to whether they had kept their charge neat and clean. To this, Gargantua replied that he himself had given orders on this point, and that in all the country there was not any cleaner a lad than he.

"How is that?" inquired Grandgousier.

"I," replied Gargantua, "after long and careful experiment, have discovered a means of wiping my rump that is the most lordly, the most excellent, and the most expedient ever seen."

"What is that?" Grandgousier wanted to know.

"I'll tell you about it, straight off," said Gargantua. "I wiped myself once with a lady's velvet mask, and I found it did very nicely, for the softness of the silk gave my bottom very great pleasure. Another time, I tried a hat of hers, and it was the same. Another time, I tried a neckerchief, and another time some bright satin earpieces, but the gilt on them, like a lot of dingleberries, took all the skin off my behind—

may St. Anthony's fire burn out the rumpgut of the goldsmith that made them and the lady that wore them!

"I cured myself of this by wiping with a page's bonnet, prettily decked out with a Swiss feather. Then, doing my business behind a bush, I found a March-cat, and I wiped myself with him, but his claws exulcerated my entire perineum. I cured myself of this, the next day, by wiping on my mother's gloves, well perfumed, if not with benzoin, with smell of loin.

"Then, I wiped myself with sage, with fennel, with anet, with sweet marjoram, with roses, with gourd-leaves, with cabbages, with beets, with a vine-branch, with marshmallows, with mullein (which is arse-red), with lettuce, and with spinach-leaves—all of them did my leg a lot of good—with mercury, with parsley, with nettles, with comfrey—but from this I got the bloody flux of Lombardy, which I cured by wiping myself with my codpiece.

"Then, I wiped myself on the sheets, on the bedclothes, on the curtains, on a cushion, on a rug, on a green carpet, on a duster, on a napkin, on a handkerchief, and on a dressing gown. And I found more pleasure in all of them than mangy curs do when you scratch 'em."

"Well," said Grandgousier, "but what rump-wiper did you find the best?"

"I was coming to that," said Gargantua. "You shall know the *tu autem* right away. I wiped myself with hay, with straw, with oakum, with floss, with wool, with paper—but

"He always leaves bait on his balls
Who his dirty arse with paper mauls."

"What!" exclaimed Grandgousier, "my little jackanapes, have you been at the wine-jug, that you're making rhymes already?"

"Yea, verily, Your Majesty," replied Gargantua, "I'm quite a rhymer, I am; I often rhyme till I get rummy. Listen to what our privy has to say to the folks that come there to do their business:

Squirthard,
Farthard,
Turd in us;

>   Your lard
>   Bombard,
>   Discard
>   On us.
>   Clutter us,
>   Splutter us,
>   Guttur us,
>
> But with St. Anthony's fire be charred,
>
>   If a muss
>   You leave with us,
>   You ornery cuss.
>
> Wipe your arse, or you are barred.

"Do you want to hear more?"
"Yes, indeed," replied Grandgousier.
"All right, then," said Gargantua, "here goes:

A ROUNDELAY

> In dunging t'other day, I felt
> The debt I to my arse did owe:
> The odor was not orchard-blow:
> It was the worst that I had smelt.
>   Oh, if fate had but kindly dealt,
> And sent a little one I know,
>   While I was dunging.
>   Down on my knees I'd not have knelt,
> But, quite naïvely, would have stopped her flow,
> While with her fingers, back below,
> She kept me clean where turds did melt,
>   While I was dunging.

"Now, tell me I'm not a poet. But *mer Dé*—Mother of God, or *merde* to you! I didn't make 'em up, at all. Hearing this old grandmother that you see here recite 'em, I stuffed 'em into the bag of my memory."

"But," said Grandgousier, "let's go back to what we were talking about."

"What," said Gargantua, "dunging?"

"No," said Grandgousier, "wiping the rump."

"Look," said Gargantua, "will you bet me a half-keg of Breton wine that I don't make a monkey out of you over this?"

"That I will, right enough," said Grandgousier.

"Well, then," said Gargantua, "there's no need to wipe your rump unless it's dirty; it can't be dirty, unless you've been dunging; so therefore, you have to dung before you wipe your rump."

"My, my," said Grandgousier, "what good sense you have, my little lad! One of these fine days, by God, I'm going to have you made a Doctor of Jovial Science, for you're a good deal wiser than your years. And now, please, go on with your rump-wiping discourse; and by my beard, in place of a half-keg, you shall have sixty barrels, and it's real Breton wine I mean, the kind that grows, not in Brittany, but in the good land of Verron."

"I wiped myself afterward," Gargantua went on, "with a kerchief, with a pillow, with a slipper, with a purse, with a basket—but, oh, what an unpleasant rump-wiper that was—and finally with a hat—and make a note of this, that some hats are shorn, others shaggy, others velvety, others of taffeta, and still others of satin. The best of all are the shaggy ones, for the reason that they make a very neat abstersion of the fecal matter.

"Then, I wiped myself with a hen, with a rooster, with a pullet, with a calf's skin, with a hare, with a pigeon, with a cormorant, with a lawyer's bag, with a chin-band, with a hood, with a decoy-bird. But in conclusion, I will state and maintain that there is no rump-wiper like a good downy goose, providing that you hold its head between your legs. And you may believe me, on my word of honor, that you will feel in your bunghole a miraculous pleasure, from the softness of the down as well as from the moderate heat of the goose, which is readily communicated to the rump-gut and other intestines, until it reaches the region of the heart and brain. And do not think that the beatitude of the heroes and demigods in the Elysian Fields comes from their asphodel or their ambrosia or their nectar, as these old women tell us. In my humble opinion, it comes from the fact that they wipe their arses with the neck of a goose. And such, also, is the opinion of Master John of Scotland.

How do you "feel" about this selection from Rabelais? Did you laugh at any part of it? Did it strike you as dirty? In what ways is Rabelais deliberately kidding you? What is he saying about you as a human being?

Aldous Huxley's *Brave New World* (1939) is a frightening novel about a future dominated by an efficient, soulless technology. One of the devices to keep the citizens happy and tranquil is the "feely," a movie house that provides the sensations of smell and touch along with sight and sound. You are here exposed to your first feely.

The scent organ was playing a delightfully refreshing Herbal Capriccio—rippling arpeggios of thyme and lavender, of rosemary, basil, myrtle, tarragon; a series of daring modulations through the spice keys into ambergris; and a slow return through sandalwood, camphor, cedar and newmown hay (with occasional subtle touches of discord—a whiff of kidney pudding, the faintest suspicion of pig's dung) back to the simple aromatics with which the piece began. The final blast of thyme died away; there was a round of applause; the lights went up. In the synthetic music machine the sound-track roll began to unwind. It was a trio for hyper-violin, super-cello and oboe-surrogate that now filled the air with its agreeable languor. Thirty or forty bars—and then, against this instrumental background, a much more than human voice began to warble; now throaty, now from the head, now hollow as a flute, now charged with yearning harmonics, it effortlessly passed from Gaspard's Forster's low record on the very frontiers of musical tone to a trilled bat-note high above the highest C to which (in 1770, at the Ducal opera of Parma, and to the astonishment of Mozart) Lucrezia Ajugari, alone of all the singers in history, once piercingly gave utterance.

Sunk in their pneumatic stalls, Lenina and the Savage sniffed and listened. It was now the turn also for eyes and skin.

The house lights went down; fiery letters stood out solid and as though self-supported in the darkness. THREE WEEKS IN A HELICOPTER. AN ALL-SUPER-SINGING, SYNTHETIC-TALKING, COLOURED, STEREOSCOPIC FEELY. WITH SYNCHRONIZED SCENT-ORGAN ACCOMPANIMENT.

"Take hold of those metal knobs on the arms of your chair," whispered Lenina. "Otherwise you won't get any of the feely effects."

The Savage did as he was told.

Those fiery letters, meanwhile, had disappeared; there were ten seconds of complete darkness; then suddenly, dazzling and incomparably more solid-looking than they would have seemed in actual flesh and blood, far more real than reality, there stood the stereoscopic images, locked in one another's arms, of a gigantic negro and a golden-haired young brachycephalic Beta-Plus female.

The Savage started. That sensation on his lips! He lifted a hand to his mouth; the titillation ceased; let his hand fall back on the metal knob; it began again. The scent organ, meanwhile, breathed pure musk. Expiringly, a sound-track super-dove cooed "Oo-ooh"; and vibrating only thirty-two times a second, a deeper than African bass made answer: "Aa-aah." "Ooh-ah! Ooh-ah!" the stereoscopic lips came together again, and once more the facial erogenous zones of the six thousand spectators in the Alhambra tingled with almost intolerable galvanic pleasure. "Ooh . . ."

The plot of the film was extremely simple. A few minutes after the first Oohs and Aahs (a duet having been sung and a little love made on that famous bearskin, every hair of which—the Assistant Predestinator was perfectly right—could be separately and distinctly felt), the negro had a helicopter accident, fell on his head. Thump! what a twinge through the forehead! A chorus of *ow's* and *aie's* went up from the audience.

The concussion knocked all the negro's conditioning into a cocked hat. He developed for the Beta blonde an exclusive and maniacal passion. She protested. He persisted. There were struggles, pursuits, an assault on a rival, finally a sensational kidnapping. The Beta blonde was ravished away into the sky and kept there, hovering, for three weeks in a wildly anti-social *tête-à-tête* with the black madman. Finally, after a whole series of adventures and much aerial acrobacy three handsome young Alphas succeeded in rescuing her. The negro was packed off to an Adult Re-conditioning Centre and the film ended happily and decorously, with the Beta blonde becoming the mistress of all her three rescuers. They interrupted themselves for a moment to sing a synthetic quartet, with full super-orchestral accompaniment and gardenias on the scent organ. Then the bearskin made a final appearance and, amid a blare of sexophones, the last stereoscopic kiss faded into darkness, the last electric titillation died on the lips like a dying moth that quivers, quivers, ever more feebly, ever more faintly, and at last is quiet, quite still.

Feelies may not be so far in the future. Here is an account by Gene Youngblood of an evening at Cerebrum in New York City.

An evening at Cerebrum follows from Form to Structure to Place. You get out of the cab in a sleazy slum neighborhood and ring a buzzer. The door opens automatically and closes behind you, locking. You find yourself in a small black cubicle about four feet square. A hidden speaker asks your name, and after a few minutes one of the walls opens. You are led to an anteroom where you are asked to remove your shoes. A boy and a girl, obviously nude beneath diaphanous flowing gowns, lead you down a narrow corridor to a large white rectangular space.

This is the Form level: from a dark closet to a larger room, down a narrow hallway to an open space. Next comes the Structural experience: the floor actually is a raised, carpeted platform sectioned into geometrical islands inset with electronic control panels. These islands are approximately three feet above the real floor, and you are forced to pay close attention to where you step.

The guides lead you to a particular island (there are about ten of them, each accommodating four persons). You are instructed to put on a gown, and are invited to remove beneath it as much of your clothing as you desire. Glancing around, it becomes obvious that nearly everyone is nude beneath his gown, so you strip. The sensation is delicious, especially for men, who are not accustomed to being naked beneath a long silk gown. One is immediately self-conscious, but not embarrassed; one simply becomes fascinated with the feel of one's own body in its silken envelope.

89

The first half-hour of the three-hour "session" is spent adjusting to the environment, staring at bodies as they pass in silhouette, wondering what to do with yourself, and finally venturing off your island to walk among the other guests, feeling the air on your skin: this is the Place experience. A noticeably eclectic selection of music (from polkas to swing-era ballads, ragas, rock, symphonies) seems to come from nowhere in particular, and a cool passive light show plays ambiently across the walls and ceiling. Eventually, the guides pass around tambourines, gongs, triangles, and flutes, encouraging everyone to play along with the Muzak.

During this time I began to notice what for me was the most interesting aspect of the experience. People began to act out their fantasies, get into their own realities, perform anonymous little psychodramas. One refined-looking, silver-haired, middle-aged gentleman knelt and gazed lovingly at his matronly wife as she danced before him like Scheherazade, palms pressed together over her head, hips swaying in silhouette. It was, perhaps, a fantasy they had never realized in the privacy of their own bedroom.

Elsewhere, a beautiful young girl who wouldn't remove her panties was "raped" by her husband, who peeled them off beneath her gown as his friend held her arms. She squealed in mock anger and false modesty, but an hour later could be seen twirling about the room like a ballerina, her gown flying far above her shapely hips.

Thus, for some, Cerebrum becomes an excuse to do and say things they might not otherwise attempt. The two examples I've cited occurred rather anonymously, and probably went unnoticed by most of the guests. The nature of Cerebrum is such that it would be difficult to create an unpleasant scene.

I found the unisex effect of the gowns quite stimulating. At one point male guides came around with mint-flavored menthol ice that they smeared on our lips with their fingertips. "What does it taste like?" they inquired softly, as though not expecting an answer. This intimate contact with a complete stranger in a relatively "public" setting was a challenging experience, particularly for men, who are not as disposed as women to physical intimacies in public. The young men were followed by girls who daubed our foreheads with a similar skin-tingling substance. These sensual encounters had an ethereal, gentle, transcendental effect. One appreciates the delicacy and poise necessary to accomplish them without embarrassment.

Then the guides began collecting guests together in groups of six. They instructed us to form circles and clasp hands in the center, like spokes of a wheel. They squirted hand cream into the tangle of fingers as we closed our eyes and felt our hands melt into others, rubbing and squeezing anonymous flesh. We then lay on our backs, feet touching in the center of the circle, and wiggled our toes against one another as the guide squirted them with the slippery cream. The effect was extraordinarily erotic.

At one point a scented fog was released from beneath the platforms, filling the space with an eerie haze through which one could see ghostly figures moving and dancing. Needles of light from a mirror-globe cut through the fog like electrons in a cloud chamber; it was beautiful. Next a huge parachute was spread out; half of the guests lay on the floor beneath the parachute as the other half stood around its circumference, raising and lowering it to form a suction that lifted gowns, and exposed bodies, but no one cared; we just closed our eyes and enjoyed the sensation, rather like dreaming that one's bed is flying away.

All the senses were stimulated in various subtle ways: the touch and taste of the camphor ice on the lips, the slippery intermingling of hands and feet, the scent of the vapors, the kinetic stimulation of the light show and parachute, the visual alterations in the general level of luminosity that also affected one's perception of forms and distances. Bits of melon and fruit were passed around, as well as a communal mug of Coke. There was no sensation-numbing alcohol.

A kind of hypnotic centering took place when a giant balloon, anchored to an outlet in the center of the floor, began inflating slowly with a loud steady hiss. The balloon was illuminated from a spotlight on the floor beneath it and glowed eerily as the houselights were dimmed. Everyone sat in the lotus position and gazed as the luminescent sphere loomed above our heads. Then it was deflated just as slowly. A simple but effective experience.

Write a scene for a feely of your own, giving the directions for sight, sound, smell, taste, and touch.

A term that describes the sense-expanding experiences of a feely is *synaesthesia*. It means perceiving something with several senses at once, or perceiving something through the sense not normally used—for instance, hearing a color or smelling a sound. This sentence from Richard Hughes's *A Moment of Time* is an example.

He gradually melted into the Infinite—already his bodily senses were left behind, or at any rate all mixed up: so that the little green tables of the café only penetrated to him as a tinkling arpeggio to the blaring bass of the sunlight, the booming sky outside: while the rattle of a passing bullock-cart was translated into a series of vivid flashes of colour, and the discomfort of the rickety chair he sat on smelt bitter in his nostrils. . . .

93

Write a synaesthetic paragraph that suggests you are depressed. Write one that suggests you are exhilarated.

you

your sense of

YOU

YOUR SENSE OF

You have been asked to experiment with what and how you see, hear, smell, taste, touch. Most of what you did concentrated on one of these five senses, but at least indirectly almost every exercise involved all your senses, all of you. Now you are asked to investigate yourself, you as a whole: first by looking inward, then by seeing yourself in relation to your family and society, and finally by viewing yourself in relation to the universe. These three categories overlap with each other and with what you have already done, but since all of us are more than just the sum of our parts, this overlapping should enable you to see yourself more fully. Though many of your perceptions about yourself will be similar to what others have seen and described about themselves, much of what you perceive will also be unique.

YOU AND YOUR

SELF

This inkblot was made completely at random by spilling some ink on absorbent paper.

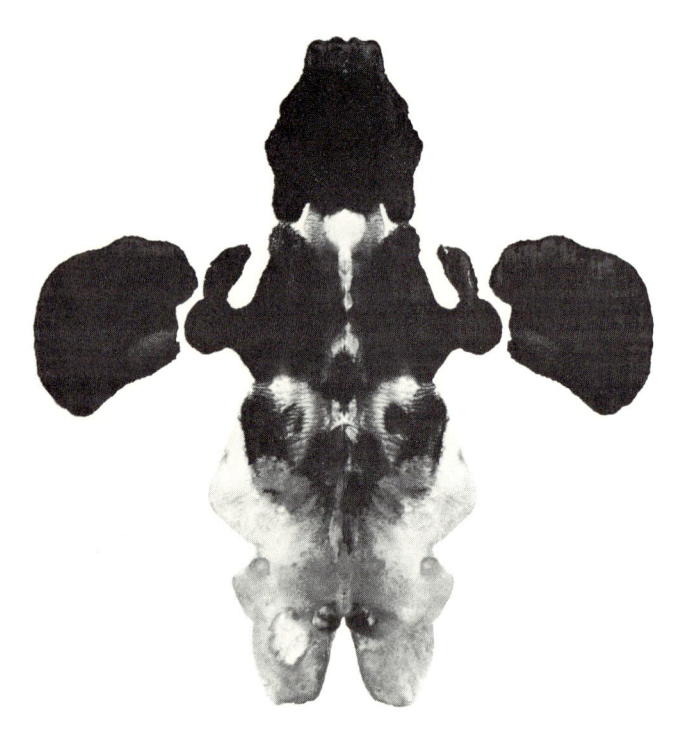

100

What picture do you see in this inkblot? What emotions do you feel when you look at it? Are there any events in your past life of which it reminds you? Write a sentence that evokes emotions similar to those you feel when you look at it.

Allegedly, one way of getting to see more deeply into yourself is through the use of drugs. Arlene Sklar-Weinstein, the painter of this picture, has experimented with drugs and she is here deliberately trying to expand both her own and the viewer's consciousness.

Arlene Sklar-Weinstein, *Between Heaven and Hell No. II,* 1967

What do you see in this painting? What emotions do you feel when you look at it? Does the title strike you as appropriate?

A graduate student in anthropology at UCLA, Carlos Castañeda, wrote this account of his first experience with peyote. Don Juan, an elderly Indian from Mexico, here introduces his pupil to "nonordinary reality."

from

THE TEACHINGS OF DON JUAN

CARLOS CASTAÑEDA

Monday, August 7, 1961

I arrived at don Juan's house in Arizona about seven o'clock on Friday night. Five other Indians were sitting with him on the porch of his house. I greeted him and sat waiting for them to say something. After a formal silence one of the men got up, walked over to me, and said, "Buenas noches." I stood up and answered, "Buenas noches." Then all the other men got up and came to me and we all mumbled "buenas noches" and shook hands either by barely touching one another's fingertips or by holding the hand for an instant and then dropping it quite abruptly.

We all sat down again. They seemed to be rather shy—at a loss for words, although they all spoke Spanish.

It must have been about half past seven when suddenly they all got up and walked toward the back of the house. Nobody had said a word for a long time. Don Juan signaled me to follow and we all got inside an old pickup truck parked there. I sat in the back with don Juan and two younger men. There were no cushions or benches and the metal floor was painfully hard, especially when we left the highway and got onto a dirt road. Don Juan whispered that we were going to the house of one of his friends who had seven mescalitos for me.

I asked him, "Don't you have any of them yourself, don Juan?"

"I do, but I couldn't offer them to you. You see, someone else has to do this."

"Can you tell me why?"

"Perhaps you are not agreeable to 'him' and 'he' won't like you, and then you will never be able to know 'him' with affection, as one should; and our friendship will be broken."

"Why wouldn't he like me? I have never done anything to him."

"You don't have to *do* anything to be liked or disliked. He either takes you, or throws you away."

"But, if he doesn't take me, isn't there anything I can do to make him like me?"

The other two men seemed to have overheard my question and laughed.

"No! I can't think of anything one can do," don Juan said.

He turned half away from me and I could not talk to him anymore.

We must have driven for at least an hour before we stopped in front of a small house. It was quite dark, and after the driver had turned off the headlights I could make out only the vague contour of the building.

A young woman, a Mexican, judging by her speech inflection, was yelling at a dog to make him stop barking. We got out of the truck and walked into the house. The men mumbled "Buenas noches" as they went by her. She answered back and went on yelling at the dog.

The room was large and was stacked up with a multitude of objects. A dim light from a very small electric bulb rendered the scene quite gloomy. There were quite a few chairs with broken legs and sagging seats leaning against the walls. Three of the men sat down on a couch, which was the largest single piece of furniture in the room. It was very old and had sagged down all the way to the floor; in the dim light it seemed to be red and dirty. The rest of us sat in chairs. We sat in silence for a long time.

One of the men suddenly got up and went into another room. He was perhaps in his fifties, dark, tall, and husky. He came back a moment later with a coffee jar. He opened the lid and handed the jar to me; inside there were seven odd-looking items. They varied in size and consistency. Some of them were almost round, others were elongated. They felt to the touch like the pulp of walnuts, or the surface of cork. Their brownish color made them look like hard, dry nutshells. I handled them, rubbing their surfaces for quite some time.

"This is to be chewed [*esto se masca*]," don Juan said in a whisper.

I had not realized that he had sat next to me until he spoke. I looked at the other men, but no one was looking at me; they were talking among themselves in very low voices. This was a moment of acute indecision and fear. I felt almost unable to control myself.

"I have to go to the bathroom," I said to him. "I'll go outside and take a walk."

He handed me the coffee jar and I put the peyote buttons in it. I was leaving the room when the man who had given me the jar stood up, came to me, and said he had a toilet bowl in the other room.

The toilet was almost against the door. Next to it, nearly touching the toilet, was a large bed which occupied more than half of the room. The woman was sleeping there. I stood motionless at the door for a while, then I came back to the room where the other men were.

The man who owned the house spoke to me in English: "Don Juan says you're from South America. Is there any mescal there?" I told him that I had never even heard of it.

They seemed to be interested in South America and we talked about the Indians for a while. Then one of the men asked me why I wanted to eat peyote. I told him that I wanted to know what it was like. They all laughed shyly.

Don Juan urged me softly, "Chew it, chew it [*Masca, masca*]."

My hands were wet and my stomach contracted. The jar with the peyote buttons was on the floor by the chair. I bent over, took one at random, and put it in my mouth. It had a stale taste. I bit it in two and started to chew one of the pieces. I felt a strong, pungent bitterness; in a moment my whole mouth was numb. The bitterness increased as I kept on chewing, forcing an incredible flow of saliva. My gums and the inside of my mouth felt as if I had eaten salty, dry meat or fish, which seems to force one to chew more. After a while I chewed the other piece and my mouth was so numb I couldn't feel the bitterness anymore. The peyote button was a bunch of shreds, like the fibrous part of an orange or like sugarcane, and I didn't know whether to swallow it or spit it out. At that moment the owner of the house got up and invited everybody to go out to the porch.

We went out and sat in the darkness. It was quite comfortable outside, and the host brought out a bottle of tequila.

The men were seated in a row with their backs to the wall. I was at the extreme right of the line. Don Juan, who was next to me, placed the jar with the peyote buttons between my legs. Then he handed me the bottle, which was passed down the line, and told me to take some of the tequila to wash away the bitterness.

I spat out the shreds of the first button and took a sip. He told me not to swallow it, but to just rinse out my mouth with it to stop the saliva. It did not help much with the saliva, but it certainly helped to wash away some of the bitterness.

Don Juan gave me a piece of dried apricot, or perhaps it was a dried fig—I couldn't see it in the dark, nor could I taste it—and told me to chew it thoroughly and slowly, without rushing. I had difficulty swallowing it; it felt as if it would not go down.

After a short pause the bottle went around again. Don Juan handed me a piece of crispy dried meat. I told him I did not feel like eating.

"This is not eating," he said firmly.

The pattern was repeated six times. I remember having chewed six peyote buttons when the conversation became very lively; although I could not distinguish what language was spoken, the topic of the conversation, in which everybody participated, was very interesting, and I attempted to listen carefully so that I could take part. But when I tried to speak I realized I couldn't; the words shifted aimlessly about in my mind.

I sat with my back propped against the wall and listened to what the men were saying. They were talking in Italian, and repeated over and over one phrase about the stupidity of sharks. I thought it was a logical, coherent topic. I had told don Juan earlier that the Colorado River in Arizona was called by the early Spaniards "el rio de los tizones [the river of charred wood]"; and someone misspelled or misread "tizones," and the river was called "el rio de los tiburones [the river of the sharks]." I was sure they were discussing that story, yet it never occurred to me to think that none of them could speak Italian.

I had a very strong desire to throw up, but I don't recall the actual act. I asked if somebody would get me some water. I was experiencing an unbearable thirst.

Don Juan brought me a large saucepan. He placed it on the ground next to the wall. He also brought a little cup or can. He dipped it into the pan and handed it to me, and said I could not drink but should just freshen my mouth with it.

The water looked strangely shiny, glossy, like a thick varnish. I wanted to ask don Juan about it and laboriously I tried to voice my thoughts in English, but then I realized he did not speak English. I experienced a very confusing moment, and became aware of the fact that although there was a clear thought in my mind, I could not speak. I wanted to comment on the strange quality of the water, but what followed next was not speech; it was the feeling of my unvoiced thoughts coming out of my mouth in a sort of liquid form. It was an effortless sensation of vomiting without the contractions of the diaphragm. It was a pleasant flow of liquid words.

I drank. And the feeling that I was vomiting disappeared. By that time all noises had vanished and I found I had difficulty focusing my eyes. I looked for don Juan and as I turned my head I noticed that my field of vision had diminished to a circular area in front of my eyes. This feeling was neither frightening nor discomforting, but, quite to the contrary, it was a novelty; I could literally sweep the ground by focusing on one spot and then moving my head slowly in any direction. When I had first come out to the porch I had noticed it was all dark except for the distant glare of the city lights. Yet within the circular area of my vision everything was clear. I forgot about my concern with don Juan and the other men, and gave myself entirely to exploring the ground with my pinpoint vision.

I saw the juncture of the porch floor and the wall. I turned my head slowly to the right, following the wall, and saw don Juan sitting against it. I shifted my head to the left in order to focus on the water. I found the bottom of the pan; I raised my head slightly and saw a medium-size black dog approaching. I saw him coming toward the water. The dog began to drink. I raised my hand to push him away from my water; I focused my pinpoint vision on the dog to carry on the movement, and suddenly I saw him become transparent. The water was a shiny, viscous liquid. I saw it going down the dog's throat into his body. I saw it flowing evenly through his entire length and then shooting out through each one of the hairs. I saw the iridescent fluid traveling along the length of each individual hair and then projecting out of the hairs to form a long, white, silky mane.

At that moment I had the sensation of intense convulsions, and in a matter of instants a tunnel formed around me, very low and narrow, hard and strangely cold. It felt to the touch like a wall of solid tinfoil. I found I was sitting on the tunnel floor. I tried to stand up, but hit my head on the metal roof, and the tunnel compressed itself until it was suffocating me. I remember having to crawl toward a sort of round point where the tunnel ended; when I finally arrived, if I did, I had forgotten all about the dog, don Juan, and myself. I was exhausted. My clothes were soaked in a cold, sticky liquid. I rolled back and forth trying to find a position in which to rest, a position where my heart would not pound so hard. In one of those shifts I saw the dog again.

Every memory came back to me at once, and suddenly all was clear in my mind. I turned around to look for don Juan, but I could not distinguish anything or anyone. All I was capable of seeing was the dog becoming iridescent; an intense light radiated from his body. I saw again the water flowing through him, kindling him like a bonfire. I got to the water, sank my face in the pan, and drank with him. My hands were in front of me on the ground and, as I drank, I saw the fluid running through my veins setting up hues of red and yellow and green. I drank more and more. I drank until I was all afire; I was all aglow. I drank until the fluid went out of my body through each pore, and projected out like fibers of silk, and I too acquired a long, lustrous, iridescent mane. I looked at the dog and his mane was like mine. A supreme happiness filled my whole body, and we ran together toward a sort of yellow warmth that came from some indefinite place. And there we played. We played and wrestled until I knew his wishes and he knew mine. We took turns manipulating each other in the fashion of a puppet show. I could make him move his legs by twisting my toes, and every time he nodded his head I felt an irresistible impulse to jump. But his most impish act was to make me scratch my head with my foot while I sat; he did it by flapping his ears from side to side. This action was to me utterly, unbearably funny. Such a touch of grace and irony; such mastery, I thought. The euphoria that possessed me was indescribable. I laughed until it was almost impossible to breathe.

I had the clear sensation of not being able to open my eyes; I was looking through a tank of water. It was a long and very painful state filled with the anxiety of not being able to wake up and yet being awake. Then slowly the world became clear and in focus. My field of vision became again very round and ample, and with it came an ordinary conscious act, which was to turn around and look for that marvelous being. At this point I encountered the most difficult transition. The passage from my normal state had taken place almost without my realizing it: I was aware; my thoughts and feelings were a corollary of that awareness; and the passing was smooth and clear. But this second change, the awakening to serious, sober consciousness, was genuinely shocking.

I had forgotten I was a man! The sadness of such an irreconcilable situation was so intense that I wept.

Saturday, August 5, 1961

Later that morning, after breakfast, the owner of the house, don Juan, and I drove back to don Juan's place. I was very tired, but I couldn't go to sleep in the truck. Only after the man had left did I fall asleep on the porch of don Juan's house.

When I woke up it was dark; don Juan had covered me up with a blanket. I looked for him, but he was not in the house. He came later with a pot of fried beans and a stack of tortillas. I was extremely hungry.

After we had finished eating and were resting he asked me to tell him all that had happened to me the night before. I related my experience in great detail and as accurately as possible.

When I finished he nodded his head and said, "I think you are fine. It is difficult for me to explain now how and why. But I think it went all right for you. You see, sometimes he is playful, like a child; at other times he is terrible, fearsome. He either frolics, or he is dead serious. It is impossible to know beforehand what he will be like with another person. Yet, when one knows him well—sometimes. You played with him tonight. You are the only person I know who has had such an encounter."

"In what way does my experience differ from that of others?"

"You're not an Indian; therefore it is hard for me to figure out what is what. Yet he either takes people or rejects them, regardless of whether they are Indians or not. That I know. I have seen numbers of them. I also know that he frolics, he makes some people laugh, but never have I seen him play with anyone."

"Can you tell me now, don Juan, how does peyote protect . . ."

He did not let me finish. Vigorously he touched me on the shoulder.

"Don't you ever name him that way. You haven't seen enough of him yet to know him."

"How does Mescalito protect people?"

"He advises. He answers whatever questions you ask."

"Then Mescalito is real? I mean he is something you can see?"

He seemed to be baffled by my question. He looked at me with a sort of blank expression.

"What I meant to say, is that Mescalito . . ."

"I heard what you said. Didn't you see him last night?"

I wanted to say that I saw only a dog, but I noticed his bewildered look.

"Then you think what I saw last night was him?"

He looked at me with contempt. He chuckled, shook his head as though he couldn't believe it, and in a very belligerent tone he added, "A poco crees que era tu—mamá [Don't tell me you believe it was your—mama]?" He paused before saying "mamá" because what he meant to say was "tu chingada madre," an idiom used as a disrespectful allusion to the other party's mother. The word "mamá" was so incongruous that we both laughed for a long time.

Then I realized he had fallen asleep and had not answered my question.

Sunday, August 6, 1961

I drove don Juan to the house where I had taken peyote. On the way he told me that the name of the man who had "offered me to Mescalito" was John. When we got to the house we found John sitting on his porch with two young men. All of them were extremely jovial. They laughed and talked with great ease. The three of them spoke English perfectly. I told John that I had come to thank him for having helped me.

I wanted to get their views on my behavior during the hallucinogenic experience, and told them I had been trying to think of what I had done that night and that I couldn't remember. They laughed and were reluctant to talk about it. They seemed to be holding back on account of don Juan. They all glanced at him as though waiting for an affirmative cue to go on. Don Juan must have cued them, although I did not notice anything, because suddenly John began to tell me what I had done that night.

He said he knew I had been "taken" when he heard me puking. He estimated that I must have puked thirty times. Don Juan corrected him and said it was only ten times.

John continued: "Then we all moved next to you. You were stiff, and were having convulsions. For a very long time, while lying on your back, you moved your mouth as though talking. Then you began to bump your head on the floor, and don Juan put an old hat on your head and you stopped it. You shivered and whined for hours, lying on the floor. I think everybody fell asleep then; but I heard you puffing and groaning in my sleep. Then I heard you scream and I woke up. I saw you leaping up in the air, screaming. You made a dash for the water, knocked the pan over, and began to swim in the puddle.

"Don Juan brought you more water. You sat quietly in front of the pan. Then you jumped up and took off all your clothes. You were kneeling in front of the water, drinking in big gulps. Then you just sat there and stared into space. We thought you were going to be there forever. Nearly everybody was asleep, including don Juan, when suddenly you jumped up again, howling, and took after the dog. The dog got scared and howled too, and ran to the back of the house. Then everybody woke up.

"We all got up. You came back from the other side still chasing the dog. The dog was running ahead of you barking and howling. I think you must have gone twenty times around the house, running in circles, barking like a dog. I was afraid people were going to be curious. There are no neighbors close, but your howling was so loud it could have been heard for miles."

One of the young men added, "You caught up with the dog and brought it to the porch in your arms."

John continued: "Then you began to play with the dog. You wrestled with him, and the dog and you bit each other and played. That, I thought, was funny. My dog does not play usually. But this time you and the dog were rolling on each other."

"Then you ran to the water and the dog drank with you," the young man said. "You ran five or six times to the water with the dog."

"How long did this go on?" I asked.

"Hours," John said. "At one time we lost sight of you two. I think you must have run to the back. We just heard you barking and groaning. You sounded so much like a dog that we couldn't tell you two apart."

"Maybe it was just the dog alone," I said.

They laughed, and John said, "You were barking there, boy!"

"What happened next?"

The three men looked at one another and seemed to have a hard time deciding what happened next. Finally the young man who had not yet said anything spoke up.

"He choked," he said, looking at John.

"Yes, you certainly choked. You began to cry very strangely, and then you fell to the floor. We thought you were biting your tongue; don Juan opened your jaws and poured water on your face. Then you started shivering and having convulsions all over again. Then you stayed motionless for a long time. Don Juan said it was all over. By then it was morning, so we covered you with a blanket and left you to sleep on the porch."

He stopped there and looked at the other men who were obviously trying not to laugh. He turned to don Juan and asked him something. Don Juan smiled and answered the question. John turned to me and said, "We left you here on the porch because we were afraid you were going to piss all over the rooms."

They all laughed very loudly.

"What was the matter with me?" I asked. "Did I . . ."

"Did you?" John sort of mimicked me. "We were not going to mention it, but don Juan says it is all right. You pissed all over my dog!"

"What did I do?"

"You don't think the dog was running because he was afraid of you, do you? The dog was running because you were pissing on him."

There was general laughter at this point. I tried to question one of the young men, but they were all laughing and he didn't hear me.

John went on: "My dog got even though; he pissed on you too!"

This statement was apparently utterly funny because they all roared with laughter, including don Juan. When they had quieted down, I asked in all earnestness, "Is it really true? This really happened?"

Still laughing, John replied: "I swear my dog really pissed on you."

What do you think Castañeda learned about himself from this trip? Did the descriptions of pissing and vomiting have any effect on how you viewed his experience? What did you learn about yourself from reading his account? Which is more real to you: what he "saw" or what the Indians observed? Describe your own sense of "nonordinary reality."

Psychoanalysis is another method of self-exploration. One of the major tools of psychoanalysis, the interpretation of dreams, can help you to see things in yourself that you are not aware of when you are awake and functioning as your own censor.

Try to analyze a dream you remember, using some of the hints given by Sigmund Freud in this letter on dream interpretation. This, of course, is not an invitation for you to become your own psychoanalyst, but a heightened awareness of your unconscious self can lead you to a heightened awareness of your conscious self.

To Oskar Pfister, March 18, 1909

(*A comment on a dream of one of Pfister's patients called Dietrich.*)

"The first dream runs: The girl jumped into the lake. I wanted to plunge in after her, but she held herself upright above the water and emerged quite dry.

"Dreams with this content are, as doubtless you have long known, *birth dreams*. The stork fetches children out of water. The piece of biological reality behind this is familiar to us all, hence the motive in giving this 'explanation.' To come out of water, therefore, is the same as being born, with the corresponding obverse to enter water—to give birth. (Here we see a result of the insoluble connection between death and sexuality. When a poor woman wishes to escape from life she does so only by way of symbolically carrying out a sexual phantasy. She throws herself into water, i.e. she gives birth; or she leaps from a height, i.e. she drops; or she poisons herself, i.e. she becomes pregnant.)

"Because of the ease of 'representation by its opposite' the symbolisms of giving birth and being born are often exchanged. In the well-known exposure myths of Sargon, Moses, Romulus, etc., the exposure in a basket or in water signifies the same as the subsequent rescuing out of the water. Both refer to birth. . . .

"In Dietrich's dream it runs that he wants to spring after the maiden who had thrown herself into the water, but she holds herself up alone and comes out of the water alone. Since this maiden is the Madonna, this trait means that he wants to help her to bear a child, but the Madonna bears the child as a virgin without any contribution from a man. Hence the allusion that follows: she is quite dry, the Immaculate Conception. The hesitation at the end of the dream, the doubt whether it is she, can only correspond to the dreamer's doubt about the Catholic doctrine, which he would like to accept, about the possibility of such an Immaculate Conception and Virgin Birth.

"Dietrich's statement that the dream was nothing new, that he had dreamed things of that kind before, agrees well with our interpretations. For it often happens that one sees a landscape in a dream and has the feeling: I have been here before. This landscape is then always the mother's genital organ, of which one can maintain more assuredly than of anywhere else that one has once been there; otherwise one would not be in the world. 'I have dreamed this dream before' has the same significance."

According to Freud, we suppress many thoughts that for one reason or another are unacceptable to our conscious minds. Partly as a result of his discoveries, today most of us are less inhibited and more open about sex. Yet censorship of yourself by yourself and of yourself by others remains a fact of life. So, read this Mother Goose rhyme aloud.

> **A dillar, a dollar,**
> **A ten-o'clock scholar,**
> **What makes you ——— so soon?**
> **You used to ——— at ten o'clock,**
> **And now you ——— at noon.**

Did you fill in the blanks with the words you remembered from childhood or did you supply "censorable" words? Do you now see this verse as "dirty"? What does your reaction to this "censorship" tell you about yourself?

A third way of getting to see more deeply into yourself—and the method this book is devoted to—is to talk and write about yourself. Though all art is ultimately autobiographical, overt autobiography can be especially revealing to someone searching for his own identity. What does Antonio Frasconi say about himself in this self-portrait? In "Fern Hill" Dylan Thomas nostalgically recalls and re-creates his growing up on a farm in Wales.

FERN HILL—DYLAN THOMAS

Now as I was young and easy under the apple boughs
About the lilting house and happy as the grass was green,
    The night above the dingle starry,
        Time let me hail and climb
    Golden in the heydays of his eyes,
And honored among wagons I was prince of the apple towns
And once below a time I lordly had the trees and leaves
        Trail with daisies and barley
    Down the rivers of the windfall light.

And as I was green and carefree, famous among the barns
About the happy yard and singing as the farm was home,
    In the sun that is young once only,
        Time let me play and be
    Golden in the mercy of his means,
And green and golden I was huntsman and herdsman, the calves
Sang to my horn, the foxes on the hills barked clear and cold,
        And the sabbath rang slowly
    In the pebbles of the holy streams.

All the sun long it was running, it was lovely, the hay
Fields high as the house, the tunes from the chimneys, it was air
        And playing, lovely and watery
            And fire green as grass.
        And nightly under the simple stars
As I rode to sleep the owls were bearing the farm away,
All the moon long I heard, blessed among stables, the night-jars
        Flying with the ricks, and the horses
            Flashing into the dark.

And then to awake, and the farm, like a wanderer white
With the dew, come back, the cock on his shoulder: it was all
      Shining, it was Adam and maiden,
          The sky gathered again
      And the sun grew round that very day.
So it must have been after the birth of the simple light
In the first, spinning place, the spellbound horses walking warm
      Out of the whinnying green stable
          On to the fields of praise.

And honored among foxes and pheasants by the gay house
Under the new made clouds and happy as the heart was long,
      In the sun born over and over,
          I ran my heedless ways,
      My wishes raced through the house high hay
And nothing I cared, at my sky blue trades, that time allows
In all his tuneful turning so few and such morning songs
      Before the children green and golden
          Follow him out of grace,

Nothing I cared, in the lamb white days, that time would take me
Up to the swallow thronged loft by the shadow of my hand,
      In the moon that is always rising,
          Nor that riding to sleep
      I should hear him fly with the high fields
And wake to the farm forever fled from the childless land.
Oh as I was young and easy in the mercy of his means,
      Time held me green and dying
      Though I sang in my chains like the sea.

What do you find that is happy in this poem? What, if anything, that is sad? How do you feel about the child you used to be? Write a poem about a significant scene or incident from your own childhood.

Other childhood memories may not be as pleasant as those recounted by Dylan Thomas. Oscar Lewis, an anthropologist, tape recorded a series of interviews with a poor boy growing up in Mexico City. Though Lewis did some editing to eliminate repetitions, you can still hear, see, and maybe understand this very alive adolescent.

ROBERTO

OSCAR LEWIS

I started stealing things from my own house when I was small. I saw something I liked and swiped it without asking anybody's permission. Just like that. I began by stealing an egg. It wasn't that I was starving, see? because my mother fed us well. It was just for the fun of filching it, and sharing it with my friends in the courtyard, and feeling important.

I stole twenty *centavos* from my mother when I was just a little fellow, five or six, more or less. Twenty *centavos* at that time was like ten *pesos* today. My father gave us five *centavos* every day, but all my life I've always wanted more, and when I saw a twenty *centavo* piece on the cupboard, well, there wasn't anybody around and I thought I might as well take it. I bought some candy and it was my bad luck that they gave me a lot of change, all single *centavos*.

So I had a lot of money in my pocket, right? When I got home in the evening, they began to ask about the missing coin. I thought, "*Caramba!* as soon as they get the idea of fishing me they'll find the money and I'll get a licking I won't forget for ten years. I'd better go to the toilet."

The toilet, which was right inside the house, had only a half-door, so when I threw the *centavos* into the toilet bowl it made a hell of a big noise and they knew what I did. Even though I flushed the coins away forever, they knew. Now, wasn't that something? Like I said, I was a bad egg from the time I was born. So I got a real thrashing that day. My mother, my father, and my mother's mother, may she rest in peace, gave me my punishment so I wouldn't do it again.

My mother took good care of us. She was loving to me, but she loved Manuel the most. She rarely hit me, and I know she loved me a lot because she always took me with her wherever she went, me more than the others. She used to say, "Roberto, let's go and get the cake trimmings."

"All right, *mamá*, sure, let's go."

My mother and father usually got along well, except for one terrible quarrel which left a lasting impression on me. My father was hollering at my mother, may she rest in peace, and, well, he was pretty mad. My mother's mother and my aunt Guadalupe kept him from hitting her. His key ring fell on the floor during the fight and I grabbed it and ran out. It had a razor blade on it and since my father was very quick-tempered, I thought he might want to use it on my mother.

My aunt, my granny Pachita, and the servant,

Sofía, all jumped in and held him off. When I came back to the house, the fight was over. My father took me with him to the Villa where he prayed to the Virgin. I saw him cry and I cried with him. Then he quieted down and bought me a *taco*.

Every year the Three Kings came on the sixth of January and left us toys in the flowerpot stand where my mother kept her favorite plants. But one sixth of January the Three Kings were unable to come to our poor house, and I felt I was the unluckiest child in the world. We children got up early, like all children do on that day, to look for our toys. We went looking in the flowerpot stand; then we looked in the brazier to see if the Kings left something for us in the ashes and charcoal. Unfortunately they didn't, so all that was left for us to do was to go out to the courtyard and watch our friends play with their toys. When they asked, "What did the Kings bring you?" Manuel and I said, "They didn't bring us anything."

It was the last sixth of January my mother spent with us before she died. After that I cried for years.

We were living in one room on Tenochtitlán Street. My father and mother slept in one bed, Manuel, Consuelo and I slept in the other. When Marta was older she slept with us too. We slept crosswise, first Manuel, then Consuelo, then Marta, then me, always in that order.

I had a real problem. I always wet the bed, right up to the age of nine or ten. They called me the champion bed-wetter in the house. I wasn't the only bed-wetter, because Manuel and Consuelo also did it sometimes. On account of this habit of mine, my father and mother gave me several whalings and threatened to bathe me in cold water in the morning. Once my mother actually did. Of course, I'm not blaming her; she did it to break me of the habit, but it stayed with me for a long time.

I was about six when my mother died in my father's arms early one morning. Her death was a shock and a torment to me all my life, because I feel I was to blame. The day before she died, we all had gone to the Basilica with my aunt and my uncles, Alfredo and José. We were very happy. My blessed mother was always celebrating our Saint's Day and we ate pork and stuff like that, which you know are not good for you. They bring on attacks, and my mother came down with an attack on account of me.

Actually, what happened was that later that day she asked me to bring the bird cages down from the roof. My mother was very fond of birds, understand? She kept the walls covered with bird cages, just because she loved the little creatures. So I climbed on the roof and some dirt dropped over to our neighbor's side and the woman there began to throw water on me.

"You brat, why don't you watch what you're doing?"

My mother ran out to defend me and had an argument with the neighbor. If she hadn't had the argument, my *mamá* would not have died. Anyway, whether I feel guilty or not, that's what happened.

They woke us up at about 2:00 A.M. I didn't want to get up because I had wet the bed and was afraid they would punish me. But we saw my father crying and we got up frightened. I knew something bad was happening because my father had my mother in his arms. We were all crying at the head of the bed when the doctor came. Our relatives tried to get us out of the house but I fought to stay.

I didn't want to believe that my mother was dead. They laid her out and that night I secretly got into bed with her. They were looking for me, and I was sleeping next to my mother under the sheet they had covered her with. At that age I already knew that dying meant the person left this world forever, though I told my brother and sister,

"Don't cry, *mamá* is just sleeping." And I went close to my mother and said, "*Mamá, mamá,* you're sleeping, aren't you?" I touched her face, but I knew she would never wake up again.

I missed my mother then, and I still miss her. Since her death I felt I could never be happy again. Some people feel relieved when they talk about their troubles, but I've told this to many people and it has never helped. I feel calm only when I run away, when I go off as a vagabond, when I am alone in the country or up in the mountains. I believe if my mother were still alive I'd be very different. Or perhaps I'd be worse.

When my mother died, my grandmother was a second mother to me. I followed her around all the time. I called her little grandmother with the same love that I had called my mother, *mamá.* She was always good to us, but was very strict and stern in character. After all, she was old and had been brought up in the old style. They were more upright in everything.

She came to live with us and took good care of us. She sold cake crumbs in the plaza and I used to visit her all the time. I felt an urge to be with her because she understood me and used to give me lots of advice. The rest of the family, even my aunt Guadalupe who was closest to us, used to call me *"negro cambujo"* and "devil face." I never knew what "black *cambujo*" meant but it hurt me just the same. So I always stuck close to my grandmother.

Manuel never wanted to go with her to buy the cake crumbs or the bread. I was the one who liked to go with her. I don't know why, I was only a kid, but I felt that if I went along with her early in the morning, nothing could possibly happen to her, and thank God, we never came to any harm. One time Manuel went with us and he made my grandmother very angry. A vendor was selling sugared crab apples on a stick, shouting, "*Tejocotes, tejocotes* one *centavo.*" Manuel, who was always teasing my grandmother, began to yell, "Grandmothers, one *centavo* . . . a *centavo* a grandmother . . ." Well, she scolded him and tried to grab him, but, of course, she could never catch him. He was a fast runner. He was only fooling, but he made her cry that time, and it hurt me very much.

We were living on Cuba Street at the time, yes, on Cuba Street, because my *papá* had just gotten to know Elena, and my grandmother left our house and went to live with my aunt Guadalupe. I felt even more lonely and really missed my mother then, because as long as my grandmother was there, I didn't feel as though my mother was gone.

When Elena came to be my stepmother I went to my granny Pachita to complain, telling her Elena this and Elena that. My grandmother was my crying towel in those days. I really unburdened myself with her. I even stole the plants and, well, I didn't steal them, they were my mother's and I didn't want Elena to touch them, so I would bring them to my grandmother or to my aunt. But I lost my poor little grandmother too, for she died soon after.

From the beginning, my stepmother didn't like me and I didn't like her. We did not get along very well, my young stepmother and I. For me there was only one mother in all the world, and even though a hundred others came along and wanted to act like my mother, it was not the same thing. Besides, I had learned from my friends that stepmothers were bad.

Elena was about eighteen years old, I think, or less. Anyway, she was too young and lacked experience to take care of a widower with four children. She didn't know how to get us to obey her, especially me, for I was the wildest. If she had spoken to me nicely, I would have been putty in her hands, but she always wanted to control me, to order me around, to dominate my life. Ever since I was small, I didn't like to have anyone but my mother or father order me around. If Elena laid a hand on me I would fight back. I always defended myself physically, I never knew how to defend myself with words.

One of the reasons I fought so much with Elena was because on account of her Manuel and I had to sleep on the floor. Once I heard my *papá* and Elena talking. She was saying that we had had the bed long enough and that the girls were growing up. So my father ordered Manuel and me to sleep on the floor—not exactly on the floor, because my *papá* bought straw mats for us. I guess at that time he couldn't buy a bed.

I cried a few times but never said a word to my father. It hurt and I had a feeling of anguish around my heart. I felt sad, like a dog, sleeping on the floor. I missed my *mamá* very much then. When she was alive we slept on beds and were better off. Even after she died . . . before Elena came . . . we slept in a bed, with my *papá*, in the place that Elena took.

I was very happy sleeping next to my father. What fights Manuel and I had when he took my place next to my *papá!* We would argue until my *papá* said, "Everybody shut up and go to sleep." Wham! Out would go the light, off would come his shoes, his pants would be put on the chair, and then everything was quiet.

From the beginning, one of the things that I didn't like was that Elena had been living with another man. I was very much afraid for my father, because her ex-husband might take revenge or something.

My father gave me many scoldings and beatings on account of the ideas my stepmother put into his head. She was not entirely wrong but she embroidered the truth and twisted things. And many times she provoked me into being bad. If I jumped on the bed and got it dirty, she said, "Get off, *negro cambujo!*" That would hurt me and I answered, "You filthy old bag, why do you call me black? If I am black it is because God made me that way." Then she would hit me and I would hit her back and make her cry.

When my father came home, instead of saying "hello," she heaped it all up on him. So my father, who was all worn out from the day's work, would become exasperated and wouldn't even listen to me. He just beat me. The next day I tangled with Elena again.

My poor father! How much money my quarrels with that woman cost him! How many fifty's, hundred's, three hundred's of *pesos*, how many coats, shoes and dresses, to content the *señora*. How mad it made me! She saved the money and I sometimes stole it from her because of the way she got it from my *papá*.

Although I haven't been able to show it, I not only love my father, I idolize him. I used to be his pride and joy when I was a kid. He liked me more than my brother, because when he'd go anywhere, he took me first. Many times just the two of us would go to the Basilica or to the movies or just take a walk in the evening. He still loves me with the same deep love, except that he doesn't show it any more because I don't deserve it.

My father was always very dry with us; he didn't talk much and we could never discuss our problems with him. I tried to be close to him. I wanted him to treat us in a special way, like other *papás*, to talk with us, to fuss over us. I liked so much the way we used to kiss his hand when he came home, or hug him. I felt my father understood me better in those days, although even then I missed a sign of affection, a word of encouragement.

Only twice in my life did my father speak intimately to me. He asked me, "Son, what troubles you? What is the matter? Tell me your troubles." I felt the most important and happy person in the world to hear him call me "son" so affectionately. Usually he called me Roberto or "you," and scolded me with bad words.

I have always disliked it when a son raises his voice to his father. Whenever my father scolded us or even just talked to us, it was impossible to look him in the eye, because he had a fierce expression. When I wanted to explain myself or at least clear up the truth a bit, he would not let me speak. "You, shut your mouth," and, "The only thing you are good for is this or that." I have never answered him back when he bawled me out. Instead I reproached myself. I told my brother and sisters that if my father was not good with us it was our fault. A father is sacred, especially mine. He is a good, fine person. There isn't another like him.

My father never beat us unless there was a good reason. He hit us with a broad belt he still wears. It was double thick and he'd hit us hard, especially me. He whacked us so much we sort of got hardened and didn't feel it any more, even though when he was angry he laid it on. Unfortunately for me, I had the damndest habit. When I was being whipped, I'd knock my head against the wall or the wardrobe or something else. I kept whacking myself on the head, without knowing why.

Then, when I was about ten years old, my father took to using an electric cord, a very thick one, two meters long. He folded it in four parts and tied a knot in it. Wow! then we could feel the punishment. Every time he gave us a lash, it raised a welt. And my father wasn't the type who stopped with the one who did it, he went after both of us alike. He was impartial that way.

My father always urged me to go to school. How stupid I was not to have listened to him! I could never explain to myself why I didn't like school. When my classmates were sent to the blackboard they did their exercises quickly and were sure of themselves, but when I was called up, I felt a weight on my back because I knew everybody's eyes were on me. I thought they were whispering about me. I wanted to be way ahead of them and because of this I couldn't concentrate and it took me longer.

My mother, my aunt, or my grandmother would take me to school; sometimes they had to drag me there. I had a feeling of desperation about them leaving me alone with all those boys and girls. I felt inferior compared to so many people.

I was in the first grade for four years, not because I was stupid but because I played hooky. I did second grade in one year but when I passed to the third grade I attended only two or three months and never returned. Because of my friends and perhaps because I had so little liberty in my home, I enjoyed playing hooky and often went to Chapultepec Park. My father was notified when I missed school and would be waiting for me with the strap when I got home.

When we were children, my brother and I were closer to each other. He always protected me; for years Manuel was the handkerchief I dried my tears on. I used to be quite a coward and a crybaby, very *rajón*, as we say in Mexico, because if somebody would just shout at me, I'd start crying. I was afraid of the older boys. They'd threaten me and I'd cry; if anyone touched me, I'd scream. Right off I'd go running to my brother and he, poor fellow, had a lot of fighting to do on account of me.

I was in the third grade when Manuel graduated. I didn't have the courage to face all those boys without him and that is why I quit school.

I don't know why but I have always felt less than a nobody. Never in my whole life did I feel that there was anyone who paid attention to me. I have always been sneered at . . . belittled. I always wanted to be something in life, to do whatever I felt like and not have to take orders from anyone. I wanted to make a kite of my life and fly it in any field.

I wanted to be somebody in athletics, to be a great automobile driver or motorcyclist and compete in races. I have always wanted to be an aviator. One day my *papá* took me to the Lagunilla Market to buy me a cap. He said, "Which cap do you want?" I immediately asked for one with goggles, the kind aviators use.

When I played with my friends, the game was always aviation. To make it more real, I would lower my goggles and go up on the roof to run there like a plane. Or I would go running around the courtyard. I'd tie ropes to the water pipes and make a swing. That was my airplane and I really felt as if I were flying. That was one of my dreams. Whenever a plane flew by, even to this day, I keep watching it, longing to fly one some day.

My head was cracked open because I wanted to fly. My cousin Salvador, my aunt Guadalupe's son, may he rest in peace, was very playful and liked to fool around with us. One time I asked him to give me an airplane ride, that is, to swing me around and around. He always did whatever we wanted and so he took hold of my wrist and ankle and began to whirl me around. He suddenly lost control, and wham! I was dashed against the wall. My head was opened and when I came to, my *mamá* and *papá* and everybody were very alarmed. I was covered with blood but I didn't get scared. Actually, I enjoyed the fact that I was bleeding. It left a scar here on my head.

I am full of scars. I was always getting banged up. My head was opened other times, by falling off the roof or getting hit in stone fights, in wars, with my friends. Once I nearly lost an eye and I bled so much I thought I was going to die. I was running and fell on a sharp little toy shovel I was carrying. It went right into my left eye, but they took me to a doctor and I can still see out of it pretty well. The worst scar and one of the worst frights of my life was when I was bitten on the arm by a dog.

I learned to swim before my brother did even though he had gone often with his friends. I sort of hung around them hoping they would take me. I used to play hooky to go swimming in a pool not far from my house. There was an attendant there, Josué, whom I admired very much because he was a good swimmer and a nice guy. He was tall, strong and very husky. I don't mind telling you, he had some body. I wanted to be like him, nice, big, strong, and able to get some recognition. He used to talk to us about how he had been all over the Republic.

Once, when I was eight years old, I didn't have money for a ticket to the pool. Manuel, his friend Alberto, the Donkey, and I were standing outside the gate trying to scrape together money, when a drunk came by. This man gave Manuel and the Donkey the money they needed. So I said, "What about me? Aren't you going to give me some, too?" He just started off, and I said, "Listen, *señor*, won't you give me what I need for a ticket?"

"Who are you?" he says.

"I'm the brother of one of the boys you just gave some money to." And I told him how many *centavos* I needed to get in.

"No, you little son-of-a-bitch. Get out of here. You're too black."

That hurt me very much. My brother and Alberto went in without me, leaving me feeling desperate and humiliated.

When I played hooky, or when my father sent me to the Lagunilla Market to carry home the things he bought, I got into the habit of taking my little sister Marta with me. I have always liked her better than the others. I don't know whether it was because she had never known our mother or because she followed me wherever I went.

I taught Marta how to hitch rides by jumping on to the bumper of the trolley and holding tight. I used to take a little white dog from the Casa Grande too, because he followed me everywhere. There we would be, comfortable and happy, sticking like flies to the back of the trolley, with the dog running after us. Everybody would stop to look at us, people would put their heads out of the cars and buses to see the spectacle. I thought they were admiring us and I enjoyed it.

I liked to jump while the trolley went at full speed. Marta was very brave and learned to do it too. I not only risked my life, I risked hers, but she enjoyed it so much that it made quite an impression on me. I believe that's why I preferred her to Consuelo and Manuel.

I used to take her with me to Chapultepec Park and to the Villa where we would climb the steepest hills. I would braid three cords together to make a strong rope and I tied one end around my waist and the other around hers. I picked out the most dangerous cliffs and would climb up first, and pull her after me. She loved it and never complained.

I want to make it clear that I always respected Marta as a sister. Contact with a woman aroused my natural feelings, right? But it's very different with my sisters. It pained me that sometimes my father would act suspicious when he found out we went here or there. He would ask, "And why did you go? And what did you do?" and he would question Marta to see if we had done anything bad. I had worked once in a bakery at the Military Hospital where they paid me with bread and rolls. Later, it occurred to me to take Marta there to see if they would give us some rolls to eat. The hospital was very far out and when my father learned that I took her there, he gave me a terrific beating.

There was a big difference between Marta and Consuelo. Consuelo was more intelligent and persistent and liked to study. When she decided to do something she stuck to it. She never played with boys like Marta and was very reserved even with girls. She was nice and quiet, and very thin and frightened-looking.

When we were little, I got along well with Consuelo. Later, I was surprised at how my sister changed. She blew up at practically nothing and would create a tempest in a glass of water. She had an uneven temperament and seemed to me to be unsociable, secretive and irritable. She was very dry and didn't have much to do with people. But apart from that, she was good, all good.

The trouble between Consuelo and me began after my stepmother came to live with my father. I ate breakfast late, after the others, because, I don't know why but ever since I was little, I was ashamed to sit at the table without doing some chore. I always did work around the house, like lighting the charcoal fire, putting up the coffee, cleaning the bird cages and feeding the birds. No one told me to, but it pained me not to do something before I ate.

After the family had eaten, I'd hunt around the kitchen for food. Many times, right in front of me, Consuelo or Elena would pour the leftover coffee down the drain, or crush up my bread. I would say, "Ha, ha! you make me laugh! I'm not even hungry." I would grab one of the bananas we fed the birds and would go out. I'd send them to the devil, not out of anger but out of hurt feelings. The truth is that when they destroyed my breakfast like that, I felt great anxiety in my heart and a lump in my throat. I would cry, not in front of them, but in one of the little shower rooms in the courtyard. I tried to keep quiet about these things because I knew if I told my father, he'd scold them and maybe even punish them with the strap. He did scold Consuelo at times, but she didn't change.

But I have always been a brother to my sisters. I have never punished them without a reason, like if they didn't obey me, or because they talked back to my *papá*, or called me "lousy black." I am heartbroken at the thought of how many times I have beaten them. I want to ask their pardon, but when I see them I lose my courage. It makes me suffer, because a man shouldn't beat a woman. But I only slapped them with the palm or the back of my hand. And when I slapped, it was only on the arm or the back, or the head.

But when my father came home Consuelo would tell him that I had kicked her or hit her on the lung. *Ay!* my God! Those weren't caresses my father gave me because of those lies! On my word! I speak from the heart, that I never hit her like that. She was a little liar then, and it was Elena's fault that, well, the blessed woman is now at peace, God has her in heaven, but when she and my sister accused me and exaggerated, my *papá* thrashed me with that doubled electric cable that had a copper wire inside and a knot on the end.

How difficult Consuelo and Elena made life for me! I felt that they were against me and that I constantly had to be on guard. And my father favored the women. He had always taken better care of them and it seemed to me that he loved my sisters more. Rather, he loved us all equally, but only they had the privilege of having him demonstrate it to them. He had always preferred women. I never paid attention to it, it never bothered me. On the contrary, I liked it because that way I was more sure of my sisters, that is, the way I see it, they could never say as an excuse that they had missed their father's love . . .

I'll tell you why I hit my sisters. It wasn't because I felt any hatred or bitterness toward them. It was that I never liked my sisters to play with boys. But they didn't pay any attention to me and it's logical, isn't it? because, well, little girls naturally have to play with little boys.

I had this feeling because ever since I was small I've been very mean toward little girls, as mean as they make them. I was full of malice. Sometimes I would take a little girl to the toilet when nobody was home. I always tried to find a way so that we wouldn't be seen, and then I'd begin to feel her up, with her consent, of course. I was only about five or six, and even after my mother died, when I was eight or nine, I still did it. That's why I didn't want my sisters to play with boys, because I figured the boys could do the same thing to them. Just feel them up, as we say, that's all I ever did to the little girls.

When we were older, Manuel, my cousin Matilde, my cousin Julia, and I began to play. My brother went off with Julia in one direction, and I went off in another with Matilde. She was the stepdaughter of my uncle Alfredo, so she was not actually related to me. Unfortunately, ever since I was little and even now that I am grown-up just the slightest contact with a woman, if I would just touch a woman or shake hands with her, stimulates my natural feelings so that I cannot control myself. It's the same with all men, I suppose.

So I had the idea of going to the bathroom with Matilde. There were no inside toilets in the *vecindad* where she lived; they were out in the courtyard, so it was convenient for what I wanted to do.

I convinced her and we went. I told her to lie down in the corner. I lifted up her dress and pulled down her panties, and at that time I couldn't call what I had a member, it was just barely sprouting, but I put it between her legs. I really couldn't do anything and I didn't even know where it should go, but with her consent, there were the two of us, trying to do it this way and that, playing *papá* and *mamá*.

So I did this shameful thing with my cousin and that's why I was always trying to watch over my sisters.

How does Roberto's voice differ from that of Dylan Thomas in "Fern Hill"? Do you find Roberto's feelings contradictory? Do you have similar conflicting memories of love-and-hate from your own adolescence? To what extent has your life been shaped by the forces that operated in Roberto's life—poverty, skin color, jealousy? What do you think happened to Roberto in his later years?

You can learn about yourself by remembering your past, but you can also learn something by speculating about your future. Describe what you think you will be doing, thinking, and feeling ten years from now. Then, from the vantage point of now, evaluate your projection of yourself.

The next two selections invite you to take a further look at your future self. George Orwell's *1984* (the year is now alarmingly closer than it was in 1949 when the novel was first published) describes a totalitarian future in which the individual is completely the slave of the state. The book's protagonist, Winston Smith, has been physically and mentally tortured. What follows is the climax of that methodical breaking of the human spirit.

from
1984
george orwell

He was much better. He was growing fatter and stronger every day, if it was proper to speak of days.

The white light and the humming sound were the same as ever, but the cell was a little more comfortable than the others he had been in. There were a pillow and a mattress on the plank bed, and a stool to sit on. They had given him a bath, and they allowed him to wash himself fairly frequently in a tin basin. They even gave him warm water to wash with. They had given him new underclothes and a clean suit of overalls. They had dressed his varicose ulcer with soothing ointment. They had pulled out the remnants of his teeth and given him a new set of dentures.

Weeks or months must have passed. It would have been possible now to keep count of the passage of time, if he had felt any interest in doing so, since he was being fed at what appeared to be regular intervals. He was getting, he judged, three meals in the twenty-four hours; sometimes he wondered dimly whether he was getting them by night or by day. The food was surprisingly good, with meat at every third meal. Once there was even a packet of cigarettes. He had no matches, but the never-speaking guard who brought his food would give him a light. The first time he tried to smoke it made him sick, but he persevered, and spun the packet out for a long time, smoking half a cigarette after each meal.

They had given him a white slate with a stump of pencil tied to the corner. At first he made no use of it. Even when he was awake he was completely torpid. Often he would lie from one meal to the next almost without stirring, sometimes asleep, sometimes waking into vague reveries in which it was too much trouble to open his eyes. He had long grown used to sleeping with a strong light on his face. It seemed to make no difference, except that one's dreams were more coherent. He dreamed a great deal all through this time, and they were always happy dreams. He was in the Golden Country, or he was sitting among enormous, glorious, sunlit ruins, with his mother, with Julia, with O'Brien—not doing anything, merely sitting in the sun, talking of peaceful things. Such thoughts as he had when he was awake were mostly about his dreams. He seemed to have lost the power of intellectual effort, now that the stimulus of pain had been removed. He was not bored; he had no desire for conversation or distraction. Merely to be alone, not to be beaten or questioned, to have enough to eat, and to be clean all over, was completely satisfying.

By degrees he came to spend less time in sleep, but he still felt no impulse to get off the bed. All he cared for was to lie quiet and feel the strength gathering in his body. He would finger himself here and there, trying to make sure that it was not an illusion that his muscles were growing rounder and his skin tauter. Finally it was established beyond a doubt that he was growing fatter; his thighs were now definitely thicker than his knees. After that, reluctantly at first, he began exercising himself regularly. In a little while he could walk three kilometers, measured by pacing the cell, and his bowed shoulders were growing straighter. He attempted more elaborate exercises, and was astonished and humiliated to find what things he could not do. He could not move out of a walk, he could not hold his stool out at arm's length, he could not stand on one leg without falling over. He squatted down on his heels, and found that with agonizing pains in thigh and calf he could just lift himself to a standing position. He lay flat on his belly and tried to lift his weight by his hands. It was hopeless; he could not raise himself a centimeter. But after a few more days—a few more mealtimes—even that feat was accomplished. A time came when he could do it six times running. He began to grow actually proud of his body, and to cherish an intermittent belief that his face also was growing back to normal. Only when he chanced to put his hand on his bald scalp did he remember the seamed, ruined face that had looked back at him out of the mirror.

His mind grew more active. He sat down on the plank bed, his back against the wall and the slate on his knees, and set to work deliberately at the task of re-educating himself.

He had capitulated; that was agreed. In reality, as he saw now, he had been ready to capitulate long before he had taken the decision. From the moment when he was inside the Ministry of Love—and yes, even during those minutes when he and Julia had stood helpless while the iron voice from the telescreen told them what to do—he had grasped the frivolity, the shallowness of his attempt to set himself up against the power of the Party. He knew now that for seven years the Thought Police had watched him like a beetle under a magnifying glass. There was no physical act, no word spoken aloud, that they had not noticed, no train of thought that they had not been able to infer. Even the speck of whitish dust on the cover of his diary they had carefully replaced. They had played sound tracks to him, shown him photographs. Some of them were photographs of Julia and himself. Yes, even ... He could not fight against the Party any longer. Besides, the Party was in the right. It must be so: how could the immortal, collective brain be mistaken? By what external standard could you check its judgments? Sanity was statistical. It was merely a question of learning to think as they thought. Only—!

The pencil felt thick and awkward in his fingers. He began to write down the thoughts that came into his head. He wrote first in large clumsy capitals:

FREEDOM IS SLAVERY.

Then almost without a pause he wrote beneath it:

TWO AND TWO MAKE FIVE.

But then there came a sort of check. His mind, as though shying away from something, seemed unable to concentrate. He knew that he knew what came next, but for the moment he could not recall it. When he did recall it, it was only by consciously reasoning out what it must be; it did not come of its own accord. He wrote:

GOD IS POWER

He accepted everything. The past was alterable. The past never had been altered. Oceania was at war with Eastasia. Oceania had always been at war with Eastasia. Jones, Aaronson, and Rutherford were guilty of the crimes they were charged with. He had never seen the photograph that disproved their guilt. It had never existed; he had invented it. He remembered remembering contrary things, but those were false memories, products of self-deception. How easy it all was! Only surrender, and everything else followed. It was like swimming against a current that swept you backwards however hard you struggled, and then suddenly deciding to turn round and go with the current instead of opposing it. Nothing had changed except your own attitude; the predestined thing happened in any case. He hardly knew why he had ever rebelled. Everything was easy, except—!

Anything could be true. The so-called laws of nature were nonsense. The law of gravity was nonsense. "If I wished," O'Brien had said, "I could float off this floor like a soap bubble." Winston worked it out. "If he *thinks* he floats off the floor, and if I simultaneously *think* I see him do it, then the thing happens." Suddenly, like a lump of submerged wreckage breaking the surface of water, the thought burst into his mind: "It doesn't really happen. We imagine it. It is hallucination." He pushed the thought under instantly. The fallacy was obvious. It presupposed that somewhere or other, outside oneself, there was a "real" world where "real" things happened. But how could there be such a world? What knowledge have we of anything, save through our own minds? All happenings are in the mind. Whatever happens in all minds, truly happens.

He had no difficulty in disposing of the fallacy, and he was in no danger of succumbing to it. He realized, nevertheless, that it ought never to have occurred to him. The mind should develop a blind spot whenever a dangerous thought presented itself. The process should be automatic, instinctive. *Crimestop*, they called it in Newspeak.

He set to work to exercise himself in crimestop. He presented himself with propositions—"the Party says the earth is flat," "the Party says that ice is heavier than water"—and trained himself in not seeing or not understanding the arguments that contradicted them. It was not easy. It needed great powers of reasoning and improvisation. The arithmetical problems raised, for instance, by such a statement as "two and two make five" were beyond his intellectual grasp. It needed also a sort of athleticism of mind, an ability at one moment to make the most delicate use of logic and at the next to be unconscious of the crudest logical errors. Stupidity was as necessary as intelligence, and as difficult to attain.

All the while, with one part of his mind, he wondered how soon they would shoot him. "Everything depends on yourself," O'Brien had said; but he knew that there was no conscious act by which he could bring it nearer. It might be ten minutes hence, or ten years. They might keep him for years in solitary confinement; they might send him to a labor camp; they might release him for a while, as they sometimes did. It was perfectly possible that before he was shot the whole drama of his arrest and interrogation would be enacted all over again. The one certain thing was that death never came at an expected moment. The tradition—the unspoken tradition: somehow you knew it, though you never heard it said—was that they shot you from behind, always in the back of the head, without warning, as you walked down a corridor from cell to cell.

One day—but "one day" was not the right expression; just as probably it was in the middle of the night: once—he fell into a strange, blissful reverie. He was walking down the corridor, waiting for the bullet. He knew that it was coming in another moment. Everything was settled, smoothed out, reconciled. There were no more doubts, no more arguments, no more pain, no more fear. His body was healthy and strong. He walked easily, with a joy of movement and with a feeling of walking in sunlight. He was not any longer in the narrow white corridors of the Ministry of Love; he was in the enormous sunlit passage, a kilometer wide, down which he had seemed to walk in the delirium induced by drugs. He was in the Golden Country, following the foot track across the old rabbit-cropped pasture. He could feel the short springy turf under his feet and the gentle sunshine on his face. At the edge of the field were the elm trees, faintly stirring, and somewhere beyond that was the stream where the dace lay in the green pools under the willows.

Suddenly he started up with a shock of horror. The sweat broke out on his backbone. He had heard himself cry aloud:

"Julia! Julia! Julia, my love! Julia!"

For a moment he had had an overwhelming hallucination of her presence. She had seemed to be not merely with him, but inside him. It was as though she had got into the texture of his skin. In that moment he had loved her far more than he had ever done when they were together and free. Also he knew that somewhere or other she was still alive and needed his help.

He lay back on the bed and tried to compose himself. What had he done? How many years had he added to his servitude by that moment of weakness?

In another moment he would hear the tramp of boots outside. They could not let such an outburst go unpunished. They would know now, if they had not known before, that he was breaking the agreement he had made with them. He obeyed the Party, but he still hated the Party. In the old days he had hidden a heretical mind beneath an appearance of conformity. Now he had retreated a step further: in the mind he had surrendered, but he had hoped to keep the inner heart inviolate. He knew that he was in the wrong, but he preferred to be in the wrong. They would understand that—O'Brien would understand it. It was all confessed in that single foolish cry.

He would have to start all over again. It might take years. He ran a hand over his face, trying to familiarize himself with the new shape. There were deep furrows in the cheeks, the cheekbones felt sharp, the nose flattened. Besides, since last seeing himself in the glass he had been given a complete new set of teeth. It was not easy to preserve inscrutability when you did not know what your face looked like. In any case, mere control of the features was not enough. For the first time he perceived that if you want to keep a secret you must also hide it from yourself. You must know all the while that it is there, but until it is needed you must never let it emerge into your consciousness in any shape that could be given a name. From now onwards he must not only think right; he must feel right, dream right. And all the while he must keep his hatred locked up inside him like a ball of matter which was part of himself and yet unconnected with the rest of him, a kind of cyst.

One day they would decide to shoot him. You could not tell when it would happen, but a few seconds beforehand it should be possible to guess. It was always from behind, walking down a corridor. Ten seconds would be enough. In that time the world inside him could turn over. And then suddenly, without a word uttered, without a check in his step, without the changing of a line in his face—suddenly the camouflage would be down and bang! would go the batteries of his hatred. Hatred would fill him like an enormous roaring flame. And almost in the same instant bang! would go the bullet, too late, or too early. They would have blown his brain to pieces before they could reclaim it. The heretical thought would be unpunished, unrepented, out of their reach forever. They would have blown a hole in their own perfection. To die hating them, that was freedom.

He shut his eyes. It was more difficult than accepting an intellectual discipline. It was a question of degrading himself, mutilating himself. He had got to plunge into the filthiest of filth. What was the most horrible, sickening thing of all? He thought of Big Brother. The enormous face (because of constantly seeing it on posters he always thought of it as being a meter wide), with its heavy black mustache and the eyes that followed you to and fro, seemed to float into his mind of its own accord. What were his true feelings toward Big Brother?

There was a heavy tramp of boots in the passage. The steel door swung open with a clang. O'Brien walked into the cell. Behind him were the waxen-faced officer and the black-uniformed guards.

"Get up," said O'Brien. "Come here."

Winston stood opposite him. O'Brien took Winston's shoulders between his strong hands and looked at him closely.

"You have had thoughts of deceiving me," he said. "That was stupid. Stand up straighter. Look me in the face."

He paused, and went on in a gentler tone:

"You are improving. Intellectually there is very little wrong with you. It is only emotionally that you have failed to make progress. Tell me, Winston—and remember, no lies; you know that I am always able to detect a lie—tell me, what are your true feelings toward Big Brother?"

"I hate him."

"You hate him. Good. Then the time has come for you to take the last step. You must love Big Brother. It is not enough to obey him; you must love him."

He released Winston with a little push toward the guards.

"Room 101," he said.

At each stage of his imprisonment he had known, or seemed to know, whereabouts he was in the windowless building. Possibly there were slight differences in the air pressure. The cells where the guards had beaten him were below ground level. The room where he had been interrogated by O'Brien was high up near the roof. This place was many meters underground, as deep down as it was possible to go.

It was bigger than most of the cells he had been in. But he hardly noticed his surroundings. All he noticed was that there were two small tables straight in front of him, each covered with green baize. One was only a meter or two from him; the other was further away, near the door. He was strapped upright in a chair, so tightly that he could move nothing, not even his head. A sort of pad gripped his head from behind, forcing him to look straight in front of him.

For a moment he was alone, then the door opened and O'Brien came in.

"You asked me once," said O'Brien, "what was in Room 101. I told you that you knew the answer already. Everyone knows it. The thing that is in Room 101 is the worst thing in the world."

The door opened again. A guard came in, carrying something made of wire, a box or basket of some kind. He set it down on the further table. Because of the position in which O'Brien was standing, Winston could not see what the thing was.

"The worst thing in the world," said O'Brien, "varies from individual to individual. It may be burial alive, or death by fire, or by drowning, or by impalement, or fifty other deaths. There are cases where it is some quite trivial thing, not even fatal."

He had moved a little to one side, so that Winston had a better view of the thing on the table. It was an oblong wire cage with a handle on top for carrying it by. Fixed to the front of it was something that looked like a fencing mask, with the concave side outwards. Although it was three or four meters away from him, he could see that the cage was divided lengthways into two compartments, and that there was some kind of creature in each. They were rats.

"In your case," said O'Brien, "the worst thing in the world happens to be rats."

A sort of premonitory tremor, a fear of he was not certain what, had passed through Winston as soon as he caught his first glimpse of the cage. But at this moment the meaning of the masklike attachment in front of it suddenly sank into him. His bowels seemed to turn to water.

"You can't do that!" he cried out in a high cracked voice. "You couldn't, you couldn't! It's impossible."

"Do you remember," said O'Brien, "the moment of panic that used to occur in your dreams? There was a wall of blackness in front of you, and a roaring sound in your ears. There was something terrible on the other side of the wall. You knew that you knew what it was, but you dared not drag it into the open. It was the rats that were on the other side of the wall."

"O'Brien!" said Winston, making an effort to control his voice. "You know this is not necessary. What is it that you want me to do?"

O'Brien made no direct answer. When he spoke it was in the schoolmasterish manner that he sometimes affected. He looked thoughtfully into the distance, as though he were addressing an audience somewhere behind Winston's back.

"By itself," he said, "pain is not always enough. There are occasions when a human being will stand out against pain, even to the point of death. But for everyone there is something unendurable—something that cannot be contemplated. Courage and cowardice are not involved. If you are falling from a height it is not cowardly to clutch at a rope. If you have come up from deep water it is not cowardly to fill your lungs with air. It is merely an instinct which cannot be disobeyed. It is the same with the rats. For you, they are unendurable. They are a form of pressure that you cannot withstand, even if you wished to. You will do what is required of you."

"But what is it, what is it? How can I do it if I don't know what it is?"

O'Brien picked up the cage and brought it across to the nearer table. He set it down carefully on the baize cloth. Winston could hear the blood singing in his ears. He had the feeling of sitting in utter loneliness. He was in the middle of a great empty plain, a flat desert drenched with sunlight, across which all sounds came to him out of immense distances. Yet the cage with the rats was not two meters away from him. They were enormous rats. They were at the age when a rat's muzzle grows blunt and fierce and his fur brown instead of gray.

"The rat," said O'Brien, still addressing his invisible audience, "although a rodent, is carnivorous. You are aware of that. You will have heard of the things that happen in the poor quarters of this town. In some streets a woman dare not leave her baby alone in the house, even for five minutes. The rats are certain to attack it. Within quite a small time they will strip it to the bones. They also attack sick or dying people. They show astonishing intelligence in knowing when a human being is helpless."

There was an outburst of squeals from the cage. It seemed to reach Winston from far away. The rats were fighting; they were trying to get at each other through the partition. He heard also a deep groan of despair. That, too, seemed to come from outside himself.

O'Brien picked up the cage, and, as he did so, pressed something in it. There was a sharp click. Winston made a frantic effort to tear himself loose from the chair. It was hopeless: every part of him, even his head, was held immovably. O'Brien moved the cage nearer. It was less than a meter from Winston's face.

"I have pressed the first lever," said O'Brien. "You understand the construction of this cage. The mask will fit over your head, leaving no exit. When I press this other lever, the door of the cage will slide up. These starving brutes will shoot out of it like bullets. Have you ever seen a rat leap through the air? They will leap onto your face and bore straight into it. Sometimes they attack the eyes first. Sometimes they burrow through the cheeks and devour the tongue."

The cage was nearer; it was closing in. Winston heard a succession of shrill cries which appeared to be occurring in the air above his head. But he fought furiously against his panic. To think, to think, even with a split second left—to think was the only hope. Suddenly the foul musty odor of the brutes struck his nostrils. There was a violent convulsion of nausea inside him, and he almost lost consciousness. Everything had gone black. For an instant he was insane, a screaming animal. Yet he came out of the blackness clutching an idea. There was one and only one way to save himself. He must interpose another human being, the *body* of another human being, between himself and the rats.

The circle of the mask was large enough now to shut out the vision of anything else. The wire door was a couple of hand-spans from his face. The rats knew what was coming now. One of them was leaping up and down; the other, an old scaly grandfather of the sewers, stood up, with his pink hands against the bars, and fiercely snuffed the air. Winston could see the whiskers and the yellow teeth. Again the black panic took hold of him. He was blind, helpless, mindless.

"It was a common punishment in Imperial China," said O'Brien as didactically as ever.

The mask was closing on his face. The wire brushed his cheek. And then—no, it was not relief, only hope, a tiny fragment of hope. Too late, perhaps too late. But he had suddenly understood that in the whole world there was just *one* person to whom he could transfer his punishment—*one* body that he could thrust between himself and the rats. And he was shouting frantically, over and over:

"Do it to Julia! Do it to Julia! Not me! Julia! I don't care what you do to her. Tear her face off, strip her to the bones. Not me! Julia! Not me!"

He was falling backwards, into enormous depths, away from the rats. He was still strapped in the chair, but he had fallen through the floor, through the walls of the building, through the earth, through the oceans, through the atmosphere, into outer space, into the gulfs between the stars—always away, away, away from the rats. He was light-years distant, but O'Brien was still standing at his side. There was still the cold touch of a wire against his cheek. But through the darkness that enveloped him he heard another metallic click, and knew that the cage door had clicked shut and not open.

What were your physical sensations as you read this? Describe your own "Room 101"—the thing you are most afraid of. Under what circumstances would you *say* that two and two make five? Under what circumstances would you *believe* that two and two make five? Do you feel that Orwell's world of 1984 may soon be realized? Would you resist it? What would you do?

W. H. Auden wrote this obituary for a citizen of the near future.

W. H. AUDEN

The Unknown Citizen

(TO JS/07/M/378
THIS MARBLE MONUMENT
IS ERECTED BY THE STATE)

He was found by the Bureau of Statistics to be
One against whom there was no official complaint,
And all the reports on his conduct agree
That, in the modern sense of an old-fashioned word, he
    was a saint,
For in everything he did he served the Greater Community.
Except for the War till the day he retired
He worked in a factory and never got fired,
But satisfied his employers, Fudge Motors Inc.

Yet he wasn't a scab or odd in his views,
For his Union reports that he paid his dues,
(Our report on his Union shows it was sound)
And our Social Psychology workers found
That he was popular with his mates and liked a drink.
The Press are convinced that he bought a paper every day
And that his reactions to advertisements were normal in
*   every way.*
Policies taken out in his name prove that he was fully insured,
And his Health-card shows he was once in hospital but left
*   it cured.*
Both Producers Research and High-Grade Living declare
He was fully sensible to the advantages of the Instalment Plan
And had everything necessary to the Modern Man,
A phonograph, a radio, a car and a frigidaire.
Our researchers into Public Opinion are content
That he held the proper opinions for the time of year;
When there was peace, he was for peace; when there was war,
*   he went.*
He was married and added five children to the population,
Which our Eugenist says was the right number for a parent of
*   his generation,*
And our teachers report that he never interfered with
*   their education.*
Was he free? Was he happy? The question is absurd:
Had anything been wrong, we should certainly have heard.

In this poem Auden seems to be deliberately saying something he does not really mean. How do you know what he means? What do the last two lines of the poem suggest about the title?

In what ways is your own life likely to become like that of JS/07/M/378? Describe yourself in statistical terms. Do you feel a person would know you after reading this description? Revise the description in such a way that a person reading it would know how you feel about being identified statistically.

you and

others
others
others
others
others
others
others
others
others

Almost any novel, play, poem, or essay could be relevant to your efforts to see yourself in relation to others. But the selections that follow are intended specifically to point up the problem of who you are in relation to those people who directly affect your life—your family, your friends, your community.

N. Scott Momaday wrote this account of a journey into his own past. The picture on page 143 was drawn by his father, Al Momaday.

from

The way to rainy mountain

N. SCOTT MOMADAY

A single knoll rises out of the plain in Oklahoma, north and west of the Wichita Range. For my people, the Kiowas, it is an old landmark, and they gave it the name Rainy Mountain. The hardest weather in the world is there. Winter brings blizzards, hot tornadic winds arise in the spring, and in summer the prairie is an anvil's edge. The grass turns brittle and brown, and it cracks beneath your feet. There are green belts along the rivers and creeks, linear groves of hickory and pecan, willow and witch hazel. At a distance in July or August the steaming foliage seems almost to writhe in fire. Great green and yellow grasshoppers are everywhere in the tall grass, popping up like corn to sting the flesh, and tortoises crawl about on the red earth, going nowhere in the plenty of time. Loneliness is an aspect of the land. All things in the plain are isolate; there is no confusion of objects in the eye, but *one* hill or *one* tree or *one* man. To look upon that landscape in the early morning, with the sun at your back, is to lose the sense of proportion. Your imagination comes to life, and this, you think, is where Creation was begun.

I returned to Rainy Mountain in July. My grandmother had died in the spring, and I wanted to be at her grave. She had lived to be very old and at last infirm. Her only living daughter was with her when she died, and I was told that in death her face was that of a child.

I like to think of her as a child. When she was born, the Kiowas were living the last great moment of their history. For more than a hundred years they had controlled the open range from the Smoky Hill River to the Red, from the headwaters of the Canadian to the fork of the Arkansas and Cimarron. In alliance with the Comanches, they had ruled the whole of the southern Plains. War was their sacred business, and they were among the finest horsemen the world has ever known. But warfare for the Kiowas was preeminently a matter of disposition rather than of survival, and they never understood the grim, unrelenting advance of the U.S. Cavalry. When at last, divided and ill-provisioned, they were driven onto the Staked Plains in the cold rains of autumn, they fell into panic. In Palo Duro Canyon they abandoned their crucial stores to pillage and had nothing then but their lives. In order to save themselves, they surrendered to the soldiers at Fort Sill and were imprisoned in the old stone corral that now stands as a military museum. My grandmother was spared the humiliation of those high gray walls by eight or ten years, but she must have known from birth the affliction of defeat, the dark brooding of old warriors.

Her name was Aho, and she belonged to the last culture to evolve in North America. Her forebears came down from the high country in western Montana nearly three centuries ago. They were a mountain people, a mysterious tribe of hunters whose language has never been positively classified in any major group. In the late seventeenth century they began a long migration to the south and east. It was a journey toward the dawn, and it led to a golden age. Along the way the Kiowas were befriended by the Crows, who gave them the culture and religion of the Plains. They acquired horses, and their ancient nomadic spirit was suddenly free of the ground. They acquired Tai-me, the sacred Sun Dance doll, from that moment the object and symbol of their worship, and so shared in the divinity of the sun. Not least, they acquired the sense of destiny, therefore courage and pride. When they entered upon the southern Plains they had been transformed. No longer were they slaves to the simple necessity of survival; they were a lordly and dangerous society of fighters and thieves, hunters and priests of the sun. According to their origin myth, they entered the world through a hollow log. From one point of view, their migration was the fruit of an old prophecy, for indeed they emerged from a sunless world.

Although my grandmother lived out her long life in the shadow of Rainy Mountain, the immense landscape of the continental interior lay like memory in her blood. She could tell of the Crows, whom she had never seen, and of the Black Hills, where she had never been. I wanted to see in reality what she had seen more perfectly in the mind's eye, and traveled fifteen hundred miles to begin my pilgrimage.

Yellowstone, it seemed to me, was the top of the world, a region of deep lakes and dark timber, canyons and waterfalls. But, beautiful as it is, one might have the sense of confinement there. The skyline in all directions is close at hand, the high wall of the woods and deep cleavages of shade. There is a perfect freedom in the mountains, but it belongs to the eagle and the elk, the badger and the bear. The Kiowas reckoned their stature by the distance they could see, and they were bent and blind in the wilderness.

Descending eastward, the highland meadows are a stairway to the plain. In July the inland slope of the Rockies is luxuriant with flax and buckwheat, stonecrop and larkspur. The earth unfolds and the limit of the land recedes. Clusters of trees, and animals grazing far in the distance, cause the vision to reach away and wonder to build upon the mind. The sun follows a longer course in the day, and the sky is immense beyond all comparison. The great billowing clouds that sail upon it are shadows that move upon the grain like water, dividing light. Farther down, in the land of the Crows and Blackfeet, the plain is yellow. Sweet clover takes hold of the hills and bends upon itself to cover and seal the soil. There the Kiowas paused on their way; they had come to the place where they must change their lives. The sun is at home on the plains. Precisely there does it have the certain character of a god. When the Kiowas came to the land of the Crows, they could see the dark lees of the hills at dawn across the Bighorn River, the profusion of light on the grain shelves, the oldest deity ranging after the solstices. Not yet would they veer southward to the caldron of the land that lay below; they must wean their blood from the northern winter and hold the mountains a while longer in their view. They bore Tai-me in procession to the east.

A dark mist lay over the Black Hills, and the land was like iron. At the top of a ridge I caught sight of Devil's Tower upthrust against the gray sky as if in the birth of time the core of the earth had broken through its crust and the motion of the world was begun. There are things in nature that engender an awful quiet in the heart of man; Devil's Tower is one of them. Two centuries ago, because they could not do otherwise, the Kiowas made a legend at the base of the rock. My grandmother said:

Eight children were there at play, seven sisters and their brother. Suddenly the boy was struck dumb; he trembled and began to run upon his hands and feet. His fingers became claws, and his body was covered with fur. Directly there was a bear where the boy had been. The sisters were terrified; they ran, and the bear after them. They came to the stump of a great tree, and the tree spoke to them. It bade them climb upon it, and as they did so it began to rise into the air. The bear came to kill them, but they were just beyond its reach. It reared against the tree and scored the bark all around with its claws. The seven sisters were borne into the sky, and they became the stars of the Big Dipper.

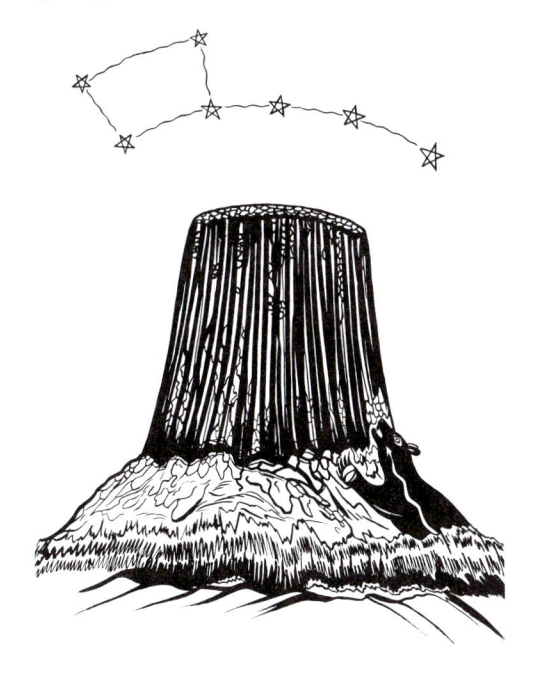

From that moment, and so long as the legend lives, the Kiowas have kinsmen in the night sky. Whatever they were in the mountains, they could be no more. However tenuous their well-being, however much they had suffered and would suffer again, they had found a way out of the wilderness.

My grandmother had a reverence for the sun, a holy regard that now is all but gone out of mankind. There was a wariness in her, and an ancient awe. She was a Christian in her later years, but she had come a long way about, and she never forgot her birthright. As a child she had been to the Sun Dances; she had taken part in those annual rites, and by them she had learned the restoration of her people in the presence of Tai-me. She was about seven when the last Kiowa Sun Dance was held in 1887 on the Washita River above Rainy Mountain Creek. The buffalo were gone. In order to consummate the ancient sacrifice—to impale the head of a buffalo bull upon the medicine tree—a delegation of old men journeyed into Texas, there to beg and barter for an animal from the Goodnight herd. She was ten when the Kiowas came together for the last time as a living Sun Dance culture. They could find no buffalo; they had to hang an old hide from the sacred tree. Before the dance could begin, a company of soldiers rode out from Fort Sill under orders to disperse the tribe. Forbidden without cause the essential act of their faith, having seen the wild herds slaughtered and left to rot upon the ground, the Kiowas backed away forever from the medicine tree. That was July 20, 1890, at the great bend of the Washita. My grandmother was there. Without bitterness, and for as long as she lived, she bore a vision of deicide.

Now that I can have her only in memory, I see my grandmother in the several postures that were peculiar to her: standing at the wood stove on a winter morning and turning meat in a great iron skillet; sitting at the south window, bent above her beadwork, and afterwards, when her vision failed, looking down for a long time into the fold of her hands; going out upon a cane, very slowly as she did when the weight of age came upon her; praying. I remember her most often at prayer. She made long, rambling prayers out of suffering and hope, having seen many things. I was never sure that I had the right to hear, so exclusive were they of all mere custom and company. The last time I saw her she prayed standing by the side of her bed at night, naked to the waist, the light of a kerosene lamp moving upon her dark skin. Her long, black hair, always drawn and braided in the day, lay upon her shoulders and against her breasts like a shawl. I do not speak Kiowa, and I never understood her prayers, but there was something inherently sad in the sound, some merest hesitation upon the syllables of sorrow. She began in a high and descending pitch, exhausting her breath to silence; then again and again—and always the same intensity of effort, of something that is, and is not, like urgency in the human voice. Transported so in the dancing light among the shadows of her room, she seemed beyond the reach of time. But that was illusion; I think I knew then that I should not see her again.

Houses are like sentinels in the plain, old keepers of the weather watch. There, in a very little while, wood takes on the appearance of great age. All colors wear soon away in the wind and rain, and then the wood is burned gray and the grain appears and the nails turn red with rust. The windowpanes are black and opaque; you imagine there is nothing within, and indeed there are many ghosts, bones given up to the land. They stand here and there against the sky, and you approach them for a longer time than you expect. They belong in the distance; it is their domain.

Once there was a lot of sound in my grandmother's house, a lot of coming and going, feasting and talk. The summers there were full of excitement and reunion. The Kiowas are a summer people; they abide the cold and keep to themselves, but when the season turns and the land becomes warm and vital they cannot hold still; an old love of going returns upon them. The aged visitors who came to my grandmother's house when I was a child were made of lean and leather, and they bore themselves upright. They wore great black hats and bright ample shirts that shook in the wind. They rubbed fat upon their hair and wound their braids with strips of colored cloth. Some of them painted their faces and carried the scars of old and cherished enmities. They were an old council of warlords, come to remind and be reminded of who they were. Their wives and daughters served them well. The women might indulge themselves; gossip was at once the mark and compensation of their servitude. They made loud and elaborate talk among themselves, full of jest and gesture, fright and false alarm. They went abroad in fringed and flowered shawls, bright beadwork and

German silver. They were at home in the kitchen, and they prepared meals that were banquets.

There were frequent prayer meetings, and great nocturnal feasts. When I was a child I played with my cousins outside, where the lamplight fell upon the ground and the singing of the old people rose up around us and carried away into the darkness. There were a lot of good things to eat, a lot of laughter and surprise. And afterwards, when the quiet returned, I lay down with my grandmother and could hear the frogs away by the river and feel the motion of the air.

Now there is a funeral silence in the rooms, the endless wake of some final word. The walls have closed in upon my grandmother's house. When I returned to it in mourning, I saw for the first time in my life how small it was. It was late at night, and there was a white moon, nearly full. I sat for a long time on the stone steps by the kitchen door. From there I could see out across the land; I could see the long row of trees by the creek, the low light upon the rolling plains, and the stars of the Big Dipper. Once I looked at the moon and caught sight of a strange thing. A cricket had perched upon the handrail, only a few inches away from me. My line of vision was such that the creature filled the moon like a fossil. It had gone there, I thought, to live and die, for there, of all places, was its small definition made whole and eternal. A warm wind rose up and purled like the longing within me.

The next morning I awoke at dawn and went out on the dirt road to Rainy Mountain. It was already hot, and the grasshoppers began to fill the air. Still, it was early in the morning, and the birds sang out of the shadows. The long yellow grass on the mountain shone in the bright light, and a scissortail hied above the land. There, where it ought to be, at the end of a long and legendary way, was my grandmother's grave. Here and there on the dark stones were ancestral names. Looking back once, I saw the mountain and came away.

What are your ancestral roots? Describe your own Rainy Mountain. How would you try to get there? How are your attitudes and actions influenced by the way your ancestors lived?

K. William Kgositsile's awareness of how his ancestors lived and the impact of their lives on his present life is expressed in this poem.

K. WILLIAM KGOSITSILE

towards a walk in the sun

THE WIND IS CARESSING
THE EVE OF A NEW DAWN
A DREAM: THE BIRTH OF
MEMORY

                Who are we? Who
were we? Things cannot go on much as
before. All night long we shall laugh
behind Time's new masks. When the moment
hatches in Time's womb we shall not complain.
Where, oh where are
The men to matches
The fuse to burn the
Snow that freezes some
Wouldbe skyward desire
    You who swallowed your balls for a piece
    Of gold beautiful from afar but far from
    Beautiful because it is colored with
    The pus from your brother's callouses
    You who creep lower than a snake's belly
    Because you swallowed your conscience
    And sold your sister to soulless vipers
    You who bleached the womb of your daughter's
    Mind to bear pale-brained freaks
    You who bleached your son's genitals to
    Slobber in the slime of missionary-eyed faggotry
    You who hide behind the shadow of your master's
    Institutionalized hypocrisy the knees of your
    Soul numbed by endless kneeling to catch

The crumbs from your master's table before
You run to poison your own mother. You too
Deballed grin you who forever tell your masters
I have a glorious past . . . I have rhythm
. . . I have this . . . I have that. . . .
Don't you know I know all your lies?
The only past I know is hunger unsatisfied
The only past I know is sweating in the sun
And a kick in the empty belly by your fatbellied master
   And rhythm don't fill an empty stomach
      Who are we? All night long
      I listen to the dream soaring
      Like the tide. I yearn to
      Slit throats and color the
      Wave with the blood of the villain
      To make a sacrifice to the gods. Yea,
      There is pain in the coil around things
Where are we? The memory . . .
And all these years all these lies!
You too over there misplaced nightmare
Forever foaming at the mouth forever
Proclaiming your anger . . . a mere
Formality because your sight is colored
With snow. What does my hunger
Have to do with a gawdamm poem?

THIS WIND YOU HEAR IS THE BIRTH OF MEMORY. WHEN THE MOMENT HATCHES IN TIME'S WOMB THERE WILL BE NO ART TALK. THE ONLY POEM YOU WILL HEAR WILL BE THE SPEARPOINT PIVOTED IN THE PUNCTURED MARROW OF THE VILLAIN; THE TIMELESS NATIVE SON DANCING LIKE CRAZY TO THE RETRIEVED RHYTHMS OF DESIRE FADING INTO MEMORY

How is this poet's reaction to his past different from Momaday's? Do you see why? Do you sympathize with the way he feels? Is there anything in your own past that would cause you to react this way? At the end of the poem what does Kgositsile say about art? What is your attitude toward the difference between words and actions? What is your attitude toward violence?

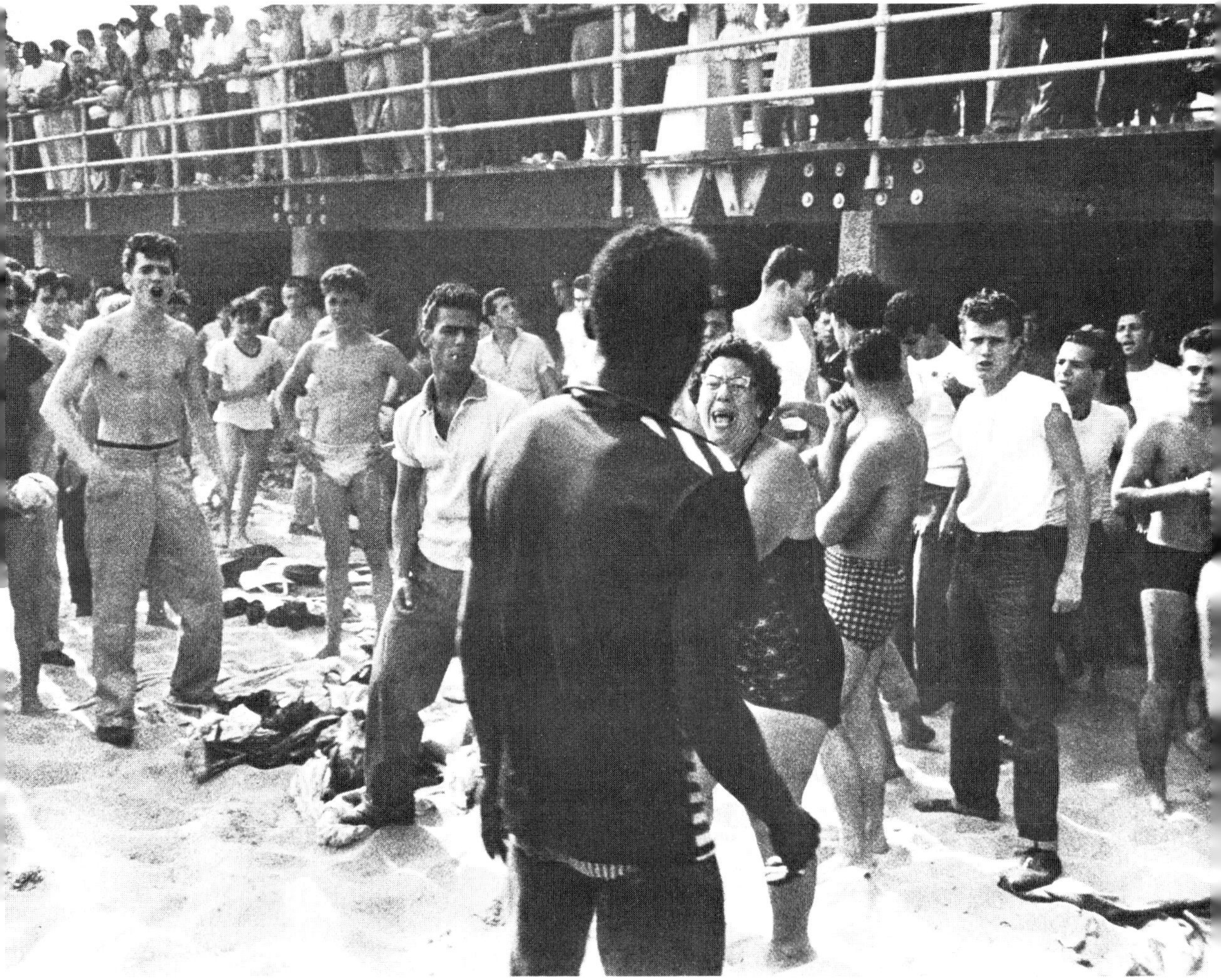

Ralph Ellison, the author of this selection, has much the same ancestry as Kgositsile, but you may find his outlook different.

RALPH ELLISON

PROLOGUE TO INVISIBLE MAN

I am an invisible man. No, I am not a spook like those who haunted Edgar Allan Poe; nor am I one of your Hollywood-movie ectoplasms. I am a man of substance, of flesh and bone, fiber and liquids—and I might even be said to possess a mind. I am invisible, understand, simply because people refuse to see me. Like the bodiless heads you see sometimes in circus sideshows, it is as though I have been surrounded by mirrors of hard, distorting glass. When they approach me they see only my surroundings, themselves, or figments of their imagination—indeed, everything and anything except me.

Nor is my invisibility exactly a matter of a bio-chemical accident to my epidermis. That invisibility to which I refer occurs because of a peculiar disposition of the eyes of those with whom I come in contact. A matter of the construction of their *inner* eyes, those eyes with which they look through their physical eyes upon reality. I am not complaining, nor am I protesting either. It is sometimes advantageous to be unseen, although it is most often rather wearing on the nerves. Then too, you're constantly being bumped against by those of poor vision. Or again, you often doubt if you really exist. You wonder whether you aren't simply a phantom in other people's minds. Say, a figure in a nightmare which the sleeper tries with all his strength to destroy. It's when you feel like this that, out of resentment, you begin to bump people back. And, let me confess, you feel that way most of the time. You ache with the need to convince yourself that you do exist in the real world, that you're a part of all the sound and anguish, and you strike out with your fists, you curse and you swear to make them recognize you. And, alas, it's seldom successful.

One night I accidentally bumped into a man, and perhaps because of the near darkness he saw me and called me an insulting name. I sprang at him, seized his coat lapels and demanded that he apologize. He was a tall blond man, and as my face came close to his he looked insolently out of his blue eyes and cursed me, his breath hot in my face as he struggled. I pulled his chin down sharp upon the crown of my head, butting him as I had seen the West Indians do, and I felt his flesh tear and the blood gush out, and I yelled, "Apologize! Apologize!" But he continued to curse and struggle, and I butted him again and again until he went down heavily, on his knees, profusely bleeding. I kicked him repeatedly, in a frenzy because he still uttered insults though his lips were frothy with blood. Oh yes, I kicked him! And in my outrage I got out my knife and prepared to slit his throat, right there beneath the lamplight in the deserted street, holding him in the collar with one hand, and opening the knife with my teeth—when it occurred to me that the man had not *seen* me, actually; that he, as far as he knew, was in the midst of a walking nightmare! And I stopped the blade, slicing the air as I pushed him away, letting him fall back to the street. I stared at him hard as the lights of a car stabbed through the darkness. He lay there, moaning on the asphalt; a man almost killed by a phantom. It unnerved me. I was both disgusted and ashamed. I was like a drunken man myself, wavering about on weakened legs. Then I was amused: Something in this man's thick head had sprung out and beaten him within an inch of his life. I began to laugh at this crazy discovery. Would he have awakened at the point of death? Would Death himself have freed him for wakeful living? But I didn't linger. I ran away into the dark, laughing so hard I feared I might rupture myself. The next day I saw his picture in the *Daily News,* beneath a caption stating that he had been "mugged." Poor fool, poor blind fool, I thought with sincere compassion, mugged by an invisible man!

Most of the time (although I do not choose as I once did to deny the violence of my days by ignoring it) I am not so overtly violent. I remember that I am invisible and walk softly so as not to awaken the sleeping ones. Sometimes it is best not to awaken them; there are few things in the world as dangerous as sleepwalkers. I learned in time though that it is possible to carry on a fight against them without their realizing it. For instance, I have been carrying on a fight with Monopolated Light & Power for some time now. I use their service and pay them nothing at all, and they don't know it. Oh, they suspect that power is being drained off, but they don't know where. All they know is that according to the master meter back there in their power station a hell of a lot of free current is disappearing somewhere into the jungle of Harlem. The joke, of course, is that I don't live in Harlem but in a border area. Several years ago (before I discovered the advantages of being invisible) I went through the routine process of buying service and paying their outrageous rates. But no more. I gave up all that, along with my apartment, and my old way of life: That way based upon the fallacious assumption that I, like other men, was visible. Now, aware of my invisibility, I live rent-free in a building rented strictly to whites, in a section of the basement that was shut off and forgotten during the nineteenth century, which I discovered when I was trying to escape in the night from Ras the Destroyer. But that's getting too far ahead of the story, almost to the end, although the end is in the beginning and lies far ahead.

The point now is that I found a home—or a hole in the ground, as you will. Now don't jump to the conclusion that because I call my home a "hole" it is damp and cold like a grave; there are cold holes and warm holes. Mine is a warm hole. And remember, a bear retires to his hole for the winter and lives until spring; then he comes strolling out like the Easter chick breaking from its shell. I say all this to assure you that it is incorrect to assume that, because I'm invisible and live in a hole, I am dead. I am neither dead nor in a state of suspended animation. Call me Jack-the-Bear, for I am in a state of hibernation.

My hole is warm and full of light. Yes, *full* of light. I doubt if there is a brighter spot in all New York than this hole of mine, and I do not exclude Broadway. Or the Empire State Building on a photographer's dream night. But that is taking advantage of you. Those two spots are among the darkest of our whole civilization—pardon me, our whole *culture* (an important distinction, I've heard)—which might sound like a hoax, or a contradiction, but that (by contradiction, I mean) is how the world moves: Not like an arrow, but a boomerang. (Beware of those who speak of the *spiral* of history; they are preparing a boomerang. Keep a steel helmet handy.) I know; I have been boomeranged across my head so much that I now can see the darkness of lightness. And I love light. Perhaps you'll think it strange that an invisible man should need light, desire light, love light. But maybe it is exactly because I *am* invisible. Light confirms my reality, gives birth to my form. A beautiful girl once told me of a recurring nightmare in which she lay in the center of a large dark room and felt her face expand until it filled the whole room, becoming a formless mass while her eyes ran in bilious jelly up the chimney. And so it is with me. Without light I am not only invisible, but formless as well; and to be unaware of one's form is to live a death. I myself, after existing some twenty years, did not become alive until I discovered my invisibility.

That is why I fight my battle with Monopolated Light & Power. The deeper reason, I mean: It allows me to feel my vital aliveness. I also fight them for taking so much of my money before I learned to protect myself. In my hole in the basement there are exactly 1,369 lights. I've wired the entire ceiling, every inch of it. And not with fluorescent bulbs, but with the older, more-expensive-to-operate kind, the filament type. An act of sabotage, you know. I've already begun to wire the wall. A junk man I know, a man of vision, has supplied me with wire and sockets. Nothing, storm or flood, must get in the way of our need for light and ever more and brighter light. The truth is the light and light is the truth. When I finish all four walls, then I'll start on the floor. Just how that will go, I don't know. Yet when you have lived invisible as long as I have you develop a certain ingenuity. I'll solve the problem. And maybe I'll invent a gadget to place my coffee pot on the fire while I lie in bed, and even invent a gadget to warm my bed—like the fellow I saw in one of the picture magazines who made himself a gadget to warm his shoes! Though invisible, I am in the great American tradition of tinkers. That makes me kin to Ford, Edison and Franklin. Call me, since I have a theory and a concept, a "thinker-tinker." Yes, I'll warm my shoes; they need it, they're usually full of holes. I'll do that and more.

Now I have one radio-phonograph; I plan to have five. There is a certain acoustical deadness in my hole, and when I have music I want to *feel* its vibration, not only with my ear but with my whole body. I'd like to hear five recordings of Louis Armstrong playing and singing "What Did I Do to Be so Black and Blue"—all at the same time. Sometimes now I listen to Louis while I have my favorite dessert of vanilla ice cream and sloe gin. I pour the red liquid over the white mound, watching it glisten and the vapor rising as Louis bends that military instrument into a beam of lyrical sound. Perhaps I like Louis Armstrong because he's made poetry out of being invisible. I think it must be because he's unaware that he *is* invisible. And my own grasp of invisibility aids me to understand his music. Once when I asked for a cigarette, some jokers gave me a reefer, which I lighted when I got home and sat listening to my phonograph. It was a strange evening. Invisibility, let me explain, gives one a slightly different sense of time, you're never quite on the beat. Sometimes you're ahead and sometimes behind. Instead of the swift and imperceptible flowing of time, you are aware of its nodes, those points where time stands still or from which it leaps ahead. And you slip into the breaks and look around. That's what you hear vaguely in Louis' music.

Once I saw a prizefighter boxing a yokel. The fighter was swift and amazingly scientific. His body was one violent flow of rapid rhythmic action. He hit the yokel a hundred times while the yokel held up his arms in stunned surprise. But suddenly the yokel, rolling about in the gale of boxing gloves, struck one blow and knocked science, speed and footwork as cold as a well-digger's posterior. The smart money hit the canvas. The long shot got the nod. The yokel had simply stepped inside of his opponent's sense of time. So under the spell of the reefer I discovered a new analytical way of listening to music. The unheard sounds came through, and each melodic line existed of itself, stood out clearly from all the rest, said its piece, and waited patiently for the other voices to speak. That night I found myself hearing not only in time, but in space as well. I not only entered the music but descended, like Dante, into its depths. And *beneath the swiftness of the hot tempo there was a slower tempo and a cave and I entered it and looked around and heard an old woman singing a spiritual as full of Weltschmerz as flamenco, and beneath that lay a still lower level on which I saw a beautiful girl the color of ivory pleading in a voice like my mother's as she stood before a group of slaveowners who bid for her naked body, and below that I found a lower level and a more rapid tempo and I heard someone shout:*

"Brothers and sisters, my text this morning is the 'Blackness of Blackness.'"

And a congregation of voices answered: "That blackness is most black, brother, most black . . ."

"In the beginning . . ."
"At the very start," they cried.
". . . there was blackness . . ."
"Preach it . . ."
". . . and the sun . . ."
"The sun, Lawd . . ."
". . . was bloody red . . ."
"Red . . ."
"Now black is . . ." the preacher shouted.
"Bloody . . ."
"I said black is . . ."
"Preach it, brother . . ."
". . . an' black ain't . . ."
"Red, Lawd, red: He said it's red!"
"Amen, brother . . ."
"Black will git you . . ."
"Yes, it will . . ."
". . . an' black won't . . ."
"Naw, it won't!"
"It do . . ."
"It do, Lawd . . ."
". . . an' it don't."
"Halleluiah . . ."
". . . It'll put you, glory, glory, Oh my Lawd, in the WHALE'S BELLY."
"Preach it, dear brother . . ."
". . . an' make you tempt . . ."
"Good God a-mighty!"
"Old Aunt Nelly!"
"Black will make you . . ."
"Black . . ."
". . . or black will un-make you."
"Ain't it the truth, Lawd?"

And at that point a voice of trombone timbre screamed at me, "Git out of here, you fool! Is you ready to commit treason?"

And I tore myself away, hearing the old singer of spirituals moaning, "Go curse your God, boy, and die."

I stopped and questioned her, asked her what was wrong.

155

"I dearly loved my master, son," she said.

"You should have hated him," I said.

"He gave me several sons," she said, "and because I loved my sons I learned to love their father though I hated him too."

"I too have become acquainted with ambivalence," I said. "That's why I'm here."

"What's that?"

"Nothing, a word that doesn't explain it. Why do you moan?"

"I moan this way 'cause he's dead," she said.

"Then tell me, who is that laughing upstairs?"

"Them's my sons. They glad."

"Yes, I can understand that too," I said.

"I laughs too, but I moans too. He promised to set us free but he never could bring hisself to do it. Still I loved him . . ."

"Loved him? You mean . . . ?"

"Oh yes, but I loved something else even more."

"What more?"

"Freedom."

"Freedom," I said. "Maybe freedom lies in hating."

"Naw, son, it's in loving. I loved him and give him the poison and he withered away like a frost-bit apple. Them boys woulda tore him to pieces with they homemade knives."

"A mistake was made somewhere," I said, "I'm confused." And I wished to say other things, but the laughter upstairs became too loud and moan-like for me and I tried to break out of it, but I couldn't. Just as I was leaving I felt an urgent desire to ask her what freedom was and went back. She sat with her head in her hands, moaning softly; her leather-brown face was filled with sadness.

"Old woman, what is this freedom you love so well?" I asked around a corner of my mind.

She looked surprised, then thoughtful, then baffled. "I done forgot, son. It's all mixed up. First I think it's one thing, then I think it's another. It gits my head to spinning. I guess now it ain't nothing but knowing how to say what I got up in my head. But it's a hard job, son. Too much is done happen to me in too short a time. Hit's like I have a fever. Ever' time I starts to walk my head gits to swirling and I falls down. Or if it ain't that, it's the boys; they gits to laughing and wants to kill up the white folks. They's bitter, that's what they is. . . ."

"But what about freedom?"

"Leave me 'lone, boy; my head aches!"

I left her, feeling dizzy myself. I didn't get far.

Suddenly one of the sons, a big fellow six feet tall, appeared out of nowhere and struck me with his fist.

"What's the matter, man?" I cried.

"You made Ma cry!"

"But how?" I said, dodging a blow.

"Askin' her them questions, that's how. Git outa here and stay, and next time you got questions like that, ask yourself!"

He held me in a grip like cold stone, his fingers fastening upon my windpipe until I thought I would suffocate before he finally allowed me to go. I stumbled about dazed, the music beating hysterically in my ears. It was dark. My head cleared and I wandered down a dark narrow passage, thinking I heard his footsteps hurrying behind me. I was sore, and into my being had come a profound craving for tranquillity, for peace and quiet, a state I felt I could never achieve. For one thing, the trumpet was blaring and the rhythm was too hectic. A tom-tom beating like heart-thuds began drowning out the trumpet, filling my ears. I longed for water and I heard it rushing through the cold mains my fingers touched as I felt my way, but I couldn't stop to search because of the footsteps behind me.

"Hey, Ras," I called. "Is it you, Destroyer? Rinehart?"

No answer, only the rhythmic footsteps behind me. Once I tried crossing the road, but a speeding machine struck me, scraping the skin from my leg as it roared past.

Then somehow I came out of it, ascending hastily from this underworld of sound to hear Louis Armstrong innocently asking,

> What did I do
> To be so black
> And blue?

At first I was afraid; this familiar music had demanded action, the kind of which I was incapable, and yet had I lingered there beneath the surface I might have attempted to act. Nevertheless, I know now that few really listen to this music. I sat on the chair's edge in a soaking sweat, as though each of my 1,369 bulbs had every one become a klieg light in an individual setting for a third degree with Ras and Rinehart in charge. It was exhausting—as though I had held my breath continuously for an hour under the terrifying serenity that comes from days of intense hunger. And yet, it was a strangely satisfying experience for an invisible man to hear the silence of sound. I had discovered unrecognized compulsions of my being—even though I could not answer "yes" to their promptings. I haven't smoked a reefer since, however; not because they're illegal, but because to *see* around corners is enough (that is not unusual when you are invisible). But to hear around them is too much; it inhibits action. And despite Brother Jack and all that sad, lost period of the Brotherhood, I believe in nothing if not in action.

Please, a definition: A hibernation is a covert preparation for a more overt action.

Besides, the drug destroys one's sense of time completely. If that happened, I might forget to dodge some bright morning and some cluck would run me down with an orange and yellow street car, or a bilious bus! Or I might forget to leave my hole when the moment for action presents itself.

Meanwhile I enjoy my life with the compliments of Monopolated Light & Power. Since you never recognize me even when in closest contact with me, and since, no doubt, you'll hardly believe that I exist, it won't matter if you know that I tapped a power line leading into the building and ran it into my hole in the ground. Before that I lived in the darkness into which I was chased, but now I see. I've illuminated the blackness of my invisibility—and vice versa. And so I play the invisible music of my isolation. The last statement doesn't seem just right, does it? But it is; you hear this music simply because music is heard and seldom seen, except by musicians. Could this compulsion to put invisibility down in black and white be thus an urge to make music of invisibility? But I am an orator, a rabble rouser—Am? I *was*, and perhaps shall be again. Who knows? All sickness is not unto death, neither is invisibility.

I can hear you say, "What a horrible, irresponsible bastard!" And you're right. I leap to agree with you. I am one of the most irresponsible beings that ever lived. Irresponsibility is part of my invisibility; any way you face it, it is a denial. But to whom can I be responsible, and why should I be, when you refuse to see me? And wait until I reveal how truly irresponsible I am. Responsibility rests upon recognition, and recognition is a form of agreement. Take the man whom I almost killed: Who was responsible for that near murder—I? I don't think so, and I refuse it. I won't buy it. You can't give it to me. *He* bumped *me*, *he* insulted *me*. Shouldn't he, for his own personal safety, have recognized my hysteria, my "danger potential"? He, let us say, was lost in a dream world. But didn't *he* control that dream world—which, alas, is only too real!—and didn't *he* rule me out of it? And if he had yelled for a policeman, wouldn't I have been taken for the offending one? Yes, yes, yes! Let me agree with you, I was the irresponsible one; for I should have used my knife to protect the higher interests of society. Some day that kind of foolishness will cause us tragic trouble. All dreamers and sleepwalkers must pay the price, and even the invisible victim is responsible for the fate of all. But I shirked that responsibility; I became too snarled in the incompatible notions that buzzed within my brain. I was a coward . . .

But what did *I* do to be so blue? Bear with me.

In what ways do you try to break away from the establishment? In what ways do you try to become invisible? How do the reactions of the narrator of this story compare with those of Winston Smith in *1984*? How do they compare with those of the speaker in "Towards a Walk in the Sun"? Why do you think these three people react differently? With which of them do you feel most sympathetic?

Though the following story was written more than a century ago, and though the events it describes took place more than two centuries ago, it still may be about you.

NATHANIEL HAWTHORNE

My Kinsman, Major Molineux

After the kings of Great Britain had assumed the right of appointing the colonial governors, the measures of the latter seldom met with the ready and general approbation which had been paid to those of their predecessors, under the original charters. The people looked with most jealous scrutiny to the exercise of power which did not emanate from themselves, and they usually rewarded their rulers with slender gratitude for the compliances by which, in softening their instructions from beyond the sea, they had incurred the reprehension of those who gave them. The annals of Massachusetts Bay will inform us, that of six governors in the space of about forty years from the surrender of the old charter, under James II, two were imprisoned by a popular insurrection; a third, as Hutchinson inclines to believe, was driven from the province by the whizzing of a musketball; a fourth, in the opinion of the same historian, was hastened to his grave by continual bickerings with the House of Representatives; and the remaining two, as well as their successors, till the Revolution, were favored with few and brief intervals of peaceful sway. The inferior members of the court party, in times of high political excitement, led scarcely a more desirable life. These remarks may serve as a preface to the following adventures, which chanced upon a summer night, not far from a hundred years ago. The reader, in order to avoid a long and dry detail of colonial affairs, is requested to dispense with an account of the train of circumstances that had caused much temporary inflammation of the popular mind.

It was near nine o'clock of a moonlight evening, when a boat crossed the ferry with a single passenger, who had obtained his conveyance at that unusual hour by the promise of an extra fare. While he stood on the landing place, searching in either pocket for the means of fulfilling his agreement, the ferryman lifted a lantern, by the aid of which, and the newly-risen moon, he took a very accurate survey of the stranger's figure. He was a youth of barely eighteen years, evidently country-bred, and now, as it should seem, upon his first visit to town. He was clad in a coarse gray coat, well worn, but in excellent repair; his under-garments were durably constructed of leather, and fitted tight to a pair of serviceable and well-shaped limbs; his stockings of blue yarn were the incontrovertible work of a mother or a sister; and on his head was a three-cornered hat, which in its better days had perhaps sheltered the graver brow of the lad's father. Under his left arm was a heavy cudgel, formed of an oak sapling, and retaining a part of the hardened root; and his equipment was completed by a wallet, not so abundantly stocked as to incommode the vigorous shoulders on which it hung. Brown, curly hair, well-shaped features, and bright, cheerful eyes, were nature's gifts, and worth all that art could have done for his adornment.

The youth, one of whose names was Robin, finally drew from his pocket the half of a little province bill of five shillings, which, in the depreciation of that sort of currency, did but satisfy the ferryman's demand, with the surplus of a sexangular piece of parchment, valued at three pence. He then walked forward into the town, with as light a step as if his day's journey had not already exceeded thirty miles, and with as eager an eye as if he were entering London city, instead of the little metropolis of a New England colony. Before Robin had proceeded far, however, it occurred to him that he knew not whither to direct his steps; so he paused, and looked up and down the narrow street, scrutinizing the small and mean wooden buildings that were scattered on either side.

"This low hovel cannot be my kinsman's dwelling," thought he, "nor yonder old house, where the moonlight enters at the broken casement; and truly I see none hereabouts that might be worthy of him. It would have been wise to inquire my way of the ferryman, and doubtless he would have gone with me, and earned a shilling from the major for his pains. But the next man I meet will do as well."

He resumed his walk, and was glad to perceive that the street now became wider, and the houses more respectable in their appearance.

He soon discerned a figure moving on moderately in advance, and hastened his steps to overtake it. As Robin drew nigh, he saw that the passenger was a man in years, with a full periwig of gray hair, a wide-skirted coat of dark cloth, and silk stockings rolled above his knees. He carried a long and polished cane, which he struck down perpendicularly before him, at every step; and at regular intervals he uttered two successive hems, of a peculiarly solemn and sepulchral intonation. Having made these observations, Robin laid hold of the skirt of the old man's coat, just when the light from the open door and windows of a barber's shop fell upon both their figures.

"Good evening to you, honored sir," said he, making a low bow, and still retaining his hold of the skirt. "I pray you tell me whereabouts is the dwelling of my kinsman, Major Molineux."

The youth's question was uttered very loudly; and one of the barbers, whose razor was descending on a well-soaped chin, and another who was dressing a Ramillies wig, left their occupations, and came to the door. The citizen, in the meantime, turned a long-favored countenance upon Robin, and answered him in a tone of excessive anger and annoyance. His two sepulchral hems, however, broke into the very centre of his rebuke, with most singular effect, like a thought of the cold grave obtruding among wrathful passions.

"Let go my garment, fellow! I tell you, I know not the man you speak of. What! I have authority, I have—hem, hem—authority; and if this be the respect you show for your betters, your feet shall be brought acquainted with the stocks by daylight, tomorrow morning!"

Robin released the old man's skirt, and hastened away, pursued by an ill-mannered roar of laughter from the barber's shop. He was at first considerably surprised by the result of his question, but, being a shrewd youth, soon thought himself able to account for the mystery.

"This is some country representative," was his conclusion, "who has never seen the inside of my kinsman's door, and lacks the breeding to answer a stranger civilly. The man is old, or verily—I might be tempted to turn back and smite him on the nose. Ah, Robin, Robin! even the barber's boys laugh at you choosing such a guide! You will be wiser in time, friend Robin."

He now became entangled in a succession of crooked and narrow streets, which crossed each other, and meandered at no great distance from the water-side. The smell of tar was obvious to his nostrils, the masts of vessels pierced the moonlight above the tops of the buildings, and the numerous signs, which Robin paused to read, informed him that he was near the centre of business. But the streets were empty, the shops were closed, and lights were visible only in the second stories of a few dwelling-houses. At length, on the corner of a narrow lane, through which he was passing, he beheld the broad countenance of a British hero swinging before the door of an inn, whence proceeded the voices of many guests. The casement of one of the lower windows was thrown back, and a very thin curtain permitted Robin to distinguish a party at supper, round a well-furnished table. The fragrance of the good cheer steamed forth into the outer air, and the youth could not fail to recollect that the last remnant of his travelling stock of provision had yielded to his morning appetite, and that noon had found, and left him, dinnerless.

"O, that a parchment three-penny might give me a right to sit down at yonder table!" said Robin, with a sigh. "But the major will make me welcome to the best of his victuals; so I will even step boldly in, and inquire my way to his dwelling."

He entered the tavern, and was guided by the murmur of voices, and the fumes of tobacco, to the public room. It was a long and low apartment, with oaken walls, grown dark in the continual smoke, and a floor, which was thickly sanded, but of no immaculate purity. A number of persons—the larger part of whom appeared to be mariners, or in some way connected with the sea—occupied the wooden benches, or leather-bottomed chairs, conversing on various matters, and occasionally lending their attention to some topic of general interest. Three or four little groups were draining as many bowls of punch, which the West India trade had long since made a familiar drink in the colony. Others, who had the appearance of men who lived by regular and laborious handicraft, preferred the insulated bliss of an unshared potation, and became more taciturn under its influence. Nearly all, in short, evinced a predilection for the Good Creature in some of its various shapes, for this is a vice to which, as Fast-day sermons of a hundred years ago will testify, we have a long hereditary claim. The only guests to whom Robin's sympathies inclined him were two or three sheepish countrymen, who were using the inn somewhat after the fashion of a Turkish caravansary; they had gotten themselves into the darkest corner of the room, and, heedless of the Nicotian atmosphere, were supping on the bread of their own ovens, and the bacon cured in their own chimney-smoke. But though Robin felt a sort of brotherhood with these strangers, his eyes were attracted from them to a person who stood near the door, holding whispered conversation with a group of ill-dressed associates. His features were separately striking almost to grotesqueness, and the whole face left a deep impression on the memory. The forehead bulged out into a double prominence, with a vale between; the nose came boldly forth in an irregular curve, and its bridge was of more than a finger's breadth; the eyebrows were deep and shaggy, and the eyes glowed beneath them like fire in a cave.

While Robin deliberated of whom to inquire respecting his kinsman's dwelling, he was accosted by the innkeeper, a little man in a stained white apron, who had come to pay his professional welcome to the stranger. Being in the second generation from a French Protestant, he seemed to have inherited the courtesy of his parent nation; but no variety of circumstances was ever known to change his voice from the one shrill note in which he now addressed Robin.

"From the country, I presume, sir?" said he, with a profound bow. "Beg leave to congratulate you on your arrival, and trust you intend a long stay with us. Fine town here, sir, beautiful buildings, and much that may interest a stranger. May I hope for the honor of your commands in respect to supper?"

"The man sees a family likeness! the rogue has guessed that I am related to the major!" thought Robin, who had hitherto experienced little superfluous civility.

All eyes were now turned on the country lad, standing at the door, in his worn three-cornered hat, gray coat, leather breeches, and blue yarn stockings, leaning on an oaken cudgel, and bearing a wallet on his back.

Robin replied to the courteous innkeeper, with such an assumption of confidence as befitted the major's relative. "My honest friend," he said, "I shall make it a point to patronize your house on some occasion when"—here he could not help lowering his voice—"when I may have more than a parchment three-pence in my pocket. My present business," continued he, speaking with lofty confidence, "is merely to inquire my way to the dwelling of my kinsman, Major Molineux."

There was a sudden and general movement in the room, which Robin interpreted as expressing the eagerness of each individual to become his guide. But the innkeeper turned his eyes to a written paper on the wall, which he read, or seemed to read, with occasional recurrences to the young man's figure.

"What have we here?" said he, breaking his speech into little dry fragments. "'Left the house of the subscriber, bounden servant, Hezekiah Mudge—had on, when he went away, gray coat, leather breeches, master's third-best hat. One pound currency reward to whosoever shall lodge him in any jail of the province.' Better trudge, boy, better trudge!"

Robin had begun to draw his hand towards the lighter end of the oak cudgel, but a strange hostility in every countenance induced him to relinquish his purpose of breaking the courteous innkeeper's head. As he turned to leave the room, he encountered a sneering glance from the bold-featured personage whom he had before noticed; and no sooner was he beyond the door, than he heard a general laugh, in which the innkeeper's voice might be distinguished, like the dropping of small stones into a kettle.

"Now, is it not strange," thought Robin, with his usual shrewdness, "is it not strange, that the confession of an empty pocket should outweigh the name of my kinsman, Major Molineux? O, if I had one of those grinning rascals in the woods, where I and my oak sapling grew up together, I would teach him that my arm is heavy, though my purse be light!"

On turning the corner of the narrow lane, Robin found himself in a spacious street, with an unbroken line of lofty houses on each side, and a steepled building at the upper end, whence the ringing of a bell announced the hour of nine. The light of the moon, and the lamps from the numerous shop windows, discovered people promenading on the pavement, and amongst them Robin hoped to recognize his hitherto inscrutable relative. The result of his former inquiries made him unwilling to hazard another, in a scene of such publicity, and he determined to walk slowly and silently up the street, thrusting his face close to that of every elderly gentleman, in search of the major's lineaments. In his progress, Robin encountered many gay and gallant figures. Embroidered garments of showy colors, enormous periwigs, gold-laced hats, and silver-hilted swords, glided past him, and dazzled his optics. Travelled youth, imitators of the European fine gentlemen of the period, trod jauntily along, half-dancing to the fashionable tunes which they hummed, and making poor Robin ashamed of his quiet and natural gait. At length, after many pauses to examine the gorgeous display of goods in the shop windows, and after suffering some rebukes for the impertinence of his scrutiny into people's faces, the major's kinsman found himself near the steepled building, still unsuccessful in his search. As yet, however, he had seen only one side of the thronged street, so Robin crossed, and continued the same sort of inquisition down the opposite pavement, with stronger hopes than the philosopher seeking an honest man, but with no better fortune. He had arrived about midway towards the lower end, from which his course began, when he overheard the approach of someone, who struck down a cane on the flagstones at every step, uttering, at regular intervals, two sepulchral hems.

"Mercy on us!" quoth Robin, recognizing the sound.

Turning a corner, which chanced to be close at his right hand, he hastened to pursue his researches in some other part of the town. His patience now was wearing low, and he seemed to feel more fatigue from his rambles since he crossed the ferry, than from his journey of several days on the other side. Hunger also pleaded loudly within him, and Robin began to balance the propriety of demanding, violently, and with lifted cudgel, the necessary guidance from the first solitary passenger whom he should meet. While a resolution to this effect was gaining strength, he entered a street of mean appearance, on either side of which a row of ill-built houses was straggling towards the harbor. The moonlight fell upon no passenger along the whole extent, but in the third domicile which Robin passed there was a half-opened door, and his keen glance detected a woman's garment within.

"My luck may be better here," said he to himself.

Accordingly, he approached the door, and beheld it shut closer as he did so; yet an open space remained, sufficing for the fair occupant to observe the stranger, without a corresponding display on her part. All that Robin could discern was a strip of scarlet petticoat, and the occasional sparkle of an eye, as if the moonbeams were trembling on some bright thing.

"Pretty mistress," for I may call her so with a good conscience, thought the shrewd youth, since I know nothing to the contrary—"my sweet pretty mistress, will you be kind enough to tell me whereabouts I must seek the dwelling of my kinsman, Major Molineux?"

Robin's voice was plaintive and winning, and the female, seeing nothing to be shunned in the handsome country youth, thrust open the door, and came forth into the moonlight. She was a dainty little figure, with a white neck, round arms, and a slender waist, at the extremity of which her scarlet petticoat jutted out over a hoop, as if she were standing in a balloon. Moreover, her face was oval and pretty, her hair dark beneath the little cap, and her bright eyes possessed a sly freedom, which triumphed over those of Robin.

"Major Molineux dwells here," said this fair woman.

Now, her voice was the sweetest Robin had heard that night, the airy counterpart of a stream of melted silver; yet he could not help doubting whether that sweet voice spoke Gospel truth. He looked up and down the mean street, and then surveyed the house before which they stood. It was a small, dark edifice of two stories, the second of which projected over the lower floor; and the front apartment had the aspect of a shop for petty commodities.

"Now truly I am in luck," replied Robin, cunningly, "and so indeed is my kinsman, the major, in having so pretty a housekeeper. But I prithee trouble him to step to the door; I will deliver him a message from his friends in the country, and then go back to my lodgings at the inn."

"Nay, the major has been a-bed this hour or more," said the lady of the scarlet petticoat; "and it would be to little purpose to disturb him tonight, seeing his evening draught was of the strongest. But he is a kind-hearted man, and it would be as much as my life's worth to let a kinsman of his turn away from the door. You are the good old gentleman's very picture, and I could swear that was his rainy-weather hat. Also he has garments very much resembling those leather small-clothes. But come in, I pray, for I bid you hearty welcome in his name."

So saying, the fair and hospitable dame took our hero by the hand;

and the touch was light, and the force was gentleness, and though Robin read in her eyes what he did not hear in her words, yet the slender-waisted woman in the scarlet petticoat proved stronger than the athletic country youth. She had drawn his half-willing footsteps nearly to the threshold, when the opening of a door in the neighborhood startled the major's housekeeper, and, leaving the major's kinsman, she vanished speedily into her own domicile. A heavy yawn preceded the appearance of a man, who, like the Moonshine of Pyramus and Thisbe, carried a lantern, needlessly aiding his sister luminary in the heavens. As he walked sleepily up the street, he turned his broad, dull face on Robin, and displayed a long staff, spiked at the end.

"Home, vagabond, home!" said the watchman, in accents that seemed to fall asleep as soon as they were uttered. "Home, or we'll set you in the stocks, by peep of day!"

"This is the second hint of the kind," thought Robin. "I wish they would end my difficulties, by setting me there tonight."

Nevertheless, the youth felt an instinctive antipathy towards the guardian of midnight order, which at first prevented him from asking his usual question. But just when the man was about to vanish behind the corner, Robin resolved not to lose the opportunity, and shouted lustily after him—"I say, friend! will you guide me to the house of my kinsman, Major Molineux?"

The watchman made no reply, but turned the corner and was gone; yet Robin seemed to hear the sound of drowsy laughter stealing along the solitary street. At that moment, also, a pleasant titter saluted him from the open window above his head; he looked up, and caught the sparkle of a saucy eye; a round arm beckoned to him, and next he heard light footsteps descending the staircase within. But Robin, being of the household of a New England clergyman, was a good youth, as well as a shrewd one; so he resisted temptation, and fled away.

He now roamed desperately, and at random, through the town, almost ready to believe that a spell was on him, like that by which a wizard of his country had once kept three pursuers wandering, a whole winter night, within twenty paces of the cottage which they sought. The streets lay before him, strange and desolate, and the lights were extinguished in almost every house. Twice, however, little parties of men, among whom Robin distinguished individuals in outlandish attire, came hurrying along; but though on both occasions they paused to address him, such intercourse did not at all enlighten his perplexity. They did but utter a few words in some language of which Robin knew nothing, and perceiving his inability to answer, bestowed a curse upon him in plain English, and hastened away. Finally, the lad determined to knock at the door of every mansion that might appear worthy to be occupied by his kinsman, trusting that perseverance would overcome the fatality that had hitherto thwarted him. Firm in this resolve, he was passing beneath the walls of a church, which formed the corner of two streets, when, as he turned into the shade of its steeple, he encountered a bulky stranger, muffled in a cloak. The man was proceeding with the speed of earnest business, but Robin planted himself full before him, holding the oak cudgel with both hands across his body, as a bar to further passage.

"Halt, honest man, and answer me a question," said he, very resolutely. "Tell me, this instant, whereabouts is the dwelling of my kinsman, Major Molineux?"

"Keep your tongue between your teeth, fool, and let me pass!" said a deep, gruff voice, which Robin partly remembered. "Let me pass, I say, or I'll strike you to the earth!"

"No, no, neighbor!" cried Robin, flourishing his cudgel, and then thrusting its larger end close to the man's muffled face. "No, no, I'm not the fool you take me for, nor do you pass till I have an answer to my question. Whereabouts is the dwelling of my kinsman, Major Molineux?"

The stranger, instead of attempting to force his passage, stepped back into the moonlight, unmuffled his face, and stared full into that of Robin.

"Watch here an hour, and Major Molineux will pass by," said he.

Robin gazed with dismay and astonishment on the unprecedented physiognomy of the speaker. The forehead with its double prominence, the broad hooked nose, the shaggy eyebrows, and fiery eyes, were those which he had noticed at the inn, but the man's complexion had undergone a singular, or, more properly, a two-fold change. One side of the face blazed an intense red, while the other was black as midnight, the division line being in the broad bridge of the nose; and a mouth which seemed to extend from ear to ear was black or red, in contrast to the color of the cheek. The effect was as if two individual devils, a fiend of fire and a fiend of darkness, had united themselves to form this infernal visage. The stranger grinned in Robin's face, muffled his parti-colored features, and was out of sight in a moment.

"Strange things we travellers see!" ejaculated Robin.

He seated himself, however, upon the steps of the church-door, resolving to wait the appointed time for his kinsman. A few moments were consumed in philosophical speculations upon the species of man who had just left him; but having settled this point shrewdly, rationally, and satisfactorily, he was compelled to look elsewhere for his amusement. And first he threw his eyes along the street. It was of more respectable appearance than most of those into which he had wandered, and the moon, creating, like the imaginative power, a beautiful strangeness in familiar objects, gave something of romance to a scene that might not have possessed it in the light of day. The irregular and often quaint architecture of the houses, some of whose roofs were broken into numerous little peaks, while others ascended, steep and narrow, into a single point, and others again were square; the pure snow-white of some of their complexions, the aged darkness of others, and the thousand sparklings, reflected from bright substances in the walls of many; these matters engaged Robin's attention for a while, and then began to grow wearisome. Next he endeavored to define the forms of distant objects, starting away, with almost ghostly indistinctness, just as his eye appeared to grasp them; and finally he took a minute survey of an edifice which stood on the opposite side of the street, directly in front of the church-door, where he was stationed. It was a large, square mansion, distinguished from its neighbors by a balcony, which rested on tall pillars, and by an elaborate Gothic window, communicating therewith.

"Perhaps this is the very house I have been seeking," thought Robin.

Then he strove to speed away the time, by listening to a murmur which swept continually along the street, yet was scarcely audible, except to an unaccustomed ear like his; it was a low, dull, dreamy sound, compounded of many noises, each of which was at too great a distance to be separately heard. Robin marvelled at this snore of a sleeping town, and marvelled more whenever its continuity was broken by now and then a distant shout, apparently loud where it originated. But altogether it was a sleep-inspiring sound, and, to shake off its drowsy influence, Robin arose, and climbed a windowframe, that he might view the interior of the church. There the moonbeams came trembling in, and fell down upon the deserted pews, and extended along the quiet aisles. A fainter yet more awful radiance was hovering around the pulpit, and one solitary ray had dared to rest upon the opened page of the great Bible. Had nature, in that deep hour, become a worshipper in the house which man had built? Or was that heavenly light the visible sanctity of the place—visible because no earthly and impure feet were within the walls? The scene made Robin's heart shiver with a sensation of loneliness stronger than he had ever felt in the remotest depths of his native woods; so he turned away, and sat down again before the door. There were graves around the church, and now an uneasy thought obtruded into Robin's breast. What if the object of his search, which had been so often and so strangely thwarted, were at the time mouldering in his shroud? What if his kinsman should glide through yonder gate, and nod and smile to him in dimly passing by?

"O that any breathing thing were here with me!" said Robin.

Recalling his thoughts from this uncomfortable track, he sent them over forest, hill, and stream, and attempted to imagine how that evening of ambiguity and weariness had been spent by his father's household. He pictured them assembled at the door, beneath the tree, the great old tree, which had been spared for its huge twisted trunk, and venerable shade, when a thousand leafy brethren fell. There, at the going down of the summer sun, it was his father's custom to perform domestic worship, that the neighbors might come and join with him like brothers of the family, and that the wayfaring man might pause to drink at that fountain, and keep his heart pure by freshening the memory of home. Robin distinguished the seat of every individual of the little audience; he saw the good man in the midst, holding the Scriptures in the golden light that fell from the western clouds; he beheld him close the book, and all rise up to pray. He heard the old thanksgivings for daily mercies, the old supplications for their continuance, to which he had so often listened in weariness, but which were now among his dear remembrances. He perceived the slight inequality of his father's voice when he came to speak of the absent one; he noted how his mother turned her face to the broad and knotted trunk; how his elder brother scorned, because the beard was rough upon his upper lip, to permit his features to be moved; how the younger sister drew down a low hanging branch before her eyes; and how the little one of all, whose sports had hitherto broken the decorum of the scene, understood the prayer for her playmate, and burst into clamorous grief. Then he saw them go in at the door; and when Robin would have entered also, the latch tinkled into its place, and he was excluded from his home.

"Am I here, or there?" cried Robin, starting; for all at once, when his thoughts had become visible and audible in a dream, the long, wide, solitary street shone out before him.

He aroused himself, and endeavored to fix his attention steadily upon the large edifice which he had surveyed before. But still his mind kept vibrating between fancy and reality; by turns, the pillars of the balcony lengthened into the tall, bare stems of pines, dwindled down to human figures, settled again into their true shape and size, and then commenced a new succession of changes. For a single moment, when he deemed himself awake, he could have sworn that a visage—one which he seemed to remember, yet could not absolutely name as his kinsman's—was looking towards him from the Gothic window. A deeper sleep wrestled with and nearly overcame him, but fled at the sound of footsteps along the opposite pavement. Robin rubbed his eyes, discerned a man passing at the foot of the balcony, and addressed him in a loud, peevish, and lamentable cry.

"Hallo, friend! must I wait here all night for my kinsman, Major Molineux?"

The sleeping echoes awoke, and answered the voice; and the passenger, barely able to discern a figure sitting in the oblique shade of the steeple, traversed the street to obtain a nearer view. He was himself a gentleman in his prime, of open, intelligent, cheerful, and altogether prepossessing countenance. Perceiving a country youth, apparently homeless and without friends, he accosted him in a tone of real kindness, which had become strange to Robin's ears.

"Well, my good lad, why are you sitting here?" inquired he. "Can I be of service to you in any way?"

"I am afraid not, sir," replied Robin, despondingly; "yet I shall take it kindly, if you'll answer me a single question. I've been searching, half the night, for one Major Molineux; now, sir, is there really such a person in these parts, or am I dreaming?"

"Major Molineux! The name is not altogether strange to me," said the gentleman, smiling. "Have you any objection to telling me the nature of your business with him?"

Then Robin briefly related that his father was a clergyman, settled on a small salary, at a long distance back in the country, and that he and Major Molineux were brothers' children. The major, having inherited riches, and acquired civil and military rank, had visited his cousin, in great pomp, a year or two before; had manifested much interest in Robin and an elder brother, and, being childless himself, had thrown out hints respecting the future establishment of one of them in life. The elder brother was destined to succeed to the farm which his father cultivated in the interval of sacred duties; it was therefore determined that Robin should profit by his kinsman's generous intentions, especially as he seemed to be rather the favorite, and was thought to possess other necessary endowments.

"For I have the name of being a shrewd youth," observed Robin, in this part of his story.

"I doubt not you deserve it," replied his new friend, good-naturedly; "but pray proceed."

"Well, sir, being nearly eighteen years old, and well-grown, as you see," continued Robin, drawing himself up to his full height, "I thought it high time to begin the world. So my mother and sister put me in handsome trim, and my father gave me half the remnant of his last year's salary, and five days ago I started for this place, to pay the major a visit. But, would you believe it, sir! I crossed the ferry a little after dark, and have yet found nobody that would show me the way to his dwelling—only, an hour or two since, I was told to wait here, and Major Molineux would pass by."

"Can you describe the man who told you this?" inquired the gentleman.

"O, he was a very ill-favored fellow, sir," replied Robin, "with two great bumps on his forehead, a hook nose, fiery eyes—and, what struck me as the strangest, his face was of two different colors. Do you happen to know such a man, sir!"

"Not intimately," answered the stranger, "but I chanced to meet him a little time previous to your stopping me. I believe you may trust his word, and that the major will very shortly pass through this street. In the meantime, as I have a singular curiosity to witness your meeting, I will sit down here upon the steps, and bear you company."

He seated himself accordingly, and soon engaged his companion in animated discourse. It was but of brief continuance, however, for a noise of shouting, which had long been remotely audible, drew so much nearer that Robin inquired its cause.

"What may be the meaning of this uproar?" asked he. "Truly, if your town be always as noisy, I shall find little sleep, while I am an inhabitant."

"Why, indeed, friend Robin, there do appear to be three or four riotous fellows abroad tonight," replied the gentleman. "You must not expect all the stillness of your native woods, here in our streets. But the watch will shortly be at the heels of these lads, and—"

"Ay, and set them in the stocks by peep of day," interrupted Robin, recollecting his own encounter with the drowsy lantern-bearer. "But, dear sir, if I may trust my ears, an army of watchmen would never make head against such a multitude of rioters. There were at least a thousand voices went up to make that one shout."

"May not a man have several voices, Robin, as well as two complexions?" said his friend.

"Perhaps a man may; but Heaven forbid that a woman should!" responded the shrewd youth, thinking of the seductive tones of the major's housekeeper.

The sounds of a trumpet in some neighboring street now became so evident and continual, that Robin's curiosity was strongly excited. In addition to the shouts, he heard frequent bursts from many instruments of discord, and a wild and confused laughter filled up the intervals. Robin rose from the steps, and looked wistfully towards a point whither several people seemed to be hastening.

"Surely some prodigious merry-making is going on," exclaimed he. "I have laughed very little since I left home, sir, and should be sorry to lose an opportunity. Shall we step round the corner by that darkish house, and take our share of the fun?"

"Sit down again, sit down, good Robin," replied the gentleman, laying his hand on the skirt of the gray coat. "You forget that we must wait here for your kinsman; and there is reason to believe that he will pass by, in the course of a very few moments."

The near approach of the uproar had now disturbed the neighborhood; windows flew open on all sides; and many heads, in the attire of the pillow, and confused by sleep suddenly broken, were protruded to the gaze of whoever had leisure to observe them. Eager voices hailed each other from house to house, all demanding the explanation, which not a soul could give. Half-dressed men hurried towards the unknown commotion, stumbling as they went over the stone steps, that thrust themselves into the narrow foot-walk. The shouts, the laughter, and the tuneless bray, the antipodes of music, came onwards with increasing din, till scattered individuals, and then denser bodies, began to appear round a corner at the distance of a hundred yards.

"Will you recognize your kinsman, if he passes in this crowd?" inquired the gentleman.

"Indeed, I can't warrant it, sir; but I'll take my stand here, and keep a bright look-out," answered Robin, descending to the outer edge of the pavement.

A mighty stream of people now emptied into the street, and came rolling slowly towards the church. A single horseman wheeled the corner in the midst of them, and close behind him came a band of fearful wind-instruments, sending forth a fresher discord, now that no intervening buildings kept it from the ear. Then a redder light disturbed the moonbeams, and a dense multitude of torches shone along the street, concealing, by their glare, whatever object they illuminated. The single horseman, clad in a military dress, and bearing a drawn sword, rode onward as the leader, and, by his fierce and variegated countenance, appeared like war personified: the red of one cheek was an emblem of fire and sword; the blackness of the other betokened the mourning that attends them. In his train were wild figures in the Indian dress, and many fantastic shapes without a model, giving the whole march a visionary air, as if a dream had broken forth from some feverish brain, and were sweeping visibly through the midnight streets. A mass of people, inactive, except as applauding spectators, hemmed the procession in; and several women ran along the side-walk, piercing the confusion of heavier sounds with their shrill voices of mirth or terror.

"The double-faced fellow has his eye upon me," muttered Robin, with an indefinite but an uncomfortable idea that he was himself to bear a part in the pageantry.

The leader turned himself in the saddle, and fixed his glance full upon the country youth, as the steed went slowly by. When Robin had freed his eyes from those fiery ones, the musicians were passing before him, and the torches were close at hand; but the unsteady brightness of the latter formed a veil which he could not penetrate. The rattling of wheels over the stones sometimes found its way to his ear, and confused traces of a human form appeared at intervals, and then melted into the vivid light. A moment more, and the leader thundered a command to halt: the trumpets vomited a horrid breath, and then held their peace; the shouts and laughter of the people died away, and there remained only a universal hum, allied to silence. Right before Robin's eyes was an uncovered cart. There the torches blazed the brightest, there the moon shone out like day, and there, in tar-and-feathery dignity, sat his kinsman Major Molineux!

He was an elderly man, of large and majestic person, and strong, square features, betokening a steady soul; but steady as it was, his enemies had found means to shake it. His face was pale as death, and far more ghastly; the broad forehead was contracted in his agony, so that his eyebrows formed one grizzled line; his eyes were red and wild, and the foam hung white upon his quivering lip. His whole frame was agitated by a quick and continual tremor, which his pride strove to quell, even in those circumstances of overwhelming humiliation. But perhaps the bitterest pang of all was when his eyes met those of Robin; for he evidently knew him on the instant, as the youth stood witnessing the foul disgrace of a head grown gray in honor. They stared at each other in silence, and Robin's knees shook, and his hair bristled, with a mixture of pity and terror. Soon, however, a bewildering excitement began to seize upon his mind; the preceding adventures of the night, the unexpected appearance of the crowd, the torches, the confused din and the hush that followed, the spectre of his kinsman reviled by that great multitude—all this, and, more than all, a perception of tremendous ridicule in the whole scene, affected him with a sort of mental inebriety. At that moment a voice of sluggish merriment saluted Robin's ears; he turned instinctively, and just behind the corner of the church stood the lantern-bearer, rubbing his eyes, and drowsily enjoying the lad's amazement. Then he heard a peal of laughter like the ringing of silvery bells; a woman twitched his arm, a saucy eye met his, and he saw the lady of the scarlet petticoat. A sharp, dry cachinnation appealed to his memory, and, standing on tiptoe in the crowd, with his white apron over his head, he beheld the courteous little innkeeper. And lastly, there sailed over the heads of the multitude a great, broad laugh, broken in the midst by two sepulchral hems; thus, "Haw, haw, haw—hem, hem—haw, haw, haw, haw!"

The sound proceeded from the balcony of the opposite edifice, and thither Robin turned his eyes. In front of the Gothic window stood the old citizen, wrapped in a wide gown, his gray periwig exchanged for a night-cap, which was thrust back from his forehead, and his silk stockings hanging about his legs. He supported himself on his polished cane in a fit of convulsive merriment, which manifested itself on his solemn old features like a funny inscription on a tomb-stone. Then Robin seemed to hear the voices of the barbers, of the guests of the inn, and of all who had made sport of him that night. The contagion was spreading among the multitude, when, all at once, it seized upon Robin, and he sent forth a shout of laughter that echoed through the street—every man shook his sides, every man emptied his lungs, but Robin's shout was the loudest there. The cloud-spirits peeped from their silvery islands, as the congregated mirth went roaring up the sky! The Man in the Moon heard the far bellow; "Oh," quoth he, "the old earth is frolicksome tonight!"

When there was a momentary calm in that tempestuous sea of sound, the leader gave the sign, the procession resumed its march. On they went, like fiends that throng in mockery around some dead potentate, mighty no more, but majestic still in his agony. On they went, in counterfeited pomp, in senseless uproar, in frenzied merriment, trampling all on an old man's heart. On swept the tumult, and left a silent street behind.

"Well, Robin, are you dreaming?" inquired the gentleman, laying his hand on the youth's shoulder.

Robin started, and withdrew his arm from the stone post to which he had instinctively clung, as the living stream rolled by him. His cheek was somewhat pale and his eye not quite as lively as in the earlier part of the evening.

"Will you be kind enough to show me the way to the ferry?" said he, after a moment's pause.

"You have, then, adopted a new subject of inquiry?" observed his companion, with a smile.

"Why, yes, sir," replied Robin, rather dryly. "Thanks to you, and to my other friends, I have at last met my kinsman, and he will scarce desire to see my face again. I begin to grow weary of a town life, sir. Will you show me the way to the ferry?"

"No, my good friend Robin—not tonight, at least," said the gentleman. "Some few days hence, if you wish it, I will speed you on your journey. Or, if you prefer to remain with us, perhaps, as you are a shrewd youth, you may rise in the world without the help of your kinsman, Major Molineux."

Why, at the end of the story, does Robin laugh? Would you have laughed? In what ways is this a story about any young person leaving home and starting a new life—about you?

You may also find this story pertinent to you as you begin college. It is about one of your professors—and somewhere on campus there *is* a Dovisch.

Dovisch in the wilderness
HERBERT WILNER

Call me Dovisch, another wanderer survived to tell a story.

I mean it. Since I saw you last Wednesday, I had an American misadventure. I find myself obligated to share it with you, a class in American Literature, Early Period. Yes, I know what you are here for: because I announced last week this hour is set aside to talk with you about your final examination. Thus come all the bright faces at eight in the morning at the end of May in yet another Spring in a part of California that has only weather and no climate, thus no season, hence no time. Except finals time. What kind of questions will Dovisch ask on his final exam? A short route to a high grade to know beforehand the kind of questions. So no one is absent today. Perfect attendance for the first time in—how many weeks? Let it be so.

Nevertheless, I shall share this experience with you. I promise it will be preparation enough for your finals. I share it with you fresh and unrehearsed, because it didn't end till two o'clock this very morning. Six hours ago. No, that's not right. Today is for a flyer, but it is also for facts. My colleagues would remind me: dates, figures, facts—toughness. At the bottom of all knowledge and every wisdom, a fact. It is the gossip of the corridors, what my colleagues accuse me of. And some of you have heard it in the corridors, or over coffee, or in your other classes. I know how they accuse me, leavening it with an intolerable affection: Dovisch, the rainbowmaker. So the hard fact of it is that my misadventure did not come to its end at two this morning. It continues still, because I am obligated to share it with you, and I am going to share it with you, delicacies notwithstanding. And you will not learn from it because you will not see the immediate profit to yourselves because you will not imagine it can have anything to do with your final exam. You begin already to put down the ballpoints, to close the notebooks, and on some of your faces I see that smile reserved for moments like this when you know I am about to go the long way around. There goes Dovisch again, the rainbowmaker on another flyer. Students of Early American Literature, Section 2, listen to me. Take notes. My little misadventure *is* your finals. And thus I begin, Dovisch fashion, learned from Emerson, accented by way of the Bronx, inflected not a little by a history somewhat older than the American, the inflection slightly exaggerated this morning.

I went last week to Pyramid Lake. I went

179

alone after my last class on Wednesday. I went in my car. I curse cars every day of my life, but I went to Pyramid Lake to be alone, to hold conversations with no one, so the car was a matter of free choice. For those of you not from this part of the country, know that Pyramid Lake is thirty miles north and slightly east of Reno. It is thirty miles long and ten miles wide. I went to Pyramid Lake to test myself in the experience of solitude, and to know at first hand the distinctions to be made between solitude and isolation. I had four whole days to spend there. It will come to some of you as no surprise that I had never in all my life sustained a period, however brief, of true solitude. Isolation, yes—isolation always—but not solitude. So the four days, seized from my work and my family, seemed time enough for a deliberate test. I took a sleeping bag, which I preferred to buy for the occasion rather than borrow from a colleague. I knew too well not their unwillingness to lend but their looks upon lending. Dovisch in a sleeping bag? I took a sweater, a flannel shirt, changes of socks, and so forth; also canned fruits and a can opener, and boxes of zwieback borrowed from my daughter. I have a credit card, so I needed no money even for gas. I took fifty cents for bridge tolls, and no more. And my checkbook. I must explain this.

I did not start out intending to make things difficult. I wanted, if possible, to experience joy in my solitude, not hardship. Thus my food arrangement. I was not going to test self-reliance in the form of survival. That's not what Emerson meant. Thoreau either. I was going to test solitude, in which self-reliance was a mere consequence. I can't fish. I have never in my life gone fishing. And if I did fish and caught a fish, I could not trust myself to build a fire. And if I caught a fish and built a fire, I would have had to have brought along the fishing equipment. Also a pot for cooking. No, I was altogether less encumbered with the canned fruits, and I admit a fondness for sweet syrups and a distaste for fish. I must insist upon the fact that I went responsibly to Pyramid Lake for pleasure, not hardship. I left out money not because I sneer at it. I am Puritan enough to know its grace. But in my wallet it would remind me always of purchase, and that would imply some other person who sells, and though he might through all my stay be absent, the money in my wallet would be an emblem of his implication in my life and a diminishment of my solitude. I took the checkbook because solitude is the essence of responsibility and has nothing in common with thoughtlessness. I have a wife and four little children. There are emergencies in such a world. I will come soon to tell you of some of them.

Be advised also that I took no books, magazines or newspapers. I took no paper and no writing implements. I must correct again the easy assumption some of you begin to make that I went to Pyramid Lake on a merely literary impulse borrowed from those very books I refused to take. "Life is our dictionary," Emerson said, *American Scholar,* 1837, and you imagine I set aside books the better to experience real life. It is not what Emerson meant. It is not what I intended. He wanted us to possess and not be oppressed by what we read. Reading was an extension of the active life by which he challenged all Americans. For my own part, I disavowed books because they implicate a voice roaring at me, a diminishment of solitude. I disavowed writing. It implicates my untalented efforts to roar at someone else. Another diminishment. You see—I tried to be practical in everything.

So, directly to it. The time goes. This is our last meeting. I must get it all in. I tell you, I see America now. I can open my fist and watch it dance. Rainbows, Dovisch, rainbows. Facts, dates—

I arrived at Pyramid Lake on Wednesday at five-thirty in the evening, having traveled east to find the West. I went through Reno and then north. Motels, restaurants, gas stations, domiciles for the divorced, the divorcing, the gamblers. Scarlet letters in every face, branded in the flesh. The un-epic frontier of our present time. Then northward through the desert mountains. Sagebrush and female slopes and hollows. Late sunlight shifting colors, purple and violet and blue and a flare of red, shimmering, shifting. Mountains shifting in the light. The windshield danced. A curve in the road, a descent, and there to the right, below the lowering line of the desert mountain, Pyramid Lake. Brilliant even for a polished stone. Water polished by water. A table top in a naked world. Not a tree. Not a cloud. The whole lake in one turn of the head. A great belt of not quite water under a balloon of sky. Into which enters, into that universe of silence, the *phtt phtt* of the old Plymouth, inside of which is Dovisch, Professor of American Literature. Specialist in Emerson; seminars offered also, for a touch of the old country, in Dostoevski. Inside of Dovisch, before this naked world all in silence, the heart empties with a gush, a roar reaching into the corners of *our* Promised Land.

Terrifying landscape. Perfection for solitude. I must impress you with it through *my* eyes, but I have no power for such description. From where would I get it? Born forty-two years ago in the Bronx, Simon Dovisch, second son to Morris and Esther Dovisch, immigrants from Russia, that eastern world tilting off Europe, related also to uncles of Oriental countenance to make a boy wonder from which angle the wanderers first began to wander, to cohabit with what strange ancestors along the way. Raised on the fourth floor rear, sharing his brother's room with a view opening to other windows on the fourth floor with coal-smoked bricks between, and raised in the streets, down there on the dark concrete bottom of what *your* Whitman called the clefts of streets, raised to games of ball, at which he was inept, and among the squealings and the yawpings of those to whom solitude would be death and for whom isolation was a way of life. Who learned sex on the corners under lampposts and fumbled at its practice in night-time backyards and on tenement roofs, filled with it by a guilt the whole tribe of Mathers could not have endured because it derived from the shame of poverty and not from a mere redemptive sin.

So with much to prove through the years, and with books already the only means of his demonstrations. Immersed then, drowning in the vivid American history: splashed and drenched with Pilgrims and Puritans and Quakers, Revolutionists and Rationalists and opportunists, inventors and fur trappers and Indians too, Natty Bumppos and millionaires and Abolitionists and poets and novelists and cowboys and presidents, prairies and mountains and deserts and oceans, gleaned, all of it, from black type on a white page, millions of pages by a light bulb on the fourth floor rear in the Bronx. Later in libraries. Here now on the Western shore, a Professor of American Literature.

That literature beginning, as I have told you, in a bitter romance with God for the possession by His grace of an endless wealth of wilderness to be ravished in love, goaded into the love of primitive instincts, and shamed by those instincts into savagery itself, which is the worship of the thing. So they found emblems of it everywhere, the thing: witches, kites and keys, scarlet letters, a whale, a ferry, a river, things celebrated by the very prophets who saw the doom in them. And all the while even the most ignorant of them learning in their blood what Dovisch from the Bronx, professing American literature, cannot infuse into the blood, melt down the books how he will.

Things. Things. Things. To fish, to hunt, to build a house, to farm, to conduct a business, to repair a car, to predict a season. To name a tree, to name a flower, to name a fish, a bird, to control a single practical art—to build, say, a fire. To repair, say, a car, a damned, cursed old Plymouth. Things. Things. In them resides the power of all description.

Dovisch alone at Pyramid Lake, in a naked world of silence, seeking solitude, testing whether he can so late in life experience it at all, in order to understand by experience one of the conditions of what he teaches.

Students, I take pride in telling you I remained at the lake all my allotted time. You must understand what it was for me if you are to share my experience of what came to pass at the end of it. That first night. Arrivals are stunning. Impressions are immediate. You never know again all that lives in the first encounter. And now, a mere four days later, I cannot recover those first minutes of coming upon the lake. Because none of what followed—

Look. I did this the first day. I arrived in the evening at five-thirty. I drove on. I did not want to stay where the highway came directly to the lake. There was something like a diner there. Hot dogs, soda, so forth. Closed and deserted, it could nevertheless be a point of gathering. I follow the lake road some miles farther. The sun glaring. Barren everywhere. I park the car. I open a can of stewed pears, a box of zwiebacks, and I have my supper at the lake. I sit and stare. Dovisch alone. Later, the sun going down. A dish of flame. Thoughts of my family in our Metropolitan Life Housing Project. Thoughts of my students, of you. Thoughts of America. Then a chill, the sudden cold. I put on my flannel shirt, my sweater. The growing darkness. I prepare the sleeping bag. Ah, that first night of trying to sleep in that wretched sack. Smile all you want, but one thing all of you can learn from the Bronx is the nature of a true mattress. Here at the lake, rocks and stones underneath. And I told them in the shop where I purchased the sleeping bag. Look at me, I told them. A tall man, feet like canoes. Ample room, ample room he assured me. American entrepreneurs. The human contact gone, the cash register everything. I was too big for the bag, the bag too small for me. In physical discomfort begins the wilderness of imaginings. The enemy of sleep.

In the total darkness, in the universe of silence, what else, what vast night life crawls and slithers here? Snakes? Rattlers? Spiders? Tarantulas? Calm yourself, Dovisch! Achieve solitude. I ransack such knowledge as I have of flora and fauna. Miserable knowledge. I could have written all that I knew on a part of one zwieback and have made a supper of the part remaining. So I confess. The first night was full of imagined horrors. I have from a cockroach childhood on the fourth floor a loathing of crawling things.

You can imagine, then, the depths of my self-contempt when I commenced to believe I would not even make it through the first night. Not only the lumps and clumps of stones beneath me, but the wretched sleeping bag too small. Not only the stones and the sleeping bag, but my eyeglasses too. If the stones and the bedding should keep me awake, I should at least enjoy the stars. When in his life did Dovisch sleep with the stars? But with his eyeglasses off, who could see the stars?

With his eyeglasses on, how sleep at all? And if the stones and the sleeping bag and the eyeglasses were not enough, comes now the wild imaginings of crawling things. Thoughts, then, of retreating to the car. It was not that much of a cheat on my idea of solitude, but something in me argued against it as a mere disguise for an early withdrawal. Besides, if a crawling thing had made its way into the car while I had unloaded? Wouldn't that be worse? The crawling thing and myself made natural enemies by being confined together in an artificial compartment. Wouldn't the thing then seek artificial revenge on me, whereas it might in the open space, with a whole Western desert in which to conduct its slithering life, might it not merely crawl away from me as a nuisance to be avoided?

Ultimately, I resigned myself. In the middle of the night I offered myself the following proposition. If it was my fate to succumb to a venomous bite, if a snake or a spider with thousands of square barren miles to crawl in chooses the few inches of my exposed face, then God's will be done. I surrendered. I can report to you I overcame my imaginings. Ultimately, I slept.

Came then the first of my pink dawns at the lake. Morning is when I am awake and there is a dawn in me, said Thoreau, echoes Dovisch now, who ordinarily, by old Bronx habit and by way of avoiding noisy children in the morning, leads the Dostoevski life of the underground world after the midnight hour when the soul, losing God, finds the psychiatrist. Let me summarize those blessed days. Let me give you the light and the tone and the angle. You squirm. You ask yourselves; of what relevance? Is there at least a story? But the story is also the arrangements to be made? Didn't Hawthorne arrange? Didn't Melville? Know then that I sat for long hours in sun-bright places at the other side of the lake. That I walked for miles along the rim of the water, my pants rolled, feet naked, naked head to the naked sun. My eye grew accustomed to naked distance. My mind thereafter sought relief from panoramic registrations. It ordered my eyes to closer recognitions. I forced myself to look for long uninterrupted sequences at nearer things. At pebbles, rocks, pools of water, boulders that were porous, at the pores of boulders, at brush; at silence itself I looked and listened. I spent a whole hour tossing one pebble into shallow water retrieving it each time. I spent a whole hour watching a large bird flying high in great circles—watching me, perhaps. Crow, eagle, hawk, falcon—who am I to know the names of birds? For a whole hour we were hundreds of feet apart, but eyeball to eyeball. And I knew its great power of sight compared to my weakness of vision. Easy then to make factual what I have told you again and again as mere surmise: the object seen is in the image of the eyes, not the object. Never again ask me, where is it—the Oversoul? Of what size, what shape? Know then what I mean when I ask in turn: of what size and shape is your eye?

Look—picture my days at Lake Pyramid this way. Know that my days were symmetrical. Know that I lived inside them with great precision. Picture me there from up close as a tall, gross-featured, big-footed, clumsy man, alien to where he stood and what he gazed at, reddening in the sun, his hidden heart slipping into the thrill of un-isolation. Picture him there from afar as but another sparrow in the great void, not without a little grace, a small addition of human design against the barren mountains overlooking the blue and stony water under the height of the sky. Hear me whistling Mozart melodies into the Nevada air.

Students, in this landscape so strange to me, I learned how I loved the great, secret, mythical history of my country. Yes, *my* country too. Removed by the solitude itself from all isolation, I would have laid down my life for my country's secret heart. Yes, Dovisch on a flyer, but fly with me if you can. Solitude is the experience of the idea itself. It is the racial nostalgia reducing the baggage of our life's factuality—even the fourth floor rear and its crazy summons to books. But in the thingness of time, the idea vanishes. It had to be lost. Long before cars and jets and bombs and rockets. Lost even as far back as whaling time, as *Walden* time, as *Leaves of Grass* time. But history is the aspiration as well as the loss.

The idea and the fact and the emblem between. I could not wait to get back to share some of this with you in the beginning of this hour, to give you a particle of my new feeling. But how would I say it, since it was itself only another idea? More Dovisch rainbows. But fate waited. Nothing is wasted. My misadventure waited. The facts themselves waited. So—the arrangements made and the story at last.

My time was up, and I threw my litter into the car. I left not one trace of my presence there. The bird who had watched me was long since gone. Would its eyes in the future remember Dovisch? Who knows? It was Sunday. It was yesterday. It was two in the afternoon. I was exuberant. I had stayed out my time. I had learned. Which of you cannot by now picture Dovisch in his exuberance? I almost could not find my keys. Trembling fingers fumbling in pockets. The beginning of panic. Voluntary solitude is one thing, but who am I to confront an enforced one? Calm, calm, I urged myself. There were the keys in the glove compartment where I had with good forethought left them. The return home then.

I turn the key. I press the pedal. Nothing. A little *erk-erk* noise in the big silence, and then nothing. Calm, calm, I urge myself. First the fuel. But how should it be the fuel when I had filled up in Truckee with just such a precaution in mind? I am almost afraid to look. If there was a leak and in three days it all ran out, where should I walk now for gas? I turn the key and look. Plenty of fuel. The needle almost to the three-quarters. It was a mistake. A clumsiness of the fingers. My excitement to get home. To see you here this morning, to tell you. Again, then, on the pedal. Again nothing. *Erk-erk-erk,* and nothing more. In the middle of nowhere with a car that won't start on a Sunday afternoon with a lecture class to meet on the next morning, having promised, given my word to review for the finals, not to mention a devoted family, the oldest child only seven, but who knows already how to worry. Calm yourself. A voice into the panic, into the silence, into another *erk-erk,* another and another. I ransack such facts as I have gathered of cars that will not start. Another zwieback full. Gathered from the general mechanic atmosphere and previous car catastrophes, like old people in hospitals who know their organs in proportion to the number of survived diseases therein. So a car that won't start: wet spark plugs? How could that be in a desert? Once with an old Studebaker there was trouble with the vacuum advance. A vacuum advance. Who could remember what it was? Where in the engine would I find it? Once with an old Ford there was trouble with a voltage regulator. Again, who knows where such a thing is to be found in an engine? Would you believe me when I confess I do not even know what voltage is? I would tell you back what you tell me of the Oversoul. I can't see it, so why should I believe in it? Is a voltage regulator something to believe in? Tinker Toys for children. Apparatus. But if the ignorance derived from a lack of faith should cost you your life in a desert? or attendance at your job? or the peace of mind of your family? There's the rub.

So smile at me and my car pickle. Do you pause ever to count up all the things to which you have delivered faith and are ignorant of? Girls here who drive cars to campus. Do you know what makes them go? Gasoline. Is that an answer? Then food alone would keep alive a dying man. Do you know, when you press a button, why the elevator should close a door and go up or down to the designated floor and not through the top of the building or through the bottom of the cellar? Do you know why an airplane should fly? Why these senseless tubes in the ceiling should light up when I press a button? Not to mention computers. Or X-rays. Or a radio. Or television. Listen—our Benjamin Franklin, whom I treated so scantily in the first semester. Sandwiched between Puritans and Emerson, who could afford to pause there? But who would deny he was one of those who lived with his feet on the ground? That I despise the man is another story.

The battery. Of course I thought of the battery. Three days and I had not once used the car. But the battery was only three months old and the guarantee was for eighteen. So go cash in a guarantee at Lake Pyramid. A million eighteen-month batteries, and Dovisch gets the lemon. Another old story. The question was a push. Where could I find another car to push me in that sand and sage where I had pulled mine off the road? Calm. Calm. Perhaps not the whole battery. A cable connection, perhaps. I too had heard of such things. For luck I try once more. *Erk-erk,* and then nothing. I open the hood. I see the battery and the cables thereto, one with the plus and one with the minus. What all that means, I never knew. Gingerly, I touch the wires. My heart leaps. Indeed, one seems loose. I turn a little, and it tightens. I rush back to the car, turn the ignition. *Erk-erk,* nothing more. I go out again. Again with the cables—pinching, stroking, prodding, pushing, punching at last, punching the senseless cable, the stupid battery, and for good measure the hot fender. *Erk-erk.*

Listen—the hour flies. To make it short: I need a push and the solitude is over for me, but not for where I am. To walk then and return in a car with help. I take the keys. I walk. I walk and walk. At last a sign. Four miles to Nixon. It is already an hour since I first tried to start the car. Three o'clock now and who ever heard of Nixon? A community, a hamlet, and people nevertheless. Nixon in an hour, I assure myself, and perhaps a car I can flag down along the way before then. I am a good walker, an old Manhattan tramper. A deep breath for fortitude, and off I go, driven by hatred of cars, hurried by my anxiety about driving at night on highways.

There is no time to give you the hike in the hot desert sun. Fill in as you will. All history is incomplete. Only imagine the anger, the distress, the reasonable panic. A cool head, says Melville, betrays an icy heart. The sweat, the dust. The beginning of trees, an oasis. The sight at last of a car on the highway. I get out in the lane. Exultant, I wave my arms. How lucky that I so soon see a car! Would you believe it that they nearly ran me down? A gang of boys, maybe college boys, car-tinkerers. Maybe any one of them could have helped me. Am I innocent to believe any one of them would have if I had had the opportunity to explain to him what it was all about? But can I make a speech to a rocket? Seventy, eighty miles an hour they went past me, swerving into the other lane in the last minute, and at the same time I leaped into a thicket of sage on my side. One of them had the gall to stick a head out the window and shake a fist at me.

I brushed myself off and resumed walking. Only then did I think for the first time of the appearance I presented to others. Since the Wednesday morning of my departure, I had not shaved. My nose and forehead, I knew from old experience, would be shining like a McIntosh apple—sunburn. My khaki pants were some other color now, and no end of wrinkles everywhere from struggles with the undersized sleeping bag. My T-shirt smeared from where I leaned under the hood of the car, and my hands all dirt and grease from playing with the battery cable. What sort of welcome could I expect at the first house I came to? Bedraggled and begrimed, how would I be received on someone's property, uninvited on a Sunday afternoon?

Came then the first house. Not a house, a shack. Albeit under a few trees and with a porch, and before the porch not one but three cars. Not a person in sight. Behind the dwelling place, on a small slope, cows, cattle—it was not then the time to discriminate. But on the other side of the road, another shack, and only one car. I decide for that one. Three cars on a Sunday before such a small dwelling place means company, visitors. Not, it seemed to me, an encouraging atmosphere for a plea of distress, a call for help. I crossed the road, noticing the newness of the car. A shack to live in, but a new car for leaving and returning. Another small porch. Three, four steps, the wood answering back to my feet. Good, I tell myself: for the door to the right of the steps is half open, and the noise of my approach forewarns them I don't come in stealth. Outside, the brilliant sun; inside, all dark. And already a foul odor. Better that way, I encourage myself. Poverty and even filth will be less offended by my own appearance. I knock, not timidly, not too loudly. Good luck to you here, Dovisch, I announce to myself, implore. Then I tell myself at once: Ask only to use the telephone, to call the nearest service station.

There is no answer to my knocking. I knock again, somewhat louder. I wait. No answer. There is the odor, definitely foul, reminiscent for me of dark corners in schoolyards, of relief stations on certain desolate subway stops. Also sounds—a chair scraping, perhaps. But no footsteps, no speech. I call out: "Anyone at home?" And that, in four days' time, is the first spoken language I have addressed to a listener. Do you know the experience of separation from your own voice? Do you know how it accounts in Thoreau for the initial acid of his Walden tones, the isolation invading solitude? But yesterday at that moment I was not looking for insights into Thoreau. I thought: should I push the door open the rest of the way or knock again? I push. Not vigorously—politely. The light from outside floods in. They are standing there blinking at the light, watching me.

A man and a woman. Puerto Ricans, I tell myself. No, Mexicans. What would Puerto Ricans be doing there? Short and thick and swarthy, wide foreheads, wide noses, like Gauguins—but no sparkle: sullen, suspicious. They keep blinking at the light. They look at me, and they look at each other. Dark black hair, both of them. The man in a sort of crew cut, but not cut down enough. The hairs standing up like quills, and greasy. The woman's too, but lank, uncombed. He wears dungarees and one of those faded blue worker's-farmer's shirts, also denim. She is bare-armed in a dress that merely hangs from her, that needs a belt, a collar, or something. Will they even understand English, I wonder, as I begin my introduction, my explanation, my need.

Students, I am not a good reporter, not a good observer to begin with. Furniture I am blind to. I can stare at stuff in the house of a stranger or friend and not remember the very next day what was there. But did you need to be Henry James or even Dreiser to stand where I stood yesterday afternoon on the threshold of that shack (no one had yet invited me in) and not know at once as you tried to explain your predicament that there could be no telephone in such a place? Perhaps there was not even electricity. Between the two of them, where they stood, there was a little table on skinny legs—a bridge table—piled with dishes and beer cans, and on the table was a thick, half-burned candle. So you see how I had to shift my explanation toward a plea for direct help. What I do remember is a potbellied stove with a tilted flue, clothes on hooks on one of the walls, and in a corner, by itself, nothing near it, like a museum piece, a single contour chair on those pipe legs. Sears, Roebuck modern. Red yet.

So—were they in all those exchanges of looks between them, understanding a word of what I said about my car, my plight, my explanation and apology for my ragged appearance? I must confess I said nothing of my professional occupation. Instinctively I imagined it would make no impression, or it would actually run a risk. Anywhere in Europe it would have been my first announcement. Put that in your notebooks and make of it what you will. I ended with a mention of my children and my wife, and the worry my certain absence from dinner tonight would cause them until I could get the car started and find a telephone. Did they understand? Another exchange of looks between the two of them. Then at last the man speaks. One word.

"Sunday."

No accent, least of all a Mexican accent. But with spitefulness. That haughtiness of the permanently deprived addressing the temporarily deprived.

"Yes, Sunday," I say. "My wife alone on a Sunday and worrying that something has happened to me. The accidents on highways these days." I look toward the woman. I have, you noticed, dropped the plea of children. I get the impression this is a childless place. Who can guess what resentment it causes? Again the exchange of looks between them. Except for the turning of their heads and the blinking of their eyes, they remain all the while motionless. And I am still only on the threshold. He talks again. Two words now.

"How much?" he says.

"How much what?" I ask him. I look again at the woman. I am forced to say she was ugly. That stoop, that arch and thickness between the shoulder blades. The filthy hair. That sullenness, that stupefaction of face. She looks again at the man.

"Sunday," he repeats. "You pay how much?"

"How much do you want?" I say.

"How much do you give?" he asks.

"How much do you get paid an hour?" I ask him.

No response. Like wood. Nevertheless, in fairness, in fact, though I am but a poor businessman, I do admit the bargain is on his side, and, humanity apart, the right too. I cannot conceive of what I intruded upon between those two, but I am the intruder, and in need.

"Ten dollars if you get the car to start," I tell him.

Again the looks back and forth. This time a little perceptible heightening of effect. The impact of ten dollars in this place, in these lives.

"Fifteen," he says. "Fifteen for the car to start."

I smile to him, I shrug. All this from the threshold still. The smile and shrug of my people for centuries with their back against the wall. "It will take you," I tell him, "ten minutes to get there, two minutes to push, ten minutes to get back. But all right, fifteen."

"Ten anyway," he says.

"Fifteen is all right," I say. "I made a bargain. I gave my word."

"Ten anyway," he repeats. The woman moved now for the first time. She scratches.

"Anyway what?" I ask him.

"If the car don't start, ten dollars anyway."

Bitter money-sucking pessimist! Go romanticize peasants. What could I do? I agree. I refuse to contemplate the possibility that the car should not start. What could be wrong with it after bringing me all this way here without incident and sitting there undisturbed for four days, what else but a battery?

And so then to his car, the key for which he removes from a chain round his neck inside his shirt. Can you imagine? And though it was parked right outside his shack, the doors were locked. Well, I do not make much of it. Who is really to blame him? A brand new Chevy with red-leather seats. What efforts it took to buy it, the labors now to keep paying for it. Did he come all the way from Mexico—under what hardships?—to live here—in what alienation?—and not have some chrome glitter of our ways rub off on him? So let Professor Dovisch sweat blood with the old Plymouth that won't start and let the laborer of the shack have his firebox that he was driving now a wild seventy miles an hour. Compensation, Emerson called it. It was also a source of reassurance. When they drive like maniacs, they know all about cars.

He had nothing to say to me. We sat the first minute in silence. There was almost a foot between us in height—the advantage on my side. I must say it helped me to contemplate with a little less anxiety the financial arrangement I had made—the fact that I would have to pay with a check, and somewhere find a pen, and commence with identifications. And what would he make of such identifications? American Association of University Professors, Modern Language Association, New England Historical Society. He would have to settle for the gasoline credit card.

I mentioned at the beginning of the hour that I would tell my misadventure despite certain indelicacies. Let me say, then, that in the man's car on the way back to the lake and to my own car, whether from understandable tension, or from the unrelieved diet of stewed fruits whatever it was, my stomach commenced now to emit noises. To cover the awkwardness, though I had determined I could be as sullenly silent as my companion, I began to speak.

"My name is Simon Dovisch," I say to him.

He nods. No handshake. Nothing.

"And your name is—?" I ask.

"Mike," he says.

"Mike what?" I press him. Why should I alone be the vulnerable one? Why should I have given away everything and he nothing?

"Mike," he repeats. Nothing more, and stares straight ahead. A profile, I am forced to say, that looks as if it got finished off with a bang from a flat shovel.

"This is an impressive country," I remark. I confess a twinge for the stuffy ambiguity of the word I chose. "A beautiful country," I correct myself. No answer. I try again. "The kind of a country," I observe, "in which, for four days, you might say, we were almost neighbors." Like a stone he sits behind the wheel, not even a blink of the eyes. An elbow on his door where the window is open, the arm up, the fingers drumming on the roof. With one hand seventy miles an hour, seventy-five. What else can I try with him

in this simple way that's demanded of decent human exchange? Can I offer a hint of what I was doing at the lake? How would he understand it? From where do human connections come anyway? Must language always fail except among the limited few who have formed a corporation to study from it, but also without connection and only until finals time, and then the corporation dissolved, finished? Am I committed forever to my alienation? Is it my fault, or the others? Who was alien in the car that I should talk and he shouldn't answer and that ten inches between us should be a whole Mississippi? Do I make mistakes not knowing country ways? Is there a right subject for conversation with him that I have not the instinct for? The colors on the hills? Or even Reno: gambling? Or something personal—a compliment to his car? Or something more manly, albeit speculative, about the common labor before us of starting my car, and by which, if he would respond, I could sneakily test his air of authority over such matters as batteries and vacuum advances? Or something historical, as, for instance, not too long ago Indians had lived here?

Indians!

I had no sooner shaped the word in my head when my eyes gave it back again, in type, recollected all at once from the road map I had used on the way up. Near Pyramid Lake, Nixon. Printed next to Nixon, each word under the other inside the lines designating borders of the allotted land, the words: Pyramid Lake Piute Indian Reservation. An Indian! Not a Puerto Rican, not a Mexican—a

Piute Indian. Simon Dovisch in a car in the Far West with an American Indian.

"You're an Indian!" I exclaimed.

Students of American Literature, Early Period, I call on you to appreciate that moment. I am not one of those who hides his faults. I leave myself open. I do not hedge on the personal if it will but throw a particle of light on the common subject. But I call on you now to admit with me, would I, could I, am I the one to shout out "You're an Indian!" and mean it as a curse? What was it if not plain and unchecked Dovisch enthusiasm? A joy for an unexpected enthusiasm, this embodied experience, new at least to me, of meeting and traveling and about to labor with, an American Indian—Piute. Could I have meant anything but a form of my own congratulation for his identity? Did he have to at seventy-five miles an hour slam on the brakes? Did he have to nearly kill us both, the car screaming and squealing and twisting on the highway and not stopping till I had jammed one hand on my side of the dash trying to brace myself and skinned an elbow on the door handle? Did he have to turn on me then and show his teeth for the first time in a snarl God meant only for creatures of the jungle who go on four feet with heads turned down. He holds out his hand to me.

"Five dollars till here," he says.

"What's the matter?" I plead. "What did you do that for?"

"Five dollars till here," he repeats.

I can feel the heat of his eyes, and though I have done nothing I dare not look at them.

"You could have killed us," I say, and thought to say, Do you run a taxi, the mileage and fare and destination based on unfounded resentments along the way? Bending my wrist, rubbing the elbow on my thigh, I try to explain. But how? But how? Can I bring him into the exuberance out of which I spoke. Can I tell him that, on the contrary, I love Indians? How shall I love Indians? I never met an Indian before. And if he who sat there snarling at me with his hand out was a prototype of his race, or even his tribe, why should I pretend to love them?

To make it short, I apologized. I had said nothing for which I had to be guilty, but there was no other way. On top of the apology, I offered five dollars more. Twenty now to get the car started. Thus Dovisch, the rainbow-maker, is also a man of bribes. That flicker appeared in his eyes again. We resumed. This time I chose silence. Dovisch, I told myself, let the facts stand for themselves, their own essence toward their own emblem.

Come we at last to my car, there as I had left it, hood up, no one else in sight, a forlorn object: a machine which doesn't work. Immediately, then, another disagreement. I want him to push. He wants to look. I explain how it could be nothing but the battery. He looks under the hood. I look with him. He orders me into the car.

"Start it," he says.

What do I know of cars to quarrel with him? Perhaps he is a man of craft, after all. But if I could start it, would I have walked all those miles to find him, Indian or not? Into the car then, the hood up before my vision like a metal wing. My head out the window to hear signals from a body I no longer see. "Start it," he says. Again, *erk-erk*. "Stop it," he says. "The battery?" I suggest. "A push?" I plead. "Start it," he says. And this time a variation, an *erk-erk* with a gasp at the end, an asthma. Nevertheless, a slight improvement, a promise. I see him now come past my side of the car on the way to his. His face, as he passes, a mask of sullenness and resentment. I get out to follow.

"You know what it is?" I ask him. "Is it the battery? Are you going to push?"

He stops with his hand on the door of the trunk and looks at me. If it was not a hostile look, then call me Natty Bumppo. If it is the way of his people, then too bad they learned no written language. They would have left us a great literature, for they are melancholy enough. If it was merely his own way, then my heart goes to the woman, ugly or not, he lives with in the shack.

"Fix," he says to me, leaning over the trunk. Nothing else. Then opens the trunk and rummages inside and walks off, going around me without another word, holding in his hand some kind of tool that I tell you did not inspire confidence. Too big to be a scissors, too small to be a shears, not a screwdriver, not a wrench, but almost a pliers. I follow after him. I try to summon control and decency, also a little command, and yet a degree of deference for the unhappy incident on the way here with him. Helplessness for my ignorance and plight—that, I didn't need to summon.

"Would you mind telling me what's wrong with my car and what you are going to do now?"

Delicacy set aside, the last part of my question was addressed not to his ear but to his behind. He was already gone, altogether under the hood, his body draped over its insides like a dungaree rag. Should such a man inspire confidence in the ignorant and dependent? Who's to say? Doctors also will probe and prod with gadgets on your own body and tell you nothing. But I must confess I had no confidence. Call it the prejudice of a provincial man. God knows I regard mechanical work as toy tinkering, a skill on the idiot level of man's capacity. But to each his own and from each, nevertheless, a kind of evidence, an emanation, manifesting the essence of the work itself, the man at or in his work. Thus a professor of sociology, say, shall be known by his bow tie and pipe, and the smack of brightness in his face, like an insult. And the true professor of literature, by the weariness of spirit. And so with auto mechanics. Also an essence. Was it that he lacked the boyish gleam of the eyes you see in the born mechanic let loose before an automobile, a refrigerator, a clock, and anything in need of repair? Was it his sullenness alone? Was it the strange implement he carried as a tool? Was it merely, finally—face it, Dovisch—my own bigoted preconception that an Indian and an engine make for no better combination than Dovisch and an engine do, admitting, as I face it, that I hold myself above such a combination and hold him not up to it? And on top of it an Indian who might be bent on spite for what he ineradicably regarded as name-calling?

I squatted down to see better what he was up to. It was already four o'clock. The instrument he had carried, I could see now. He had placed it on top of the engine. All covered with rust, between a wire cutter and a pliers. He was head down into the engine, grunting, his hands, both of them, pulling at something, yanking. Was this part of a skillful operation?

"What are you doing?" I shouted. "What are you pulling on like that?"

You must understand I was still not used to talking. How much opportunity had he given me? It was the unmodulated sound of my sudden voice that frightened him into snapping his head back. He banged it against the hood. Then he turned his head toward me, a side of his face against the engine, his eyes all white, with terror, or anger—who knows? But his hands kept on pulling. And then I heard something snap. It was as clear as a bone fracture in total silence. He began inching out of the engine, his arms working now, hauling, the way a sailor pulls in rope, a housewife a clothesline. And coming out after him, draping over the engine and then coiling on the desert floor, was half the insides of my car. Who knew a car had such insides? Bowels, I tell you. A regular vascular system. Wires and wires, black ones and red ones, and then a piece of tubing, and a piece of hose, and more wires, and some sort of chain. And he kept on hauling it all out, backing off further and further from the car and hauling it, his own face now a picture of surprise. You can imagine the horror with which I regarded this performance. From where could I find voice and words to tell him what I felt?

"Madman!" I cried. "Spiteful lunatic! You have ruined my car. Look at what you did to my car! You have pulled out all the insides. It is all there on the ground. My car will never go again."

Let me not make it a big thing, the feelings I endured. Suffice it to say I wanted to punch him. Instead, I pulled at my hair. You see, it was more than my car he destroyed. It was the whole sense of my experience, of belonging—all that I had fought for in my solitude in those terrified nights, the silent days. What recourse now? Salvage what? Was it for the car alone that there passed now, at last, some expression on his face? He glanced at me and then looked at the heap of car guts at his feet, his small eyes widening and his heavy mouth falling open in an uncomplicated look of—what shall I call it?—astonishment?

Students, listen—you are free to leave. I can't keep you, those of you due for another fifty-minute injection somewhere else—Geology, Speech for the Classroom Teacher, Spinoza. I have used up all my time, a lecturer and not a storyteller. Some could go directly in, but for Dovisch, layer by layer. Because aliveness itself is the crisis. But you know the end of the story. Here I am, I got back. Go, those who need to; stay, those who can. If I haven't come yet to that last layer which opens on at least the conditions of your final exam, then add up consequences as you will. Not a threat, not a bribe—another fact. Facts are facts. Leave your term papers here, those who go.

So then—half of you gone. More than half. Let it be so. I will not for all that change my style. A picture is also a picture, and a picture we made then, Dovisch and Mike the Piute. It's hard to believe it happened only yesterday. The time for it seems to have been histories ago. The two of us, soon to become three, and then four, and five if I may count that passive Cleopatra whose description you can relay to your fellow students who walked out.

See us then on the highway, car chained to car, Dovisch in the old Plymouth pulled by the Indian in the new Chevy, having removed a chain from his trunk and lashed us bumper to bumper. Crawling now on the highway toward Reno that follows the Truckee River along the valley in the desert through the purple-shifting hills in the growing twilight. Fancy diction, but we were on our way by my command to find an open gas station. The guts of my car stuffed back under the hood. And me staring with constant hot and maybe tearing eyes at the constant backside of the head in front that belongs to him who pulls. Always twenty feet away. And Dovisch ponders. And now I say a curse upon the analytic mind. That it kept me from resigning myself to my recognition. Which spoke this way to me, the recognition—which is the beginning of all compassion. Said to me then: Wherefore not peace in this peaceful place, albeit you are being hauled? The man who hauls you, is it not a labor for him as felt with pain as it would be if he hauled you with his back instead of an engine? Regard the slope of his shoulder that crowns his back. Heaped with humility which is born out of his very anger and spite. Born also out of remorse for the harm he did me that might have been done to revenge a mere word I spoke that he imagined was a name I called him. All the old stuff: pride and defeat and foolishness and sorrow, and damage too. From Russia to the Bronx, and from God knows where to Indian Reservation, Nixon, Nevada—an old story. A shack and slop jars and beer cans, a sputtered candle and a contour chair—red. And a woman to live with made ugly not by nature (what woman is ever by nature ugly?) but by deprivation, designation, contamination. But then is it my fault?, I plead. A Simon-come-lately to this total land, and a stranger altogether to this specific place. But for him who calls himself Mike, how shall it not be in some part my fault? For if Dovisch is a rainbow-maker, why shouldn't the mind of the other have some license to abstract? So resign then, Dovisch, to this moment given to you as a gift, and feel for him who pulls you in the desert as though he pulled you on his back. The aspiration and the loss. But comes then the needling analytic fact. A question. Does he pull me for the money? Not as we are stretched and held as men across the rack of his chain, but for twenty dollars? And if it is for money, do I owe him money who wrecked my car? And if my car is wrecked and I need some other way of getting home, does he owe me? And if he owes me, is it money? Can I collect?

With such questions the sweet elegy of dependent journey is done with, finished. Arrive we then, after miles, at the gas station, my mouth sour, the time now almost five. In two seconds flat my benefactor is out the door, has the cars unchained, and with two words justifies all the cruelty of my analysis. His hand out and his back to the station: "Fifteen dollars." See what he was up to. Because I had raised from fifteen to twenty the amount I would pay him for starting the car, he raises from ten to fifteen the amount I should pay him for not only *not* starting my car, but for destroying it. At least wait, I reply acidly. At least see what happens here. No answer. A glance toward the station, and a nervousness of face. The wide mouth twitches a little. He shifts from foot to foot, a thick, arrogant body. He holds the chain, the main length of it coiling on the asphalt, and a foot or two of it hanging from his hands. Like a weapon. This I need now to cap my quiet intention—bloody violence.

There is only one attendant I can see at this small station, a Negro. Yes, a Negro. Am I responsible for the racial distribution of Nevada? He is watching us as soon as we arrive, and he is still watching, leaning against the window of the office—whatever you call it where they keep the money and the oil. He wears one of those one piece things from the Army. His arms are folded on his chest. I said he looks at *us*. He looks at the Chevy, and he looks at the back of the Indian. There is a charge, a tension to how he looks. Even from where I stand, I can feel its current. This, too, I need: petty anthropological animosities. He gives no sign, the attendant, that he will come to us. He leans there, arms folded, glaring.

"Listen," I say to the Indian. "I solicited your help. What you did, I invited. I understand that. What your motives were, that's for a debating society. Some other time. Now, whether I pay you ten dollars or fifteen, I need first to get squared away. Surely you can wait five minutes, since, as a result of your help, I might have to wait until tomorrow. Now let me pass."

I walk around him. I walk to the attendant. I summarize the situation. I ask him finally for the use of his phone for a long distance call, collect. I need to eliminate my own anxiety for what will soon be a worried wife. I need to have the time and latitude to do whatever has to be done. There is the nagging problem of money. Not only that I don't have cash and I might confront skepticism about a check. But the checking account itself now at the end of the month will take just so much for the repair of a cursed car. Know then that all the time I told my story and endured my fears, the attendant never once looked at me. He looked always at the other one. At his back, because the Indian hadn't turned. I repeated my immediate need. I raised my voice to repeat it. "May I use your phone? It's an emergency. Can't you people see that? My wife—" Then the Indian turned. Then the attendant moved. He came off the window. He dropped his arms to his sides. Over his breast pocket in red embroidery, the name Wilbur. A lean man with a sharp moustache and ears back on his head as though they had been sewed. A little pointed also. A regular Donatello. Not a word to me. Once a glance. A slightest turning of the head and a shot with the eyes. He takes two steps forward.

"You gonna get off? You gonna beat it?"

Not to me. To the Indian. The Indian looks back at him.

"I got money now," the Indian says. "I got fifteen dollars from him."

The attendant takes two more steps. "The boss says *you* come back here, even if you have fifteen *hundred* dollars, I keep you off. You getting offa here?"

"No boss here now," says the Indian.

"Piute, me and you together makes me boss."

I run up to him. "Wilbur, I told you. My wife. I need to use your phone."

Now he spins on me. Movements like a boxer. "I call you Mister, you call me same. You don't hear me callin' you first-name basis."

Another one. In the middle of nowhere Dovisch flushes out these advocates of niceties. That I'm the one in the human crisis, that they ignore.

"Look—"

"I already looked. I see a Piute haulin' a tramp in here that—"

"Now just you wait a minute."

"—ain't too smart either. 'Cause you hired a guy to fix your car that went and wrecked your car that likely pulled a wire on it in the first place some night you were snorin away out there and now you got to pay him for it."

"Liar!"

Not the Indian's protest. Mine. If the Indian at that moment took himself to be insulted, I can't report. He merely stood there, his back almost on the door of his car, the chain still hanging from his hands. Once he turned his head to look down the road. Otherwise he looked at the attendant. Not yet with plain hatred. Something worse. His face, his whole body pinched with watching and waiting. And the Negro, arrested from his walking toward the other one by what he had stopped to tell me, was arrested still by the epithet I had impulsively flung out at him. I had to. I didn't intend by it to take sides in whatever miserable history the two of them had made together. How, anyway, could I have been on the side of the one who had done me so much harm? But to believe that the harm had been done even before I saw it? To believe that it had been done so that I couldn't see it? While I slept and dreamt, overcoming fears of animals and crawling things? While I made blueprints for an architecture of ideas about my country? It was more than I could bear. Picture now the Negro himself frozen to the spot. Confused for the moment. Confronting suddenly a second enemy. Diverted from the one idea of the Indian which was obviously all his mind could hold from the first moment he saw the cars.

So I apologized. Why not? What pride did I have at stake here? I asked once more for the use of the telephone. I called him Mister. I told him he could call me Simon. I told him all right, he could forget the telephone. Would he at least look at my car? Would he try to repair my car?

"This ain't no mechanic place," he says. "On Sunday I pump gas," he says. "I don't need no lookin' in your car," he says. "He got his hands on it you can send it back to Detroit. Take it to a dump. Maybe you get somethin' for the tires."

"To a dump? Listen, let me call my wife. Let me—"

"Boss says nobody use the phone."

"But this is an emer—"

Enter once more the Indian. Hear again the voice of love. Two words spoken with a flatness you cannot make out of speech with two such words. Not on the spot. It takes centuries. Spoken with the mouth, it goes along the ground the way a snake moves.

"Cotton picker," he says.

Goodbye Negro attendant. Like a track star, like a shot: back to the office and in the door and then out the door with a yard of iron bar in his hands they use for tires, running with it over his shoulder behind his head. Good God, murder! I say to myself as he runs past me, and I see the Indian turn sideways and brace his legs and let out two more feet of the chain and raise it to the height of his shoulder and almost close his eyes, as if he prepared himself to lash out when his hearing told him to and not his vision. Or else thinking of it as a kind of foregone conclusion, a suicide, and who wants to greet his own death with wide-open eyes? They will murder each other, I say to myself, or out loud—who knows?—and begin to close my own eyes and raise my hands to my ears to keep out the sounds of iron and bone. I raise my shoulders and lower my head and almost turn away—waiting, waiting. Nothing. The attendant has stopped in his tracks a little better than the chain length away. His iron bar is still raised. They confront each other, their chests heaving as though they had already fought. Their faces twisted with fear and hatred—nostrils and lips. Dark skin and darker skin. A madness here.

What goes through my mind, frozen there? I turn lunatic myself. I analyze: What did the Indian mean? Why did he choose that time to fling his curse? Was he on my side? Was I back again to his remorse for my plight that made him empty his sac of venom at the attendant's refusal to allow me the telephone? Or was it the mere overflow of hatred that drowned his need, his claim, his greed—whatever you want to call his idea of the fifteen, the ten dollars he could get from me? Because what he chose to say he must surely have known would provoke what it did.

So picture us. Make the tableau. It was not there for me then, but I see it now. Off the highway a little gas station with two yellow pumps and a small office. A dot in a desert country. One way with the road is back to the lake and the Indian Reservation. The other way is to Reno. The dry, tough land—Bible land—and the shifting, shimmering mountains and the miraculous stony water. Sunday at five P.M. When even solitude itself ceases to have value and all men past thirty should be home—shack, palace, or insurance-company housing project—in the tumultuous retreat of family. Picture, then, that neighbor of a bird I had looking down with hawk vision at that spot of a gas station in that vast empty land, seeing three alien specks of men inside that spot on the vast land, all of them motionless, waiting, not for the consolations of an alien man to a more alien man to the most alien of men, but for murder.

Come down from there and the bird and see it with Dovisch, who, lugging the Bronx with him, thus Europe too, finds in man himself all the universe. Dovisch looking at the other two, also men, poised with implements of murder. The hatred in their faces, which is the willingness to murder, dreadful to see. And dreadful to see, also, the fear in each face for his own murder, which is all that holds them back. Muscles in the hands, in the faces, too tight to be too long held back. Dovisch saying to himself: Outsider, alien—did you start this? Did you bring it on? But a moment for panic, not questions. Finished with analyzing. In panic, to the drowning man, the pictures, the fantasies. Picture Dovisch, then, picturing salvation. To be out of there. To be back with family, with books, back here in this classroom with you. Then cries out to himself: to hell with books! To give it all, his whole kingdom, for one skill: to repair a car. Picture him staring in dread at the two men who began at last to put the slightest pinwheel of motion into the tableau, making half circles about each other across the diameter they still fear to diminish, the weapons poised. And see Dovisch making fantasy as he looks, seeing himself in a Disney rescue, rushing to the car, opening the hood, the flash of Ben Franklin hands and the restoration of wires, tubes, hoses, chains, and in an instant in the car, the car starting, and Dovisch, all in the same timeless Disney instant, lowering the window and calling out I don't understand you. I never understood you. The lake was a lie. Gentlemen, goodbye!

Picture finally what I did do, a madman equal to them. Between an iron bar and an iron chain, and between the savage intentions born out of the heartache of their own isolations, strides Dovisch. In dirty clothes, in a four-day beard, off a diet of zwieback and stewed fruits, and in a celebration of or recoil from the hot blood of abstract insights, with his arms outstretched, one for each of them so that they could have fractured his wrists at a single impulse, offering for peace what he has taken from his wallet: identification cards. And a brief illustrating lecture that must have gone something like this.

"Madmen, what are you doing? You are going to kill each other. For what? Listen, I am no tramp. That I don't belong here, I grant you. But not a tramp. Are you Russians that you tell everything from a man's clothing? See—here. Take the cards. Look. Identification. I'm Simon Dovisch, Professor of American Literature. See this one—The New England Historical Society. And this one—The Modern Language Association. This one too, from my university—Simon Dovisch, Ph.D. That's Doctor of Philosophy. Take them. Read them. Put away the chain. Put down the bar. I only came here to recover something I lost that I never had! Take them, please! Read! Study! Peace!"

I have returned to tell you they put down their weapons. They looked at me as though I alone were the one madman, and they looked at the cards I held out the way I would have looked at tarantulas held out to me. But they took them. And they looked at them. And they looked at each other. And then at the cards again, turning them this way and that. And then they spoke to me. The Negro says, "I ain't afraid of him." The Indian says, "I pulled you. You pay fifteen dollars."

Nobody heard the new car come until it parked behind my Plymouth. I ran to it.

"You have to help me!" I begged to the window.

Right then, on the spot, I didn't notice, but now I can tell you. A Cadillac, white like the whale itself, and as long, and with fins and flukes too. Behind the wheel, lowering the window so he could hear me, this—what shall I call him? What is the term I have heard you people use against yourselves—WASP? White-Anglo-Saxon-Protestant? Well, I have never used it. I deplore it. It is your own form of Bronx snobbery injected from behind. I use it now as a shortcut from your own shorthand. I would say, rather, that he was a papermonger. Insurance, banking, credit, stocks, even publishing, even a registrar in a college—except for the Cadillac. Anything by which the management of the entity itself, people or things, is accomplished by the avoidance of the person or the thing. The paper accomplishes. So I say a papermonger to describe a face. And if you say to me a man's work does not describe his face, I say to you it is because you haven't begun to work. In his fifties he was, with silver hair, a Palm Springs sunburn, a straight nose, like a knifeblade, a tight mouth, a light-gray suit.

Later I would notice the transparent film of nail polish. But much before that—indeed a moment after I noticed him—I would notice who sat beside him, the Cleopatra I promised some while back to describe to you for the envy of your fellow students who have abandoned us.

I asked him to help me. What I then, at the first moment of his arrival, like salvation itself (yes, I confess, I was grateful at once that it came in all the pompous authority of a Cadillac)—what I then told him I can't now recall. It would have had such phrases in it as "destroyed my car," "my wife will be frantic," "murdering each other," "Professor of American Literature," "only my checkbook," "four days at the lake," "fruits and zwieback," "excuse my appearance,"—and so forth. He looked at me once while I was talking, the look of a long moment, of taking someone in. Then he never looked at me again. Dovisch summarized. But his face was alert and firm, and I must confess my heart went to calmness, rubbed and soothed by this stranger's—who in all other circumstances would have been so inimical to me—by his Cadillacs of certainty. Came then the gas-station attendant to the car. Edges me from the window. Makes at-your-service smile.

"Fill'er up?"

"Just a minute," says the stranger, like a slap across the face. And turns to the Cleopatra beside him and says, "Go ahead. Use it, now that we've stopped." She makes a reply I can't hear, and he says, "Yes, here. It won't kill you." Her door opens and she walks to the office.

I promised a description. Say only that she was no older than some of you here. Say also that she could not have been his daughter. Even a blind man could sense that right away—an essence. And let me say her hair was beautiful, and her own color, blond, like sunlight. And almost no makeup, makeup only on the eyes, but a quality in the face of something between good health and a frost that made the face more blatant than all the sticks and paints and rouges in Woolworth's could have. She wore a white dress—bare arms, bare back, bare shoulders—and was tanned as he was. Listen—we are, what is left of us, a mixed group here. Propriety is a value. Furthermore, my place here before the room and behind the desk is a position of trust. A prig is a bore, but a libertine is a coward. Suffice it to say that what she wore she filled; what she filled she wore. And say also that her walk to the office and whatever rest room she would find there was a short parade under the desert sky. The attendant watched her, the Indian watched her, I watched her. Only the stranger himself did not watch her.

When she disappeared, I edged at the attendant, nudged him from the window, and began again with the stranger on my baggage of miserable phrases.

"Yes," he said, and cut me off. He opened the door and got out. A trim man. Squash and swimming twice a week at the athletic club. Also a wedding ring. You may wonder that I notice it after my admission of my incapacity to observe. I say then, given the *mise en scène,* wait till you are forty-two. He addresses the attendant.

"Fill it with super. The oil's all right. Check the water." Then to me: "I'll take you as far as Sacramento. You can get a bus there. I'll give you the fare."

I am broken by his kindness; also with my own resentment. I mention my car, a badge of ruined shame beside his great white whale.

"You have no choice. It's Sunday." He turns to the attendant, who is already pumping gas, wiping windows. "You have this man's car towed to a mechanic tomorrow. Leave it here overnight."

"I can't do that. My boss—"

"Tell your boss a letter from my office will cancel his franchise. Tell him I can have this place closed in twenty-four hours."

So—an oil man.

The attendant stares at him, wipes the windows. End of debate. God in His wisdom, seeing my troubles, sends me not an Emerson, not a Thoreau, not even a Franklin, but a regular James Bond—or his father. Comes then the Indian, not to me, but to the stranger, and still dragging his length of chain.

"He owes me fifteen dollars," he says.

I looked once to the attendant. Will he go again for his iron bar that he had placed against the pump with the arrival of the Cadillac? No. He stops his cleaning of the windows to watch the outcome. His face is full of pleasure and deliverance. The stranger turns to me. He inquires of details. I give him details. You understand that the moral situation behind my business arrangement with the Indian is now complex. Yes, I hired him to start the car. But I stipulated for a push. The surgery was his idea. In sum, my answer to the stranger is yes and no. Shakes his head, then, the silver-haired stranger. Obviously ambiguities are outside his territory. He turns to the Indian. One sentence. A question.

"What's the name of the Indian Commissioner here?"

Exit the Indian, trailing the length of his chain. Smile on the face of the attendant as wide as vengeance. The Indian, my so-to-speak neighbor of four days, tearing off in a lamentable assertion from his exhaust pipe and a shouted obscenity one can barely hear. But for me, before he shut the door of his car, he reserved a special look: accusation, betrayal, or some secret shared—who knows? Reenters now from the Palace of Fine Arts, Miss America. Another parade. Dovisch rejoins the staring. A polite walking aside by the stranger and his possession. Hushed conference. Looks from her toward me. Dovisch shrugs. And now a look for me from the attendant, even a laying on of hands, at least a finger on the shoulder, a warm smile. But for what?

So now a trio in the car, myself in the back, the deep blackleather seats of a Cadillac. Another first for Dovisch. The stranger starts the car. No *erk-erk* here. The power of God's chosen continent in the turn of a key. Which he turns off again.

"You want to make that call home?" he asks. She turns and regards me. That mere flesh could hurl such a challenge. Another old story.

"No need now," I reply.

Off then to Sacramento. Goodbye old Plymouth. Dovisch from the rear murmurs gratitudes. Stranger from the front in brief disclaimers. Pays respects to higher education and learning. "They ought to raise salaries," he concludes. Dovisch deeper into the corner, arms over chest, bottom lip out. A long and uneventful journey back, if you exclude from eventfulness the growing frequency of exchanges of hot glances in the front seat, the sliding of thighs. Dovisch stares out the window. An intruder yes, an isolate always, but not yet a *voyeur*.

The misadventure, then, almost at an end, but not quite. I said at the beginning that I did not get home until two A.M. Wherefore, then, you should ask, all the consumed time? Departing a little past five P.M. yesterday, it is not nine hours to home. Know then, that two hours were spent in Sacramento waiting for the bus. Know that two hours before that were spent in front of a motel. Dovisch pacing like a patrolman, waiting for the two of them to get done with the business that is now the national pastime all the way from the Bronx to where we were now on the Western side of the Sierras. A factory of Hester Prynnes sewing night and day couldn't keep up with the scarlet letters needed here. It was also, from the stranger—let me credit him with his deservings—a gesture as well as a need. The need for him, with her; the gesture for me. Having rescued, having saved, having as much as said to me: Aren't you lucky that I came along instead of another Professor of American Literature? The stranger says now: So eat a little crow. Do I need to spell it out? Can't you see the rainbow finished now? Poor, thingless Dovisch is the emblem itself.

In Sacramento, after long silence in the car, the beauty asleep and the stranger quiet, and even Dovisch in a surfeit of his own, speaks now the stranger, out of nowhere addressing me.

"I took a course in Lit. once. Never knew what he was talking about."

Pronounced, of course, before the bus station, when there is time for Dovisch to retort with nothing more than another "Thanks" because the stranger turns now to put in my hand the money that is the bus fare home. Dovisch closing the door lightly not to wake the dozing Cleopatra. Goodbye, Prince of the Silver Hair and Master of All Situations. Then to the bus and the wooden bench in this midnight depository of transportation and breakage. Home then to keep up his wife all night in rehearsal of what I have told you now. Checking with her wise soul the relevance of it all for your final exams. When I make rainbows and take my flyers, she is there, bless her days, like a shining thing. And checking with her all night, too, on remaining ambiguities. Today's schedule, for instance, for the return to that American Bible landscape to retrieve my car. And my identification cards. Which means, this afternoon, another visit to that shack and the Indian. Or to let it go. Let him paste the one I gave him on the wall somewhere. Paste it over the red chair. Whichever one I gave him, let him be an honorary member of the society. And let it suffice, too, for my own resignation. Enough can be too much. And even too much is inadequate. Endure, endure—and not the least of it now, I confess frankly, is that half of you should walk out in the middle of all this Dovisch vulnerability, prior commitments notwithstanding. Well, I am not altogether drowned. I have my own survival weapons. Ishmael and his floating coffin, Dovisch and his final exam.

Listen, leave me your term papers on the way out. Your final exam? Only this. A critical appraisal of my original intention and of what befell me. Include a moral estimate of the characters involved. Answer to the question of lawful and human guilt. Discuss deprivation. Also rescue. And don't neglect the car. Support all your assessments with liberal reference to as many of the works we have studied this semester as will shed particles of light on such dark problems. References to be factual (God bless all my colleagues) and ideational (you know, rainbows).

That's all. Dovisch is finished. I'll see you at our finals.

Dovisch, Mike the Piute, and Wilbur, the gas-station attendant—in what ways is each of them alone? How do they differ from the owner of the Cadillac? How would you distinguish between isolation and solitude? Does Dovisch find out who he is? What is your Pyramid Lake? Would you take Professor Dovisch's class in American Literature, Early Period? Try to answer the question he intends to ask on his final exam: write a critical appraisal of Dovisch's experience.

Shirley Jackson seems, at first glance, to write not about the wilderness but about a small American town glowing with old-fashioned virtue. But watch out.

The Lottery

SHIRLEY JACKSON

The morning of June 27th was clear and sunny, with the fresh warmth of a full-summer day; the flowers were blossoming profusely and the grass was richly green. The people of the village began to gather in the square, between the post office and the bank, around ten o'clock; in some towns there were so many people that the lottery took two days and had to be started on June 26th, but in this village, where there were only about three hundred people, the whole lottery took less than two hours, so it could begin at ten o'clock in the morning and still be through in time to allow the villagers to get home for noon dinner.

The children assembled first, of course. School was recently over for the summer, and the feeling of liberty sat uneasily on most of them; they tended to gather together quietly for a while before they broke into boisterous play, and their talk was still of the classroom and the teacher, of books and reprimands. Bobby Martin had already stuffed his pockets full of stones, and the other boys soon followed his example, selecting the smoothest and roundest stones; Bobby and Harry Jones and Dickie Delacroix—the villagers pronounced this name "Dellacroy"—eventually made a great pile of stones in one corner of the square and guarded it against the raids of the other boys. The girls stood aside, talking among themselves, looking over their shoulders at the boys, and the very small children rolled in the dust or clung to the hands of their older brothers or sisters.

Soon the men began to gather, surveying their own children, speaking of planting and rain, tractors and taxes. They stood together, away from the pile of stones in the corner, and their jokes were quiet and they smiled rather than laughed. The women, wearing faded house dresses and sweaters, came shortly after their menfolk. They greeted one another and exchanged bits of gossip as they went to join their husbands. Soon the women, standing by their husbands, began to call to their children, and the children came reluctantly, having to be called four or five times. Bobby Martin ducked under his mother's grasping hand and ran, laughing, back to the pile of stones. His father spoke up sharply, and Bobby came quickly and took his place between his father and his oldest brother.

The lottery was conducted—as were the square dances, the teenage club, the Halloween program—by Mr. Summers, who had time and energy to devote to civic activities. He was a round-faced, jovial man and he ran the coal business, and people were sorry for him, because he had no children and his wife was a scold. When he arrived in the square, carrying the black wooden box, there was a murmur of conversation among the villagers, and he waved and called, "Little late today, folks." The postmaster, Mr. Graves, followed him, carrying a three-legged stool, and the stool was put in the center of the square and Mr. Summers set the black box down on it. The villagers kept their distance, leaving a space between themselves and the stool, and when Mr. Summers said, "Some of you fellows want to give me a hand?" there was a hesitation before two men, Mr. Martin and his oldest son, Baxter, came forward to hold the box steady on the stool while Mr. Summers stirred up the papers inside it.

The original paraphernalia for the lottery had been lost long ago, and the black box now resting on the stool had been put into use even before Old Man Warner, the oldest man in town, was born. Mr. Summers spoke frequently to the villagers about making a new box, but no one liked to upset even as much tradition as was represented by the black box. There was a story that the present box had been made with some pieces of the box that had preceded it, the one that had been constructed when the first people settled down to make a village here. Every year, after the lottery, Mr. Summers began talking again about a new box, but every year the subject was allowed to fade off without anything's being done. The black box grew shabbier each year; by now it was no longer completely black but splintered badly along one side to show the original wood color, and in some places faded or stained.

Mr. Martin and his oldest son, Baxter, held the black box securely on the stool until Mr. Summers had stirred the papers thoroughly with his hand. Because so much of the ritual had been forgotten or discarded, Mr. Summers had been successful in having slips of paper substituted for the chips of wood that had been used for generations. Chips of wood, Mr. Summers had argued, had been all very well when the village was tiny, but now that the population was more than three hundred and likely to keep on growing, it was necessary to use something that would fit more easily into the black box. The night before the lottery, Mr. Summers and Mr. Graves made up the slips of paper and put them in the box, and it was then taken to the safe of Mr. Summers' coal company and locked up until Mr. Summers was ready to take it to the square next morning. The rest of the year, the box was put away, sometimes one place, sometimes another; it had spent one year in Mr. Graves's barn and another year underfoot in the post office, and sometimes it was set on a shelf in the Martin grocery and left there.

There was a great deal of fussing to be done before Mr. Summers declared the lottery open. There were the lists to make up—of heads of families, heads of households in each family, members of each household in each family. There was the proper swearing-in of Mr. Summers by the postmaster, as the official of the lottery; at one time, some people remembered, there had been a recital of some sort, performed by the official of the lottery, a perfunctory, tuneless chant that had been rattled off duly each year; some people believed that the official of the lottery used to stand just so when he said or sang it, others believed that he was supposed to walk among the people, but years and years ago this part of the ritual had been allowed to lapse. There had been, also, a ritual salute, which the official of the lottery had had to use in addressing each person who came up to draw from the box, but this also had changed with time, until now it was felt necessary only for the official to speak to each person approaching. Mr. Summers was very good at all this; in his clean white shirt and blue jeans, with one hand resting carelessly on the black box, he seemed very proper and important as he talked interminably to Mr. Graves and the Martins.

Just as Mr. Summers finally left off talking and turned to the assembled villagers, Mrs. Hutchinson came hurriedly along the path to the square, her sweater thrown over her shoulders, and slid into place in the back of the crowd. "Clean forgot what day it was," she said to Mrs. Delacroix, who stood next to her, and they both laughed softly. "Thought my old man was out back stacking wood," Mrs. Hutchinson went on, "and then I looked out the window and the kids was gone, and then I remembered it was the twenty-seventh and came a-running." She dried her hands on her apron, and Mrs. Delacroix said, "You're in time, though. They're still talking away up there."

Mrs. Hutchinson craned her neck to see through the crowd and found her husband and children standing near the front. She tapped Mrs. Delacroix on the arm as a farewell and began to make her way through the crowd. The people separated good-humoredly to let her through; two or three people said, in voices just loud enough to be heard across the crowd, "Here comes your Missus, Hutchinson," and "Bill, she made it after all." Mrs. Hutchinson reached her husband, and Mr. Summers, who had been waiting, said cheerfully, "Thought we were going to have to get on without you, Tessie." Mrs. Hutchinson said, grinning, "Wouldn't have me leave m'dishes in the sink, now, would you, Joe?," and soft laughter ran through the crowd as the people stirred back into position after Mrs. Hutchinson's arrival.

"Well, now," Mr. Summers said soberly, "guess we better get started, get this over with, so's we can go back to work. Anybody ain't here?"

"Dunbar," several people said. "Dunbar, Dunbar."

Mr. Summers consulted his list. "Clyde Dunbar," he said. "That's right. He's broke his leg, hasn't he? Who's drawing for him?"

"Me, I guess," a woman said, and Mr. Summers turned to look at her. "Wife draws for her husband," Mr. Summers said. "Don't you have a grown boy to do it for you, Janey?" Although Mr. Summers and everyone else in the village knew the answer perfectly well, it was the business of the official of the lottery to ask such questions formally. Mr. Summers waited with an expression of polite interest while Mrs. Dunbar answered.

"Horace's not but sixteen yet," Mrs. Dunbar said regretfully. "Guess I gotta fill in for the old man this year."

"Right," Mr. Summers said. He made a note on the list he was holding. Then he asked, "Watson boy drawing this year?"

A tall boy in the crowd raised his hand. "Here," he said. "I'm drawing for m'mother and me." He blinked his eyes nervously and ducked his head as several voices in the crowd said things like "Good fellow, Jack," and "Glad to see your mother's got a man to do it."

"Well," Mr. Summers said, "guess that's everyone. Old Man Warner make it?"

"Here," a voice said, and Mr. Summers nodded.

A sudden hush fell on the crowd as Mr. Summers cleared his throat and looked at the list. "All ready?" he called. "Now, I'll read the names—heads of families first—and the men come up and take a paper out of the box. Keep the paper folded in your hand without looking at it until everyone has had a turn. Everything clear?"

The people had done it so many times that they only half listened to the directions; most of them were quiet, wetting their lips, not looking around. Then Mr. Summers raised one hand high and said, "Adams." A man disengaged himself from the crowd and came forward. "Hi, Steve," Mr. Summers said, and Mr. Adams said, "Hi, Joe." They grinned at one another humorlessly and nervously. Then Mr. Adams reached into the black box and took out a folded paper. He held it firmly by one corner as he turned and went hastily back to his place in the crowd, where he stood a little apart from his family, not looking down at his hand.

"Allen," Mr. Summers said. "Anderson. . . . Bentham."

"Seems like there's no time at all between lotteries any more," Mrs. Delacroix said to Mrs. Graves in the back row. "Seems like we got through with the last one only last week."

"Time sure goes fast," Mrs. Graves said.

"Clark. . . . Delacroix."

"There goes my old man," Mrs. Delacroix said. She held her breath while her husband went forward.

"Dunbar," Mr. Summers said, and Mrs. Dunbar went steadily to the box while one of the women said, "Go on, Janey," and another said, "There she goes."

"We're next," Mrs. Graves said. She watched while Mr. Graves came around from the side of the box, greeted Mr. Summers gravely, and selected a slip of paper from the box. By now, all through the crowd there were men holding the small folded papers in their large hands, turning them over and over nervously. Mrs. Dunbar and her two sons stood together, Mrs. Dunbar holding the slip of paper.

"Harburt. . . . Hutchinson."

"Get up there, Bill," Mrs. Hutchinson said, and the people near her laughed.

"Jones."

"They do say," Mr. Adams said to Old Man Warner, who stood next to him, "that over in the north village they're talking of giving up the lottery."

Old Man Warner snorted. "Pack of crazy fools," he said. "Listening to the young folks, nothing's good enough for *them*. Next thing you know, they'll be wanting to go back to living in caves, nobody work any more, live *that* way for a while. Used to be a saying about 'Lottery in June, corn be heavy soon.' First thing you know, we'd all be eating stewed chickweed and acorns. There's *always* been a lottery," he added petulantly. "Bad enough to see young Joe Summers up there joking with everybody."

"Some places have already quit lotteries," Mrs. Adams said.

"Nothing but trouble in *that*," Old Man Warner said stoutly. "Pack of young fools."

"Martin." And Bobby Martin watched his father go forward. "Overdyke. . . . Percy."

"I wish they'd hurry," Mrs. Dunbar said to her older son. "I wish they'd hurry."

"They're almost through," her son said.

"You get ready to run tell Dad," Mrs. Dunbar said.

Mr. Summers called his own name and then stepped forward precisely and selected a slip from the box. Then he called, "Warner."

"Seventy-seventh year I been in the lottery," Old Man Warner said as he went through the crowd. "Seventy-seventh time."

"Watson." The tall boy came awkwardly through the crowd. Someone said, "Don't be nervous, Jack," and Mr. Summers said, "Take your time, son."

"Zanini."

After that, there was a long pause, a breathless pause, until Mr. Summers, holding his slip of paper in the air, said, "All right, fellows." For a minute, no one moved, and then all the slips of paper were opened. Suddenly, all the women began to speak at once, saying, "Who is it?" "Who's got it?" "Is it the Dunbars?" "Is it the Watsons?" Then the voices began to say, "It's Hutchinson. It's Bill," "Bill Hutchinson's got it."

"Go tell your father," Mrs. Dunbar said to her older son.

People began to look around to see the Hutchinsons. Bill Hutchinson was standing quiet, staring down at the paper in his hand. Suddenly, Tessie Hutchinson shouted to Mr. Summers, "You didn't give him time enough to take any paper he wanted. I saw you. It wasn't fair."

"Be a good sport, Tessie," Mrs. Delacroix called, and Mrs. Graves said, "All of us took the same chance."

"Shut up, Tessie," Bill Hutchinson said.

"Well, everyone," Mr. Summers said, "that was done pretty fast, and now we've got to be hurrying a little more to get done in time." He consulted his next list. "Bill," he said, "you draw for the Hutchinson family. You got any other households in the Hutchinsons?"

"There's Don and Eva," Mrs. Hutchinson yelled. "Make *them* take their chance!"

"Daughters draw with their husbands' families, Tessie," Mr. Summers said gently. "You know that as well as anyone else."

"It wasn't *fair*," Tessie said.

"I guess not, Joe," Bill Hutchinson said regretfully. "My daughter draws with her husband's family, that's only fair. And I've got no other family except the kids."

"Then, as far as drawing for families is concerned, it's you," Mr. Summers said in explanation, "and as far as drawing for households is concerned, that's you, too. Right?"

"Right," Bill Hutchinson said.

"How many kids, Bill?" Mr. Summers asked formally.

"Three," Bill Hutchinson said. "There's Bill, Jr., and Nancy, and little Dave. And Tessie and me."

"All right, then," Mr. Summers said. "Harry, you got their tickets back?"

Mr. Graves nodded and held up the slips of paper. "Put them in the box, then," Mr. Summers directed. "Take Bill's and put it in."

"I think we ought to start over," Mrs. Hutchinson said, as quietly as she could. "I tell you it wasn't *fair*. You didn't give him time enough to choose. *Every*body saw that."

Mr. Graves had selected the five slips and put them in the box, and he dropped all the papers but those onto the ground, where the breeze caught them and lifted them off.

"Listen, everybody," Mrs. Hutchinson was saying to the people around her.

"Ready, Bill?" Mr. Summers asked, and Bill Hutchinson, with one quick glance around at his wife and children, nodded.

"Remember," Mr. Summers said, "take the slips and keep them folded until each person has taken one. Harry, you help little Dave." Mr. Graves took the hand of the little boy, who came willingly with him up to the box. "Take a paper out of the box, Davy," Mr. Summers said. Davy put his hand into the box and laughed. "Take just *one* paper," Mr. Summers said. "Harry, you hold it for him." Mr. Graves took the child's hand and removed the folded paper from the tight fist and held it while little Dave stood next to him and looked up at him wonderingly.

"Nancy next," Mr. Summers said. Nancy was twelve, and her school friends breathed heavily as she went forward, switching her skirt, and took a slip daintily from the box. "Bill, Jr.," Mr. Summers said, and Billy, his face red and his feet over-large, nearly knocked the box over as he got a paper out. "Tessie," Mr. Summers said. She hesitated for a minute, looking around defiantly, and then set her lips and went up to the box. She snatched a paper out and held it behind her.

"Bill," Mr. Summers said, and Bill Hutchinson reached into the box and felt around, bringing his hand out at last with the slip of paper in it.

The crowd was quiet. A girl whispered, "I hope it's not Nancy," and the sound of the whisper reached the edges of the crowd.

"It's not the way it used to be," Old Man Warner said clearly. "People ain't the way they used to be."

"All right," Mr. Summers said. "Open the papers. Harry, you open little Dave's."

Mr. Graves opened the slip of paper and there was a general sigh through the crowd as he held it up and everyone could see that it was blank. Nancy and Bill, Jr., opened theirs at the same time, and both beamed and laughed, turning around to the crowd and holding their slips of paper above their heads.

"Tessie," Mr. Summers said. There was a pause, and then Mr. Summers looked at Bill Hutchinson, and Bill unfolded his paper and showed it. It was blank.

"It's Tessie," Mr. Summers said, and his voice was hushed. "Show us her paper, Bill."

Bill Hutchinson went over to his wife and forced the slip of paper out of her hand. It had a black spot on it, the black spot Mr. Summers had made the night before with the heavy pencil in the coal-company office. Bill Hutchinson held it up, and there was a stir in the crowd.

"All right, folks," Mr. Summers said. "Let's finish quickly."

Although the villagers had forgotten the ritual and lost the original black box, they still remembered to use stones. The pile of stones the boys had made earlier was ready; there were stones on the ground with the blowing scraps of paper that had come out of the box. Mrs. Delacroix selected a stone so large she had to pick it up with both hands and turned to Mrs. Dunbar. "Come on," she said. "Hurry up."

Mrs. Dunbar had small stones in both hands, and she said, gasping for breath, "I can't run at all. You'll have to go ahead and I'll catch up with you."

The children had stones already, and someone gave little Davy Hutchinson a few pebbles.

Tessie Hutchinson was in the center of a cleared space by now, and she held her hands out desperately as the villagers moved in on her. "It isn't fair," she said. A stone hit her on the side of the head.

Old Man Warner was saying, "Come on, come on, everyone." Steve Adams was in the front of the crowd of villagers, with Mrs. Graves beside him.

"It isn't fair, it isn't right," Mrs. Hutchinson screamed, and then they were upon her.

Why do the people in the village hold the lottery? Is this lottery a primitive ritual, a current event, or both? Do you know any of the people in the story? If you lived in this village, how would you have behaved on that June 27?

Here you are asked not to assess your own behavior but to judge the guilt or innocence of another person, in this case a juggler.

Han's Crime
NAOYA SHIGA

translated by Ivan Morris

Much to everyone's astonishment, the young Chinese juggler, Han, severed his wife's carotid artery with one of his heavy knives in the course of a performance. The young woman died on the spot. Han was immediately arrested.

At the scene of the event were the director of the theatre, Han's Chinese assistant, the announcer and more than three hundred spectators. There was also a policeman who had been stationed behind the audience. Despite the presence of all these witnesses, it was a complete mystery whether the killing had been intentional or accidental.

Han's act was as follows: his wife would stand in front of a wooden board about the size of a door and, from a distance of approximately four yards, he would throw his large knives at her so that they stuck in the board about two inches apart, forming a contour around her body. As each knife left his hand, he would let out a staccato exclamation as if to punctuate his performance.

The examining judge first questioned the director of the theatre.
"Would you say that this was a very difficult act?"
"No, Your Honour, it's not as difficult as all that for an experienced performer. But to do it properly, you want steady nerves and complete concentration."
"I see. Then assuming that what happened was an accident, it was an extremely unlikely type of accident?"
"Yes, indeed, Your Honour. If accidents were not so very unlikely, I should never have allowed the act in my theatre."
"Well then, do you consider that this was done on purpose?"

"No, Your Honour, I do not. And for this reason: an act of this kind performed at a distance of twelve feet requires not only skill but at the same time a certain—well, intuitive sense. It is true that we all thought a mistake virtually out of the question, but after what has happened, I think we must admit that there was always the possibility of a mistake."

"Well, then, which do you think it was—a mistake or on purpose?"

"That I simply cannot say, Your Honour."

The judge felt puzzled. Here was a clear case of homicide, but whether it was manslaughter or premeditated murder it was impossible to tell. If murder, it was indeed a clever one, thought the judge.

Next, the judge decided to question the Chinese assistant who had worked with Han for many years past.

"What was Han's normal behaviour?" he asked.

"He was always very correct, Your Honour; he didn't gamble or drink or run after women. Besides, last year he took up Christianity. He studied English and in his free time always seemed to be reading collections of sermons—the Bible and that sort of thing."

"And what about his wife's behaviour?"

"Also very correct, Your Honour. Strolling players aren't always the most moral people, as you know. Mrs. Han was a pretty little woman and quite a few men used to make propositions to her, but she never paid the slightest attention to that kind of thing."

"And what sort of temperaments did they have?"

"Always very kind and gentle, Sir. They were extremely good to all their friends and acquaintances and never quarrelled with anyone. But . . ." He broke off and reflected a moment before continuing. "Your Honour, I'm afraid that if I tell you this, it may go badly for Han. But to be quite truthful, these two people, who were so gentle and unselfish to others, were amazingly cruel in their relations to each other."

"Why was that?"

"I don't know, Your Honour."

"Was that the case ever since you first knew them?"

"No, Your Honour. About two years ago Mrs. Han was pregnant. The child was born prematurely and died after about three days. That marked a change in their relations. They began having terrible rows over the most trivial things, and Han's face used to turn white as a sheet. He always ended by suddenly growing silent. He never once raised his hand against her or anything like that—I suppose it would have gone against his principles. But when you looked at him, Your Honour, you could see the terrible anger in his eyes! It was quite frightening at times.

"One day I asked Han why he didn't separate from his wife, seeing that things were so bad between them. Well, he told me that he had no real grounds for divorce, even though his love for her had died. Of course, she felt this and gradually stopped loving him too. He told me all this himself. I think the reason he began reading the Bible and all those sermons was to calm the violence in his heart and stop himself from hating his wife, whom he had no real cause to hate. Mrs. Han was really a pathetic woman. She had been with Han nearly three years and had travelled all over the country with him as a strolling player. If she'd ever left Han and gone back home, I don't think she'd have found it easy to get married. How many men would trust a woman who'd spent all that time travelling about? I suppose that's why she stayed with Han, even though they got on so badly."

"And what do you really think about this killing?"

"You mean, Your Honour, do I think it was an accident or done on purpose?"

"That's right."

"Well, Sir, I've been thinking about it from every angle since the day it happened. The more I think, the less I know what to make of it. I've talked about it with the announcer, and he also says he can't understand what happened."

"Very well. But tell me this: at the actual moment it did happen, did it occur to you to wonder whether it was accidental or on purpose?"

"Yes, Sir, it did. I thought, 'He's gone and killed her.'"

"On purpose, you mean?"

"Yes, Sir. However, the announcer says that he thought, 'His hands slipped.'"

"Yes, but he didn't know about their everyday relations as you did."

"That may be, Your Honour. But afterwards I wondered if it wasn't just because I did know about those relations that I thought, 'He's killed her.'"

"What were Han's reactions at the moment?"

"He cried out, 'Ha.' As soon as I heard that, I looked up and saw blood gushing from his wife's throat. For a few seconds she kept standing there, then her knees seemed to fold up under her and her body swayed forward. When the knife fell out, she collapsed on the floor, all crumpled in a heap. Of course there was nothing any of us could do—we just sat there petrified, staring at her. . . . As to Han, I really can't describe his reactions, for I wasn't looking at him. It was only when the thought struck me, 'He's finally gone and killed her' that I glanced at him. His face was dead white and his eyes closed. The stage manager lowered the curtain. When they picked up Mrs. Han's body she was already dead. Han dropped to his knees then, and for a long time he kept praying in silence."

"Did he appear very upset?"

"Yes, Sir, he was quite upset."

"Very well. If I have anything further to ask you, I shall call for you again."

The judge dismissed the Chinese assistant and now summoned Han himself to the stand. The juggler's intelligent face was drawn and pale; one could tell right away that he was in a state of nervous exhaustion.

"I have already questioned the director of the theatre and your assistant," said the judge when Han had taken his place in the witness-box. "I now propose to examine you."

Han bowed his head.

"Tell me," said the judge, "did you at any time love your wife?"

"From the day of our marriage until the child was born I loved her with all my heart."

"And why did the birth of the child change things?"

"Because I knew it was not mine."

"Did you know who the other man was?"

"I had a very good idea. I think it was my wife's cousin."

"Did you know him personally?"

"He was a close friend. It was he who first suggested that we get married. It was he who urged me to marry her."

"I presume that his relations with her occurred prior to your marriage."

"Yes, Sir. The child was born eight months after we were married."

"According to your assistant, it was a premature birth."

"That is what I told everyone."

"The child died very soon after birth, did it not? What was the cause of death?"

"He was smothered by his mother's breasts."

"Did your wife do that on purpose?"

"She said it was an accident."

The judge was silent and looked fixedly at Han's face. Han raised his head but kept his eyes lowered as he awaited the next question. The judge continued:

"Did your wife confess these relations to you?"

"She did not confess, nor did I ever ask her about them. The child's death seemed like retribution for everything and I decided that I should be as magnanimous as possible, but . . ."

"But in the end you were unable to be magnanimous?"

"That's right. I could not help thinking that the death of the child was insufficient retribution. When apart from my wife, I was able to reason calmly, but as soon as I saw her, something happened inside me. When I saw her body, my temper would begin to rise."

"Didn't divorce occur to you?"

"I often thought that I should like to have a divorce, but I never mentioned it to my wife. My wife used to say that if I left her she could no longer exist."

"Did she love you?"

"She did not love me."

"Then why did she say such things?"

"I think she was referring to the material means of existence. Her home had been ruined by her elder brother and she knew that no serious man would want to marry a woman who had been the wife of a strolling player. Also, her feet were too small for her to do any ordinary work."

"What were your physical relations?"

"I imagine about the same as with most couples."

"Did your wife have any real liking for you?"

"I do not think she really liked me. In fact, I think it must have been very painful for her to live with me as my wife. Still, she endured it. She endured it with a degree of patience almost unthinkable for a man. She used to observe me with a cold, cruel look in her eyes as my life gradually went to pieces. She never showed a flicker of sympathy as she saw me struggling in agony to escape into a better, truer sort of existence."

"Why could you not take some decisive action—have it out with her, or even leave her if necessary?"

"Because my mind was full of all sorts of ideals."

"What ideals?"

"I wanted to behave towards my wife in such a way that there would be no wrong on my side. . . . But in the end it didn't work."

"Did you never think of killing your wife?"

Han did not answer and the judge repeated his question. After a long pause, Han replied:

"Before the idea of killing her occurred to me, I often used to think it would be a good thing if she died."

"Well, in that case, if it had not been against the law, don't you think you might have killed her?"

"I wasn't thinking in terms of the law, Sir. That's not what stopped me. It was just that I was weak. At the same time I had this overmastering desire to enter into a truer sort of life."

"Nevertheless you did think of killing your wife, did you not—later on, I mean?

"I never made up my mind to do it. But, yes, it is correct to say that I did think about it once."

"How long was that before the event?"

"The previous night. . . . Or perhaps even the same morning?"

"Had you been quarrelling?"

"Yes, Sir."

"What about?"

"About something so petty that it's hardly worth mentioning."

"Try telling me about it."

"It was a question of food. I get rather short-tempered when I haven't eaten for some time. Well, that evening my wife had been dawdling and our supper wasn't ready when it should have been. I got very angry."

"Were you more violent than usual?"

"No, but afterwards I still felt worked up, which was unusual. I suppose it was because I'd been worrying so much during those past weeks about making a better existence for myself, and realising there was nothing I could do about it. I went to bed but couldn't get to sleep. All sorts of upsetting thoughts went through my mind. I began to feel that whatever I did, I should never be able to achieve the things I really wanted—that however hard I tried, I should never be able to escape from all the hateful aspects of my present life. This sad, hopeless state of affairs all seemed connected with my marriage. I desperately wanted to find a chink of light to lead me out of my darkness, but even this desire was gradually being extinguished. The hope of escape still flickered and sputtered within me, and I knew that if ever it should go out I would to all intents and purposes be a dead person.

"And then the ugly thought began flitting through my mind, 'If only she would die! If only she would die! If only she would die! Why should I not kill her?' The practical consequences of such a crime meant nothing to me any longer. No doubt I would go to prison, but life in prison could not be worse—could only be better—than this present existence. And yet somehow I had the feeling that killing my wife would solve nothing. It would have been shirking the issue, in the same way as suicide. I must go through each day's suffering as it came, I told myself; there was no way to circumvent that. That had become my true life now: to suffer.

"As my mind raced along these tracks, I almost forgot that the cause of my suffering lay beside me. Utterly exhausted, I lay there unable to sleep. I fell into a blank state of stupefaction, and as my tortured mind turned numb, the idea of killing my wife gradually faded. Then I was overcome by the sad empty feeling that follows a nightmare. I thought of all my fine resolutions for a better life, and realised that I was too weak-hearted to attain it. When dawn finally broke I saw that my wife, also, had not been sleeping. . . ."

"When you got up, did you behave normally towards each other?"

"We did not say a single word to each other."

"But why didn't you think of leaving her, when things had come to this?"

"Do you mean, Your Honour, that that would have been a solution of my problem? No, no, that too would have been a shirking of the issue! As I told you, I was determined to behave towards my wife so that there would be no wrong on my side."

Han gazed earnestly at the judge, who nodded his head as a sign for him to continue.

"Next day I was physically exhausted and of course my nerves were ragged. It was agony for me to remain still, and as soon as I had got dressed I left the house and wandered aimlessly about the deserted part of the town. Constantly the thought kept returning that I must do something to solve my life, but the idea of killing no longer occurred to me. The truth is that there was a chasm between my thoughts of murder the night before and any actual decision to commit a crime! Indeed, I never even thought about the evening's performance. If I had, I certainly would have decided to leave out the knife-throwing act. There were dozens of other acts that could have been substituted.

"Well, the evening came and finally it was our turn to appear on the stage. I did not have the slightest premonition that anything out of the ordinary was to happen. As usual, I demonstrated to the audience the sharpness of my knives by slicing pieces of paper and throwing some of the knives at the floorboards. Presently my wife appeared, heavily made up and wearing an elaborate Chinese costume; after greeting the audience with her charming smile, she took up her position in front of the board. I picked up one of the knives and placed myself at the usual distance from her.

"That's when our eyes met for the first time since the previous evening. At once I understood the risk of having chosen this particular act for that night's performance! Obviously I would have to master my nerves, yet the exhaustion which had penetrated to the very marrow of my bones prevented me. I sensed that I could no longer trust my own arm. To calm myself I closed my eyes for a moment, and I sensed that my whole body was trembling.

"Now the time had come! I aimed my first knife above her head; it struck one inch higher than usual. My wife raised her arms and I prepared to throw my next two knives under each of her arms. As the first one left the ends of my fingers, I felt as if something were holding it back; I no longer had the sense of being able to determine the exact destination of my knives. It was now really a matter of luck if the knife struck at the point intended; each of my movements had become deliberate and self-conscious.

"I threw one knife to the left of my wife's neck and was about to throw another to the right when I saw a strange expression in her eyes. She seemed to be seized by a paroxysm of fear! Did she have a presentiment that this knife, that in a matter of seconds would come hurtling towards her, was going to lodge in her throat? I do not know. All I knew was that her terrible expression of fear was reflected in my own heart. I felt dizzy as if about to faint. Forcing the knife deliberately out of my hand, I as good as aimed it into space. . . ."

The judge was silent, peering intently at Han.

"All at once the thought came to me, 'I've killed her,'" said Han abruptly.

"On purpose, you mean?"

"Yes. Suddenly I felt that I had done it on purpose."

"After that I understand you knelt down beside your wife's body and prayed in silence."

"Yes, Sir. That was a rather cunning device that occurred to me on the spur of the moment. I realized that everyone knew me as a believer in Christianity. But while I was making a pretence of praying, I was in fact carefully calculating what attitude to adopt."

"So you were absolutely convinced that what you had done was on purpose?"

"I was. But I realized at once that I should be able to pretend it had been an accident."

"And why did you think it had been on purpose?"

"I had lost all sense of judgement."

"Did you think you'd succeeded in giving the impression it was an accident?"

"Yes, though when I thought about it afterwards it made my flesh creep. I pretended as convincingly as I could to be grief-stricken, but if there'd been just one really sharp-witted person about, he'd have realized right away that I was only acting. Well, that evening I decided that there was no good reason why I should not be acquitted; I told myself very calmly that there wasn't a shred of material evidence against me. To be sure, everyone knew how badly I got on with my wife, but if I persisted in saying that it was an accident, no one could prove the contrary. Going over in my mind everything that had happened, I saw that my wife's death could be explained very plausibly as an accident.

"And then a strange question came to my mind: why did I myself believe that it had not been an accident? To be sure, the previous night I had thought about killing her, but might it not be that very fact which now caused me to think of my act as deliberate? Gradually I came to the point that I myself did not know what actually had happened! At that I became very happy—almost unbearably happy. I wanted to shout at the top of my lungs."

"Because you had come to consider it an accident?"

"No, that I can't say: because I no longer had the slightest idea as to whether it had been intentional or not. So I decided that my best way of being acquitted would be to make a clean breast of everything. Rather than deceive myself and everyone else by saying it was an accident, why not be completely honest and say I did not know what happened? I cannot declare it was a mistake; on the other hand I can't admit it was intentional. In fact, I can plead neither 'guilty' nor 'not guilty'."

Han was silent. The judge, too, remained silent for a long moment before saying softly, reflectively:

"I believe that what you have told me is true. Just one more question; do you not feel the slightest sorrow for your wife's death?"

"None at all! Even when I hated my wife most bitterly in the past, I never could have imagined I would feel such happiness in talking about her death."

"Very well," said the judge. "You may stand down."

Han silently lowered his head and left the room. Feeling strangely moved, the judge reached for his pen. On the document which lay on the table before him he wrote down the words, "Not Guilty."

Do you agree with the judge's decision? How would you justify your own verdict? What does that verdict tell you about yourself: about your own sense of guilt and innocence, your own view of justice?

This "Meditation" was written in the early seventeenth century by John Donne, an English preacher and poet.

No man is an island entire of itself; every man is a piece of the continent, a part of the main. If a clod be washed away by the sea, Europe is the less, as well as if a promontory were, as well as if a manor of thy friend's or of thine own were. Any man's death diminishes me, because I am involved in mankind, and therefore never send to know for whom the bell tolls; it tolls for thee.

Did you hear the bell toll when John F. Kennedy was assassinated? Martin Luther King? Robert Kennedy? How did you feel when the students at Kent State and Jackson State were shot? How do you feel when you read about the death of a Vietnamese child? a Pakistani peasant? a black South African miner? In the future, whose death might cause you to feel most acutely that the bell was tolling for you?

Donne says that we are all involved in mankind. Maybe today, as our planet becomes more crowded and more polluted, that involvement is turning into an enslavement. Susanne Langer's essay considers this possibility and suggests a more hopeful forecast than those found in Huxley's *Brave New World* and Orwell's *1984*.

SUSANNE K. LANGER

MAN AND ANIMAL: THE CITY AND THE HIVE

Within the past five or six decades, the human scene has probably changed more radically than ever before in history. The outward changes in our own setting are already an old story: the disappearance of horse-drawn vehicles, riders, children walking to school, and the advent of the long, low, powerful Thing in their stead; the transformation of the mile-wide farm into a ticktacktoe of lots, each sprouting a split-level dream home. These are the obvious changes, more apparent in the country than in the city. The great cities have grown greater, brighter, more mechanized, but their basic patterns seem less shaken by the new power and speed in which the long industrial revolution culminates.

The deepest change, however, is really a change in our picture of mankind, and that is most spectacular where mankind is teeming and concentrated—in the city. Our old picture of human life was a picture of local groups, each speaking its mother tongue, observing some established religion, following its own customs. It might be a civilized community or a savage tribe, but it had its distinct traditions. And in it were subdivisions, usually families, with their more special local ties and human relations.

Today, natural tribes and isolated communities have all but disappeared. The ease and speed of travel, the swift economic changes that send people in search of new kinds of work, the two wars that swept over all boundaries, have wiped out most of our traditions. The old family structure is tottering. Society tends to break up into new and smaller units —in fact, into its ultimate units, the human individuals that compose it.

This atomization of society is most obvious in a great cosmopolitan city. The city seems to be composed of millions of unrelated individuals, each scrambling for himself, yet each caught in the stream of all the others.

Discerning eyes saw this a hundred years ago, especially in industrial cities, where individuals from far or near came to do what other individuals from far or near had also come to do—each a cog in the new machine. Most of the cogs had no other relation to each other. And ever since this shake-up in society began, a new picture of society has been in the making—the picture of *human masses*, brought together by some outside force, some imposed function, into a superpersonal unit—masses of people, each representing an atom of "manpower" in a new sort of organism, the industrial state.

The idea of the state as a higher organism—the state as a superindividual—is old. But our conception of such a state is new, because our industrial civilization, which begets our atomized society, is new. The old picture was not one of masses driven by some imposed economic power, or any other outside power. The superindividual was a rational being, directed by a mind within it. The guardians of the state, the rulers, were its mind. Plato described the state as "the man writ large." Hobbes, two thousand years later, called it "Leviathan," the great creature. A city-state like ancient Athens or Sparta might be "a man writ large," but England was too big for that. It was the big fish in the big pond. The mind of Hobbes's fish was perhaps subhuman, but it was still single and sovereign in the organism.

Another couple of centuries later, Rudyard Kipling, faced with a democratic, industrialized civilization, called his allegory of England, "The Mother Hive." Here, a common will, dictated by complicated instincts, replaced even Leviathan's mind; each individual was kept in line by the blind forces of the collective life.

The image of the hive has had a great success as an ideal of collaborative social action. Every modern utopia (except the completely wishful Shangri-La) reflects the beehive ideal. Even a statesman of highest caliber, Jan Smuts, has praised it as a pattern for industrial society. Plato's personified state and Hobbes's sea monster impress us as fantasies, but the hive looks like more than a poetic figure; it seems really to buzz around us.

I think the concept of the state as a collective organism, composed of multitudes of little workers, guided by social forces that none of the little workers can fathom, and accomplishing some greater destiny, is supported by a factor other than our mechanized industry; that other factor is a momentous event in our intellectual history: the spread of the theory of evolution.

First biologists, then psychologists, and finally sociologists and moralists have become newly aware that man belongs to the animal kingdom.

The impact of the concept of evolution on scientific discovery has been immense, and it has not stopped at laboratory science; it has also produced some less sober and sound inspirations. The concept of continuous animal evolution has made most psychologists belittle the differences between man and his nonhuman relatives, and led some of them, indeed, to think of *Homo sapiens* as just one kind of primate among others, like the others in all essential respects—differing from apes and monkeys not much more than they differ from species to species among themselves. Gradually the notion of the human animal became common currency, questioned only by some religious minds. This in turn has made it natural for social theorists with scientific leanings to model their concepts of human society on animal societies, the anthill and the beehive.

Perhaps it were well, at this point, to say that I myself stand entirely in the scientific camp. I do not argue against any religious or even vitalistic doctrines; such things are not arguable. I speak not *for*, but *from*, a naturalist's point of view, and anyone who does not share it can make his own reservations in judging what I say.

Despite man's zoological status, which I wholeheartedly accept, there is a deep gulf between the highest animal and the most primitive normal human being: a difference in mentality that is fundamental. It stems from the development of one new process in the human brain—a process that seems to be entirely peculiar to that brain: the use of *symbols for ideas*. By "symbols" I mean all kinds of signs that can be used and understood whether the things they refer to are there or not. The word "symbol" has, unfortunately, many different meanings for different people. Some people reserve it for mystic signs, like Rosicrucian symbols; some mean by it *significant images*, such as Keats's "Huge cloudy symbols of a high romance"; some use it quite the opposite way and speak of "mere symbols," meaning empty gestures, signs that have lost their meanings; and some, notably logicians, use the term for mathematical signs, marks that constitute a code, a brief, concise language. In their sense, ordinary words are symbols, too. Ordinary language is a symbolism.

When I say that the distinctive function of the human brain is the use of symbols, I mean any and all of these kinds. They are all different from signs that animals use. Animals interpret signs, too, but only as pointers to actual things and events, cues to action or expectation, threats and promises, landmarks and earmarks in the world. Human beings use such signs, too, but above all they use symbols—especially words—to think and talk about things that are neither present nor expected. The words convey *ideas*, that may or may not have counterparts in actuality. This power of thinking *about* things expresses itself in language, imagination, and speculation—the chief products of human mentality that animals do not share.

Language, the most versatile and indispensable of all symbolisms, has put its stamp on all our mental functions, so that I think they always differ from even their closest analogues in animal life. Language has invaded our feeling and dreaming and action, as well as our reasoning, which is really a product of it. The greatest change wrought by language is the increased scope of awareness in speech-gifted beings. An animal's awareness is always of things in its own place and life. In human awareness, the present, actual situation is often the least part. We have not only memories and expectations; we have *a past* in which we locate our memories, and *a future* that vastly overreaches our own anticipations. Our past is a story, our future a piece of imagination. Likewise our ambient is a place in a wider, symbolically conceived place, the universe. We live in *a world*.

This difference of mentality between man and animal seems to me to make a cleft between them almost as great as the division between animals and plants. There is continuity between the orders, but the division is real nevertheless. Human life differs radically from animal life. By virtue of our incomparably wider awareness, of our power of envisagement of things and events beyond any actual perception, we have acquired needs and aims that animals do not have; and even the most savage human society, having to meet those needs and implement those aims, is not really comparable to any animal society. The two may have some analogous functions, but the essential structure must be different, because man and beast live differently in every way.

Probably the profoundest difference between human and animal needs is made by one piece of human awareness, one fact that is not present to animals, because it is never learned in any direct experience: that is our foreknowledge of death. The fact that we ourselves must die is not a simple and isolated fact. It is built on a wide survey of facts that discloses the structure of history as a succession of overlapping brief lives, the patterns of youth and age, growth and decline; and above all that, it is built on the logical insight that *one's own life is a case in point*. Only a creature that can think symbolically *about* life can conceive of its own death. Our knowledge of death is part of our knowledge of life.

What, then, do we—all of us—know about life?

Every life that we know is generated from other life. Each living thing springs from some other living thing or things. Its birth is a process of new individuation, in a life stream whose beginning we do not know.

Individuation is a word we do not often meet. We hear about individuality, sometimes spoken in praise, sometimes as an excuse for someone's being slightly crazy. We hear and read about "the individual," a being that is forever adjusting, like a problem child, to something called "society." But how does individuality arise? What makes an individual? A fundamental, biological process of *individuation*, that marks the life of every stock, plant or animal. Life is a series of individuations, and these can be of various sorts, and reach various degrees.

Most people would agree, offhand, that every creature lives its life and then dies. This might, indeed, be called a truism. But, like some other truisms, it is not true. The lowest forms of life, such as the amoebae, normally (that is, barring accidents) do not die. When they grow very large and might be expected to lay eggs, or in some other way raise a family, they do no such thing; they divide, and make two small ones ready to grow. Well now, where is the old one? It did not die. But it is gone. Its individuation was only an episode in the life of the stock, a phase, a transient form that changed again. Amoebae are individuated in space—they move and feed as independent, whole organisms—but in time they are not self-identical individuals. They do not generate young ones while they themselves grow old; they grow old and *become* young ones.

All the higher animals, however, are final individuations that end in death. They spring from a common stock, but they do not merge back into it. Each one is an end. Somewhere on its way toward death it usually produces a new life to succeed it, but its own story is finished by death.

That is our pattern, too. Each human individual is a culmination of an inestimably long line—its ancestry—and each is destined to die. The living stock is like a palm tree, a trunk composed of its own past leaves. Each leaf springs from the trunk, unfolds, grows, and dies off; its past is incorporated in the trunk, where new life has usually arisen from it. So there constantly are ends, but the stock lives on, and each leaf has that whole life behind it.

The momentous difference between us and our animal cousins is that they do not know they are going to die. Animals spend their lives avoiding death, until it gets them. They do not know it is going to. Neither do they know that they are part of a greater life, but pass on the torch without knowing. Their aim, then, is simply to keep going, to function, to escape trouble, to live from moment to moment in an endless Now.

Our power of symbolic conception has given us each a glimpse of himself as one final individuation from the great human stock. We do not know when or what the end will be, but we know that there will be one. We also envisage a past and future, a stretch of time so vastly longer than any creature's memory, and a world so much richer than any world of sense, that it makes our time in that world seem infinitesimal. This is the price of the great gift of symbolism.

In the face of such uncomfortable prospects (probably conceived long before the dawn of any religious ideas), human beings have evolved aims different from those of any other creatures. Since we cannot have our fill of existence by going on and on, we want to have *as much life as possible* in our short span. If our individuation must be brief, we want to make it complete; so we are inspired to think, act, dream our desires, create things, express our ideas, and in all sorts of ways make up by concentration what we cannot have by length of days. We seek the greatest possible individuation, or development of personality. In doing this, we have set up a new demand, not for mere continuity of existence, but for *self-realization*. That is a uniquely human aim.

But obviously, the social structure could not arise on this principle alone. Vast numbers of individualists realizing themselves with a vengeance would not make up an ideal society. A small number might try it; there is a place, far away from here, called the Self-Realization Golden World Colony. But most of us have no golden world to colonize. You can only do that south of Los Angeles.

Seriously, however, an ideal is not disposed of by pointing out that it cannot be implemented under existing conditions. It may still be a true ideal; and if it is very important we may have to change the conditions, as we will have to for the ideal of world peace. If complete individuation were really the whole aim of human life, our society would be geared to it much more than it is. It is not the golden world that is wanting, but something else; the complete individualist is notoriously not the happy man, even if good fortune permits his antics.

The fact is that *the greatest possible individuation* is usually taken to mean, "as much as is possible without curtailing the rights of others." But that is not the real measure of how much is possible. The measure is provided in the individual himself, and is as fundamental as his knowledge of death. It is the other part of his insight into nature—his knowledge of life, of the great unbroken stream, the life of the stock from which his individuation stems.

One individual life, however rich, still looks infinitesimal; no matter how much self-realization is concentrated in it, it is a tiny atom—and we don't like to be tiny atoms, not even hydrogen atoms. We need more than fullness of personal life to counter our terrible knowledge of all it implies. And we have more; we have our history, our commitments made for us before we were born, our relatedness to the rest of mankind. The counterpart of individuation from the great life of the stock is our rootedness in that life, our involvement with the whole human race, past and present.

Each person is not only a free, single end, like the green palm leaf that unfolds, grows in a curve of beauty, and dies in its season; he is like the whole palm leaf, the part inside the trunk, too. He is the culmination of his entire ancestry, and *represents* that whole human past. In his brief individuation he is an *expression* of all humanity. That is what makes each person's life sacred and all-important. A single ruined life is the bankruptcy of a long line. This is what I mean by the individual's involvement with all mankind.

All animals are unconsciously involved with their kind. Heredity governs not only their growth, color, and form, but their actions, too. They carry their past about with them in everything they do. But they do not know it. They don't need to, because they never could lose it. Their involvement with the greater life of the race is implicit in their limited selfhood.

Our knowledge that life is finite, and, in fact, precarious and brief, drives us on to greater individuation than animals attain. Our mental talents have largely freed us from that built-in behavior called instinct. The scope of our imagination gives each of us a separate world, and a separate consciousness, and threatens to break the instinctual ties of brotherhood that make all the herrings swim into one net, and all the geese turn their heads at the same moment. Yet we cannot afford to lose the feeling of involvement with our kind; for if we do, personal life shrinks up to nothingness.

The sense of involvement is our social sense. We have it by nature, originally just as animals do, and just as unconsciously. It is the direct feeling of needing our own kind, caring what happens. Social sense is an instinctive sense of being somehow one with all other people—a feeling that reflects the rootedness of our existence in a human past. Human society rests on this feeling. It is often said to rest on the need of collaboration, or on domination of the weak by the strong, or some other circumstance, but I think such theories deal with its modes, and ignore its deeper structure; at the bottom of it is the feeling of involvement, or social sense. If we lose that, no coercion will hold us to our duties, because they do not feel like commitments, and no achievements will matter, because they are doomed to be snuffed out with the individual, without being laid to account in the continuity of life.

Great individual development, such as human beings are driven by their intellectual insights to seek, does of course always threaten to break the bonds of direct social involvement, that give animal life its happy unconscious continuity. When the strain gets hard, we have social turmoil, anarchy, irresponsibility, and in private lives the sense of loneliness and infinite smallness that lands some people in nihilism and cynicism, and leads others to existentialism or less intellectual cults.

It is then that social philosophers look on animal societies as models for human society. There is no revolt, no strike, no competition, no anti-Anything party, in a beehive. As Kipling, fifty years or more ago, represented his British utopia, which he called the Mother Hive, that ideal state had a completely co-operative economy, an army that went into action without a murmur, each man with the same impulse the moment an enemy threatened to intrude, and a populace of such tribal solidarity that it would promptly run out any stranger that tried to become established in the state and disrupt its traditions. Any native individual that could not fit into the whole had to be liquidated; the loss was regrettable, but couldn't be helped, and would be made up.

Yet the beehive really has no possible bearing on human affairs, for it owes its harmonious existence to the fact that its members are *incompletely individuated*, even as animals go. None of them performs all of a creature's essential functions: feeding, food getting, nest building, mating, and procreating. The queen has to be fed and tended; she has only procreative functions. She doesn't even bring up her own children; they have nurses. The drones are born and reared only as her suitors, and when the romance is finished they are killed, like proper romantic heroes. The building, nursing, food getting, and fighting are done by sterile females who cannot procreate, amazons who do all their own housework. So there is not only division of labor, but division of organs, functional and physical incompleteness. This direct involvement of each bee with the whole lets the hive function with an organic rhythm that makes its members appear wonderfully socialized. But they are really not socialized at all, any more than the cells in our tissues are socialized; they are associated, by being unindividuated.

That is as far away from a human ideal as one can get. We need, above all, a world in which we can realize our capacities, develop and act as personalities. That means giving up our instinctive patterns of habit and prejudice, our herd instincts. Yet we need the emotional security of the greater, continuous life—the awareness of our involvement with all mankind. How can we eat that cake, and have it too?

The same mental talent that makes us need so much individuation comes to the rescue of our social involvement: I mean the peculiarly human talent of holding ideas in the mind by means of symbols. Human life, even in the simplest forms we know, is shot through and through with *social symbols*. All fantastic beliefs in a great ancestor are symbolic of the original and permanent life of the stock from which every individual life stems. The totem, the hero, the sacred cow, these are the most elementary social symbols. With a maturer view of the world, and the development of religious ideas, the symbolic image of man is usually taken up into the greater view of a divine world order and a moral law. We are sons of Adam and daughters of Eve. If Adam and Eve were simply some human couple supposed to have lived in the Near East before it was so difficult, this would be an odd way of speaking; we don't ordinarily refer to our neighbor's children as Mr. Brown's boys and Mrs. Brown's girls. But Adam is Man, and Eve is Woman (the names even mean that): and among us transient little mites, every man is Man, every woman is Woman. That is the source of human dignity, the sense of which has to be upheld at all levels of social life.

Most people have some religious ritual that supports their knowledge of a greater life, but even in purely secular affairs we constantly express our faith in the continuity of human existence. Animals provide lairs or nests for their immediate offspring. Man builds for the future—often for nothing else. His earliest great buildings were not mansions, but monuments. And not only physical edifices, but above all laws and institutions are intended for the future, and often justified by showing that they have a precedent, or are in accord with the past. They are conveniences of their day, but symbols of more than their day. They are symbols of society, and of each individual's inalienable membership in society.

What, then, is the measure of our possible individuation, without loss of social sense? It is the power of social symbolism. We can give up our actual, instinctual involvements with our kind just to the extent that we can replace them by symbolic ones. This is the prime function of social symbols, from a handshake, to the assembly of robed judges in a Supreme Court. In protocol and ritual, in the investment of authority, in sanctions and honors, lies our security against loss of involvement with mankind; in such bonds lies our freedom to be individuals.

It has been said that an animal society, like a beehive, is really an organism, and the separate bees its organic parts. I think this statement requires many reservations, but it contains some truth. The hive is an organic structure, a superindividual, something like an organism. A human city, however, is an *organization*. It is above all a symbolic structure, a mental reality. Its citizens are the whole and only individuals. They are not a "living mass," like a swarm of semi-individuated bees. The model of the hive has brought with it the concept of human masses, to be cared for in times of peace, deployed in times of war, educated for use or sacrificed for the higher good of their state. In the specious analogy of animal and human society, the hive and the city, lies, I think, the basic philosophical fallacy of all totalitarian theory, even the most sincere and idealistic—even the thoroughly noble political thought of Plato.

We are like leaves of the palm tree, each deeply embedded in the tree, a part of the trunk, each opening to the light in a final, separate life. Our world is a human world, organized to implement our highest individuation. There may be ten thousand of us working in one factory. There are several millions of us living in a city like New York. But we are not the masses; we are the public.

In your own words define what the author means by "symbolism." Why is language essential to being human? Try to imagine yourself as speechless, as not knowing any words.

Analyze the following excerpt in terms of whether you think the gift is worth the price:

We also envisage a past and future, a stretch of time so vastly longer than any creature's memory, and a world so much richer than any world of sense, that it makes our time in that world seem infinitesimal. This is the *price* of the great *gift* of symbolism.

What experiences have you had that made you feel like a bee in a beehive? What experiences have made you feel individuated? Which set of experiences do you prefer?

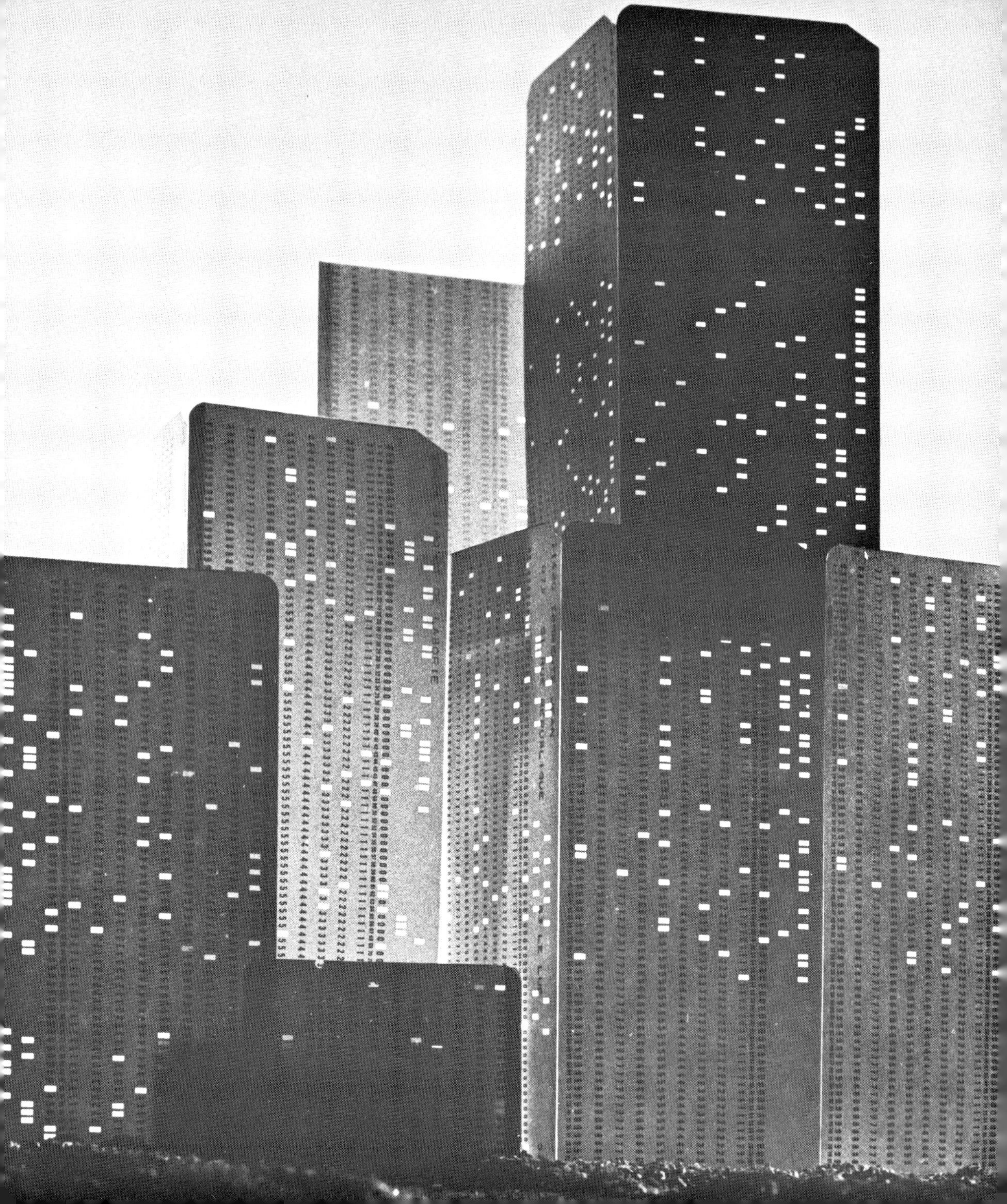

you and the

universe

When you look at yourself against the background of the universe, how do you, in the foreground, perceive yourself? In a sense you are back at the beginning of the book: how do you perceive the world around you? Yet whether you are looking up at a tree or the Milky Way or down into your own soul, what you see still ultimately depends on you.

Although we know that the world is relative to our perceptions, we still try to find absolute rules to live by. The Ten Commandments (Exodus 20:1–17) is one such code.

AND God spake all these words, saying, "I am the Lord thy God, which have brought thee out of the land of Egypt, out of the house of bondage.
Thou shalt have no other gods before me.
Thou shalt not make unto thee any graven image, or any likeness of any thing that is in heaven above, or that is in the earth beneath, or that is in the water under the earth: Thou shalt not bow down thyself to them, nor serve them: for I the Lord thy God am a jealous God, visiting the iniquity of the fathers upon the children unto the third and fourth generation of them that hate me: And showing mercy unto thousands of them that love me, and keep my commandments.
Thou shalt not take the name of the Lord thy God in vain; for the Lord will not hold him guiltless that taketh his name in vain.
Remember the sabbath day, to keep it holy. Six days shalt thou labour, and do all thy work: But the seventh day is the sabbath of the Lord thy God: in it thou shalt not do any work, thou, nor thy son, nor thy daughter, thy manservant, nor thy maidservant, nor thy cattle, nor thy stranger that is within thy gates: For in six days the Lord made heaven and earth, the sea, and all that in them is, and rested the seventh day: wherefore the Lord blessed the sabbath day, and hallowed it.
Honour thy father and thy mother: that thy days may be long upon the land which the Lord thy God giveth thee.
Thou shalt not kill.
Thou shalt not commit adultery.
Thou shalt not steal.
Thou shalt not bear false witness against thy neighbour.
Thou shalt not covet thy neighbour's house, thou shalt not covet thy neighbour's wife, nor his manservant, nor his maidservant, nor his ox, nor his ass, nor any thing that is thy neighbour's."

Whose voice do you hear uttering these prohibitions? Describe your own sense of sin. If you had to make one commandment, one prohibition, for yourself, what would it be?

Do you agree with the critic in this cartoon? Make a list of commandments for yourself that begin with "Thou shalt," rather than "Thou shalt not." Is this list more in line with your concept of morality than are the Ten Commandments?

"Generally comprehensive and incisive, but with an excessively negative tone over-all, wouldn't you say?"

How important is a belief in something absolute? A poet here looks at a world in which faith is ebbing away.

Matthew Arnold
dover beach

The sea is calm tonight.
The tide is full, the moon lies fair
Upon the straits; on the French coast the light
Gleams and is gone; the cliffs of England stand,
Glimmering and vast, out in the tranquil bay.
Come to the window, sweet is the night-air!
Only, from the long line of spray
Where the sea meets the moon-blanched land,
Listen! you hear the grating roar
Of pebbles which the waves draw back, and fling,
At their return, up the high strand,
Begin, and cease, and then again begin,
With tremulous cadence slow, and bring
The eternal note of sadness in.

Sophocles long ago
Heard it on the Aegean, and it brought
Into his mind the turbid ebb and flow
Of human misery; we
Find also in the sound a thought,
Hearing it by this distant northern sea.

The Sea of Faith
Was once, too, at the full, and round earth's shore
Lay like the folds of a bright girdle furled.
But now I only hear
Its melancholy, long, withdrawing roar,
Retreating, to the breath
Of the night-wind, down the vast edges drear
And naked shingles of the world.

Ah, love, let us be true
To one another! for the world, which seems
To lie before us like a land of dreams,
So various, so beautiful, so new,
Hath really neither joy, nor love, nor light,
Nor certitude, nor peace, nor help for pain;
And we are here as on a darkling plain
Swept with confused alarms of struggle and flight,
Where ignorant armies clash by night.

Do you agree with the last stanza? How is this poet's voice different from the one that you hear in the Ten Commandments? Is the loss of faith something that makes human love more or less significant? Do you think of love as a refuge, a shelter?

You may find John Barth's vision of love different from Arnold's. Certainly, Barth's narrator—whoever he may be—is different from the figure contemplating Dover Beach.

JOHN BARTH

night-sea journey

"One way or another, no matter which theory of our journey is correct, it's myself I address; to whom I rehearse as to a stranger our history and condition, and will disclose my secret hope though I sink for it.

"Is the journey my invention? Do the night, the sea, exist at all, I ask myself, apart from my experience of them? Do I myself exist, or is this a dream? Sometimes I wonder. And if I am, who am I? The Heritage I supposedly transport? But how can I be both vessel and contents? Such are the questions that beset my intervals of rest.

"My trouble is, I lack conviction. Many accounts of our situation seem plausible to me—where and what we are, why we swim and whither. But implausible ones as well, perhaps especially those, I must admit as possibly correct. Even likely. If at times, in certain humors—stroking in unison, say, with my neighbors and chanting with them 'Onwards! Upwards!'—I have supposed that we have after all a common Maker, Whose nature and motives we may not know, but Who engendered us in some mysterious wise and launched us forth toward some end known but to Him—if (for a moodslength only) I have been able to entertain such notions, very popular in certain quarters, it is because our night-sea journey partakes of popular absurdity. One might even say: I can believe them *because* they are absurd.

"Has that been said before?

"Another paradox: it appears to be these recesses from swimming that sustain me in the swim. Two measures onward and upward, flailing with the rest, then I float exhausted and dispirited, brood upon the night, the sea, the journey, while the flood bears me a measure back and down: slow progress, but I live, I live, and make my way, aye, past many a drowned comrade in the end, stronger, worthier than I, victims of their unremitting *joie de nager*. I have seen the best swimmers of my generation go under. Numberless the number of the dead! Thousands drown as I think this thought, millions as I rest before returning to the swim.

And scores, hundreds of millions have expired since we surged forth, brave in our innocence, upon our dreadful way. 'Love! Love!' we sang then, a quarter-billion strong, and churned the warm sea white with joy of swimming! Now all are gone down—the buoyant, the sodden, leaders and followers, all gone under, while wretched I swim on. Yet these same reflective intervals that keep me afloat have led me into wonder, doubt, despair—strange emotions for a swimmer!—have led me, even, to suspect . . . that our night-sea journey is without meaning.

"Indeed, if I have yet to join the hosts of the suicides, it is because (fatigue apart) I find it no meaningfuller to drown myself than to go on swimming.

"I know that there are those who seem actually to enjoy the night-sea; who claim to love swimming for its own sake, or sincerely believe that 'reaching the Shore,' 'transmitting the Heritage' (*Whose* Heritage, I'd like to know? And to whom?) is worth the staggering cost. I do not. Swimming itself I find at best not actively unpleasant, more often tiresome, not infrequently a torment. Arguments from function and design don't impress me: granted that we can and do swim, that in a manner of speaking our long tails and streamlined heads are 'meant for' swimming; it by no means follows—for me, at least—that we *should* swim, or otherwise endeavor to 'fulfill our destiny.' Which is to say, Someone Else's destiny, since ours, so far as I can see, is merely to perish, one way or another, soon or late. The heartless zeal of our (departed) leaders, like the blind ambition and good cheer of my own youth, appalls me now; for the death of my comrades I am inconsolable. If the night-sea journey has any justification, it is not for us swimmers ever to discover it.

"Oh, to be sure, 'Love!' one heard on every side: 'Love it is that drives and sustains us!' I translate: We don't know *what* drives and sustains us, only that we are most miserably driven and, imperfectly, sustained. *Love* is how we call our ignorance of what whips us. 'To reach the Shore,' then: but what if the Shore exists only in the fancies of us swimmers, who dream it to account for the dreadful fact that we swim, have always and only swum, and continue swimming without respite (myself excepted) until we die? Supposing even that there *were* a Shore—that, as a cynical companion of mine once imagined, we rise from the drowned to discover that all those vulgar superstitions and exalted metaphors are literal truths: the giant Maker of us all, the Shores of Light beyond our night-sea journey!—whatever would a swimmer do there? The fact is, when we imagine the Shore, what comes to mind is just the opposite of our present condition: no more night, no more sea, no more journeying. In short, the blissful estate of the drowned.

" 'Ours not to stop and think; ours but to swim and sink. . . .' Because a moment's thought reveals the pointlessness of swimming. 'No matter,' I've heard some say, even as they gulped their last: 'The night-sea journey may be absurd, but here we swim, will-we nill-we, against the flood, onward and upward, toward a Shore that may not exist and couldn't be reached even if it did.' The thoughtful swimmer's choices, then, they say, are two: give over thrashing and go under for good, or embrace the absurdity: affirm in and for itself the night-sea journey; swim on with neither motive nor destination, for the sake of swimming, and compassionate moreover with your fellow swimmer, we being all at sea and equally in the dark. I find neither course acceptable. If not even the hypothetical Shore can justify a sea full of drowned comrades, to speak of the swim-in-itself as somehow doing so strikes me as obscene. I continue to swim—but only because blind habit, blind instinct, and blind fear of drowning are still more strong than the horror of our journey. And if on occasion I have assisted a fellow thrasher, joined in the cheers and songs, even passed along to others strokes of genius from the drownèd great, it's that I shrink by temperament from making myself conspicuous. To paddle off in one's own direction, assert one's independent right-of-way, overrun one's fellows without compunction in pursuit of selfish ends, or dedicate oneself entirely to pleasures and diversions without regard for conscience—I can't finally condemn those who journey in this wise; in half my moods I envy them and despise the weak vitality that keeps me from following their example. But in reasonabler moments I remind myself that it's their very freedom and self-responsibility I reject, as more dramatically absurd, in our senseless circumstances, than tailing along in conventional fashion. Suicides, rebels, affirmers of the paradox—nay-sayers and yea-sayers alike to our fatal journey—I finally shake my head at them. And I splash sighing past their corpses, one by one, as past a hundred sorts of others: friends, enemies, brothers, fools, sages, brutes—and nobodies, million upon million. I envy them all.

"A poor irony: that I, who find abhorrent and tautological the doctrine of survival of the fittest (*fitness* meaning, in my experience, nothing more than survival ability, a talent whose only demonstration is the fact of survival, but whose chief ingredients seem to be strength, guile, and callousness), may be the sole remaining swimmer! But the doctrine is false as well as repellent: Chance drowns the worthy with the unworthy, bears up the unfit with the fit by whatever definition, and makes the night-sea journey essentially *haphazard* as well as murderous and unjustified.

"'You only swim once.' Why bother, then?

"'Except ye drown, ye shall not reach the Shore of Life.' Poppycock.

"One of my late companions—that same cynic with the curious fancy, among the first to drown—entertained us with odd conjectures while we waited to begin our journey. A favorite theory of his was that the Father does exist, and did indeed make us and the sea we swim—but not a-purpose or even consciously; He made us as it were despite Himself, as we make waves with every tail thrash, and may be unaware of our existence. Another was that He knows we're here but doesn't care what happens to us, inasmuch as He creates (voluntarily or not) other seas and swimmers at more or less regular intervals. In bitterer moments, such as just before he drowned, my friend even supposed that our Maker wished us unmade; there was indeed a Shore, he'd argue, which could save at least some of us from drowning and toward which it was our function to struggle—but for reasons unknowable to us He wanted desperately to prevent our reaching that happy place and fulfilling our destiny. Our 'Father,' in short, was our adversary and would-be killer! No less outrageous, and offensive to traditional opinion, were the fellow's speculations on the nature of our Maker: That He might well be no swimmer Himself at all, but some sort of monstrosity, perhaps even tailless; that He might be stupid, malicious, insensible, perverse, or asleep and dreaming; that the end for which He created and launched us forth, and which we flagellate ourselves to fathom, was perhaps immoral, even obscene. *Et cetera, et cetera:* there was no end to the chap's conjectures, or the impoliteness of his fancy; I have reason to suspect that his early demise, whether planned by 'our Maker' or not, was expedited by certain fellow swimmers indignant at his blasphemies.

"In other moods, however (he was as given to moods as I), his theorizing would become half-serious, so it seemed to me, especially upon the subjects of Fate and Immortality, to which our youthful conversations often turned. Then his harangues, if no less fantastical, grew solemn and obscure, and if he was still baiting us, his passion undid the joke. His objection to popular opinions of the hereafter, he would declare, was their claim to general validity. Why need believers hold that *all* the drownèd rise to be judged at journey's end, and nonbelievers that drowning is final without exception? In *his* opinion (so he'd vow at least), nearly everyone's fate was permanent death; indeed he took a sour pleasure in supposing that every 'Maker' made thousands of separate seas in His creative lifetime, each populated like ours with millions of swimmers, and that in almost every instance both sea and swimmers were utterly annihilated, whether accidentally or by malevolent design. (Nothing if not pluralistical, he imagined there might be millions and billions of 'Fathers,' perhaps in some 'night-sea' of their own!) However—and here he turned infidels against him with the faithful—he professed to believe that in possibly a single night-sea per thousand, say, one of its quarter-billion swimmers (that is, one swimmer in two-hundred-fifty billions) achieved a qualified immortality. In some cases the rate might be slightly higher; in others it was vastly lower, for just as there are swimmers of every degree of proficiency, including some who drown before the journey starts, unable to swim at all, and others created drownèd, as it were, so he imagined what can only be termed impotent Creators, Makers unable to Make, as well as uncommonly fertile ones and all grades between. And it pleased him to deny any necessary relation between a Maker's productivity and His other virtues—including, even, the quality of His creatures.

"I could go on (*he* surely did) with his elaboration of these mad notions—such as that swimmers in other night-seas needn't be of our kind; that Makers themselves might belong to different *species*, so to speak; that our particular Maker mightn't Himself be immortal, or that we might be not only His emissaries but His 'immortality,' continuing His life and our own, transmogrified, beyond our individual deaths. Even this modified immortality (meaningless to me) he conceived as relative and contingent, subject to accidental or deliberate termination: his pet hypothesis was that Makers and swimmers *each generate the other*—against all odds, their number being so great—and that any given 'immortality chain' could terminate after any number of cycles, so that what was 'immortal' (still speaking relatively) was only the cyclic process of incarnation, which itself might have a beginning and an end. Alternatively he liked to imagine cycles within cycles, either finite or infinite: for example, the 'night-sea,' as it were, in which Makers 'swam' and created night-seas and swimmers like ourselves, might be the creation of a larger Maker, Himself one of many, Who in turn, etc. Time itself he regarded as relative to our experience, like magnitude: who knew but what, with each thrash of our tails, minuscule seas and swimmers, whole eternities, came to pass—as ours, perhaps, and our Maker's Maker's, was elapsing between the strokes of some super-tail, in a slower order of time?

"Naturally I hooted with the others at this nonsense. We were young then, and had only the dimmest notion of what lay ahead; in our ignorance we imagined night-sea journeying to be a positively heroic enterprise. Its meaning and value we never questioned; to be sure, some must go down by the way, a pity no doubt, but to win a race requires that others lose, and like all my fellows I took for granted that I would be the winner. We milled and swarmed, impatient to be off, never mind where or why, only to try our youth against the realities of night and sea; if we indulged the skeptic at all it was as a droll, half-contemptible mascot. When he died in the initial slaughter, no one cared.

"And even now I don't subscribe to all his views—but I no longer scoff. The horror of our history has purged me of opinions, as of vanity, confidence, spirit, charity, hope, vitality, everything—except dull dread and a kind of melancholy, stunned persistence. What leads me to recall his fancies is my growing suspicion that I, of all swimmers, may be the sole survivor of this fell journey, tale bearer of a generation. This suspicion, together with the recent sea change, suggests to me now that nothing is impossible, not even my late companion's wildest visions, and brings me to a certain desperate resolve, the point of my chronicling.

"Very likely I have lost my senses. The carnage at our setting out; our decimation by whirlpool, poisoned cataract, and sea convulsion; the panic stampedes, mutinies, slaughters, mass suicides; the mounting evidence that none will survive the journey—add to these anguish and fatigue; it were a miracle if sanity stayed afloat. Thus I admit, with the other possibilities, that the present sweetening and calming of the sea, and what seems to be a kind of vasty presence, song, or summons from the near upstream, may be hallucinations of disordered sensibility. . . .

"Perhaps, even, I am drowned already. Surely I was never meant for the rough-and-tumble of the swim; not impossibly I perished at the outset and have only imaged the night-sea journey from some final deep. In any case I'm no longer young, and we spent old swimmers, disabused of every illusion, are most vulnerable to dreams.

"Sometimes I think I am my drownèd friend.

"Out with it: I've begun to believe, not only that *She* exists, but that She lies not far ahead, and stills the sea, and draws me Herward! Aghast, I recollect his maddest notion: that our destination (which existed, mind, in but one night-sea out of hundreds and thousands) was no Shore, as commonly conceived, but a mysterious being, indescribable except by paradox and vaguest figure: wholly different from us swimmers, yet our complement; the death of us, yet our salvation and resurrection; simultaneously our journey's end, midpoint, and commencement; not membered and thrashing like us, but a motionless or hugely gliding sphere of unimaginable dimension; self-contained, yet dependent absolutely, in some wise, upon the chance (always monstrously improbable) that one of us will survive the night-sea journey and reach . . . Her! *Her,* he called it, or *She,* which is to say, Other-than-a-he. I shake my head; the thing is too preposterous; it is myself I talk to, to keep my reason in this awful darkness. There is no She! There is no You! I rave to myself; it's Death alone that hears and summons. To the drowned, all seas are calm. . . .

"Listen: my friend maintained that in every order of creation there are two sorts of creators, contrary yet complementary, one of which gives rise to seas and swimmers, the other to the Night-which-contains-the-sea and to What-waits-at-the-journey's-end: the former, in short, to destiny, the latter to destination (and both profligately, involuntarily, perhaps indifferently or unwittingly). The 'purpose' of the night-sea journey—but not necessarily of the journeyer or of either Maker!—my friend could describe only in abstractions: *consummation, transfiguration, union of contraries, transcension of categories.* When we laughed he would shrug and admit that he understood the business no better than we, and thought it ridiculous, dreary, possibly obscene. 'But one of you,' he'd add with his wry smile, 'may be the Hero destined to complete the night-sea journey and be one with Her. Chances are, of course, you won't make it.' He himself, he declared, was not even going to try; the whole idea repelled him; if we chose to dismiss it as an ugly fiction, so much the better for us; thrash, splash, and be merry, we were soon enough drowned. But there it was, he could not say how he knew or why he bothered to tell us, any more than he could say what would happen after She and the Hero, Shore and Swimmer, 'merged identities' to become something both and neither. He quite agreed with me that if the issue of that magical union had no memory of the night-sea journey, for example, it enjoyed a poor sort of immortality; even poorer if, as he rather imagined, a swimmer-hero plus a She equalled or became merely another Maker of future night-seas and the rest, at such incredible expense of life. This being the case—he was persuaded it was—the merciful thing to do was refuse to participate; the genuine heroes, in his opinion, were the suicides, and the hero of heroes would be the swimmer who, in the very presence of the Other, refused Her proffered 'immortality' and thus put an end to at least one cycle of catastrophes.

"How we mocked him! Our moment came, we hurtled forth, pretending to glory in the adventure, thrashing, singing, cursing, strangling, rationalizing, rescuing, killing, inventing rules and stories and relationships, giving up, struggling on, but dying all, and still in darkness, until only a battered remnant was left to croak 'Onward, upward,' like a bitter echo. Then they too fell silent—victims, I can only presume, of the last frightful wave—and the moment came when I also, utterly desolate and spent, thrashed my last and gave myself over to the current, to sink or float as might be, but swim no more. Whereupon, marvelous to tell, in an instant the sea grew still! Then warmly, gently, the great tide turned, began to bear me, as it does now, onwards and upwards will-I nill-I, like a flood of joy—and I recalled with dismay my dead friend's teaching.

"I am not deceived. This new emotion is Her doing; the desire that possesses me is Her bewitchment. Lucidity passes from me; in a moment I'll cry 'Love!', bury myself in Her side, and be 'transfigured.' Which is to say, I die already; this fellow transported by passion is not I; *I am he who abjures and rejects the night-sea journey! I.* . . .

"I am all love. 'Come!' She whispers, and I have no will.

"You who I may be about to become, whatever You are; with the last twitch of my real self I beg You to listen. It is *not* love that sustains me! No; though Her magic makes me burn to sing the contrary, and though I drown even now for the blasphemy, I will say the truth. What has fetched me across this dreadful sea is a single hope, gift of my poor dead comrade: that You may be stronger-willed than I, and that by sheer force of concentration I may transmit to You, along with Your official Heritage, a private legacy of awful recollection and negative resolve. Mad as it may be, my dream is that some unimaginable embodiment of myself (or myself plus Her if that's how it must be) will come to find itself expressing, in however garbled or radical a translation, some reflection of these reflections. If against all odds this comes to pass, may You to whom, through whom I speak, do what I cannot: terminate this aimless, brutal business! Stop Your hearing against Her song! Hate love!

"Still alive, afloat, afire. Farewell then my penultimate hope: that one may be sunk for direst blasphemy on the very shore of the Shore. Can it be (my old friend would smile) that only utterest nay-sayers survive the night? But even that were Sense, and there is no sense, only senseless love, senseless death. Whoever echoes these reflections: be more courageous than their author! An end to night-sea journeys! Make no more! And forswear me when I shall forswear myself, deny myself, plunge into Her who summons, singing. . . .

"'Love! Love! Love!'"

Who is the narrator of "Night-Sea Journey"? Is this story about individual man in a mass society? Is it about man's journey through life toward death or God? What is the author saying about love? about life? about you? Why do you agree or disagree with him?

In Shakespeare's most famous play, a disillusioned Hamlet broods about the human predicament. Incidentally, these lines supplied the words to one of the songs in the popular musical *Hair*.

". . . this goodly frame the earth seems to me a sterile promontory. This most excellent canopy, the air, look you, this brave o'erhanging firmament, this majestical roof fretted with golden fire—why, it appears no other thing to me than a foul and pestilent congregation of vapors. What a piece of work is a man! How noble in reason! How infinite in faculty! In form and moving how express and admirable! In action how like an angel! In apprehension how like a god! The beauty of the world! The paragon of animals! And yet, to me, what is this quintessence of dust? Man delights not me . . ."

To what extent do you share Hamlet's view of man and the world?

If God is dead, if you are on Arnold's darkling plain or in Barth's cryptic cosmos or share Hamlet's cynical view, what new religion or philosophy can you call on to replace the faith of your ancestors? Probably the leading candidate today, at least in the Western World, is Existentialism. Albert Camus' "The Myth of Sisyphus" is an impassioned plea for human pride and dignity in a godless universe.

Albert Camus

THE MYTH OF SISYPHUS

The gods had condemned Sisyphus to ceaselessly rolling a rock to the top of a mountain, whence the stone would fall back of its own weight. They had thought with some reason that there is no more dreadful punishment than futile and hopeless labor.

If one believes Homer, Sisyphus was the wisest and most prudent of mortals. According to another tradition, however, he was disposed to practice the profession of highwayman. I see no contradiction in this. Opinions differ as to the reasons why he became the futile laborer of the underworld. To begin with, he is accused of a certain levity in regard to the gods. He stole their secrets. Ægina, the daughter of Æsopus, was carried off by Jupiter. The father was shocked by that disappearance and complained to Sisyphus. He, who knew of the abduction, offered to tell about it on condition that Æsopus would give water to the citadel of Corinth. To the celestial thunderbolts he preferred the benediction of water. He was punished for this in the underworld. Homer tells us also that Sisyphus had put Death in chains. Pluto could not endure the sight of his deserted, silent empire. He dispatched the god of war, who liberated Death from the hands of her conqueror.

It is said also that Sisyphus, being near to death, rashly wanted to test his wife's love. He ordered her to cast his unburied body into the middle of the public square. Sisyphus woke up in the underworld. And there, annoyed by an obedience so contrary to human love, he obtained from Pluto permission to return to earth in order to chastise his wife. But when he had seen again the face of this world, enjoyed water and sun, warm stones and the sea, he no longer wanted to go back to the infernal darkness. Recalls, signs of anger, warnings were of no avail. Many years more he lived facing the curve of the gulf, the sparkling sea, and the smiles of earth. A decree of the gods was necessary. Mercury came and seized the impudent man by the collar and, snatching him from his joys, led him forcibly back to the underworld, where his rock was ready for him.

You have already grasped that Sisyphus is the absurd hero. He *is*, as much through his passions as through his torture. His scorn of the gods, his hatred of death, and his passion for life won him that unspeakable penalty in which the whole being is exerted toward accomplishing nothing. This is the price that must be paid for the passions of this earth. Nothing is told us about Sisyphus in the underworld. Myths are made for the imagination to breathe life into them. As for this myth, one sees merely the whole effort of a body straining to raise the huge stone, to roll it and push it up a slope a hundred times over; one sees the face screwed up, the cheek tight against the stone, the shoulder bracing the clay-covered mass, the foot wedging it, the fresh start with arms outstretched, the wholly human security of two earth-clotted hands. At the very end of his long effort measured by skyless space and time without depth, the purpose is achieved. Then Sisyphus watches the stone rush down in a few moments toward that lower world whence he will have to push it up again toward the summit. He goes back down to the plain.

It is during that return, that pause, that Sisyphus interests me. A face that toils so close to stones is already stone itself! I see that man going back down with a heavy yet measured step toward the torment of which he will never know the end. That hour like a breathing-space which returns as surely as his suffering, that is the hour of consciousness. At each of those moments when he leaves the heights and gradually sinks toward the lairs of the gods, he is superior to his fate. He is stronger than his rock.

If this myth is tragic, that is because its hero is conscious. Where would his torture be, indeed, if at every step the hope of succeeding upheld him? The workman of today works every day in his life at the same tasks, and this fate is no less absurd. But it is tragic only at the rare moments when it becomes conscious. Sisyphus, proletarian of the gods, powerless and rebellious, knows the whole extent of his wretched condition: it is what he thinks of during his descent. The lucidity that was to constitute his torture at the same time crowns his victory. There is no fate that cannot be surmounted by scorn.

If the descent is thus sometimes performed in sorrow, it can also take place in joy. This word is not too much. Again I fancy Sisyphus returning toward his rock, and the sorrow was in the beginning. When the images of earth cling too tightly to memory, when the call of happiness becomes too insistent, it happens that melancholy rises in man's heart: this is the rock's victory, this is the rock itself. The boundless grief is too heavy to bear. These are our nights of Gethsemane. But crushing truths perish from being acknowledged. Thus, Œdipus at the outset obeys fate without knowing it. But from the moment he knows, his tragedy begins. Yet at the same moment, blind and desperate, he realizes that the only bond linking him to the world is the cool hand of a girl. Then a tremendous remark rings out: "Despite so many ordeals, my advanced age and the nobility of my soul make me conclude that all is well." Sophocles' Œdipus, like Dostoevsky's Kirilov, thus gives the recipe for the absurd victory. Ancient wisdom confirms modern heroism.

One does not discover the absurd without being tempted to write a manual of happiness. "What! by such narrow ways—?" There is but one world, however. Happiness and the absurd are two sons of the same earth. They are inseparable. It would be a mistake to say that happiness necessarily springs from the absurd discovery. It happens as well that the feeling of the absurd springs from happiness. "I conclude that all is well," says Œdipus, and that remark is sacred. It echoes in the wild and limited universe of man. It teaches that all is not, has not been, exhausted. It drives out of this world a god who had come into it with dissatisfaction and a preference for futile sufferings. It makes of fate a human matter, which must be settled among men.

All Sisyphus' silent joy is contained therein. His fate belongs to him. His rock is his thing. Likewise, the absurd man, when he contemplates his torment, silences all the idols. In the universe suddenly restored to its silence, the myriad wondering little voices of the earth rise up. Unconscious, secret calls, invitations from all the faces, they are the necessary reverse and price of victory. There is no sun without shadow, and it is essential to know the night. The absurd man says yes and his effort will henceforth be unceasing. If there is a personal fate, there is no higher destiny, or at least there is but one which he concludes is inevitable and despicable. For the rest, he knows himself to be the master of his days. At that subtle moment when man glances backward over his life, Sisyphus returning toward his rock, in that slight pivoting he contemplates that series of unrelated actions which becomes his fate, created by him, combined under his memory's eye and soon sealed by his death. Thus, convinced of the wholly human origin of all that is human, a blind man eager to see who knows that the night has no end, he is still on the go. The rock is still rolling.

I leave Sisyphus at the foot of the mountain! One always finds one's burden again. But Sisyphus teaches the higher fidelity that negates the gods and raises rocks. He too concludes that all is well. This universe henceforth without a master seems to him neither sterile nor futile. Each atom of that stone, each mineral flake of that night-filled mountain, in itself forms a world. The struggle itself toward the heights is enough to fill a man's heart. One must imagine Sisyphus happy.

Do you identify yourself with Sisyphus? How do you interpret his "lucidity"? his "scorn"? his "rock"? Do you agree with Camus' conclusion that "One must imagine Sisyphus happy"?

More familiarly, John Updike writes of your own backyard.

john updike

ECLIPSE

I went out into the backyard and the usually roundish spots of dappled sunlight underneath the trees were all shaped like feathers, crescent in the same direction, from left to right. Though it was five o'clock on a summer afternoon, the birds were singing good-bye to the day, and their merged song seemed to soak the strange air in an additional strangeness. A kind of silence prevailed. Few cars were moving on the streets of the town. Of my children only the baby dared come into the yard with me. She wore only underpants, and as she stood beneath a tree, bulging her belly toward me in the mood of jolly flirtation she has grown into at the age of two, her bare skin was awash with pale crescents. It crossed my mind that she might be harmed, but I couldn't think how. *Cancer?*

The eclipse was to be over 90 percent in our latitude and the newspapers and television for days had been warning us not to look at it. I looked up, a split-second Prometheus, and looked away. The bitten silhouette of the sun lingered redly on my retinas. The day was half-cloudy, and my impression had been of the sun struggling, amid a furious knotted huddle of black and silver clouds, with an enemy too dreadful to be seen, with an eater as ghostly and hungry as time. Every blade of grass cast a long bluish-brown shadow, as at dawn.

My wife shouted from behind the kitchen screen door that as long as I was out there I might as well burn the wastepaper. She darted from the house, eyes downcast, with the wastebasket, and darted back again, leaving the naked baby and me to wander up through the strained sunlight to the wire trash barrel. After my forbidden peek at the sun, the flames dancing transparently from the blackening paper—yesterday's Boston

Globe, a milk carton, a Hi-Ho cracker box—seemed dimmer than shadows, and in the teeth of all the warnings I looked up again. The clouds seemed bunched and twirled as if to plug a hole in the sky, and the burning afterimage was the shape of a near-new moon, horns pointed down. It was gigantically unnatural, and I lingered in the yard under the vague apprehension that in some future life I might be called before a cosmic court to testify to this assault. I seemed to be the sole witness. The town around my yard was hushed, all but the singing of the birds, who were invisible. The feathers under the trees had changed direction, and curved from right to left.

Then I saw my neighbor sitting on her porch. My neighbor is a widow, with white hair and brown skin; she has in her yard an aluminum-and-nylon-net chaise longue on which she lies at every opportunity, head back, arms spread, prostrate under the sun. Now she hunched dismally on her porch steps in the shade, which was scarcely darker than the light. I walked toward her and hailed her as a visitor to the moon might salute a survivor of a previous expedition. "How do you like the eclipse?" I called over the fence that distinguished our holdings on this suddenly lunar earth.

"I don't like it," she answered, shading her face with a hand. "They say you shouldn't go out in it."

"I thought it was just you shouldn't look at it."

"There's something in the rays," she explained, in a voice far louder than it needed to be, for silence framed us. "I shut all the windows on that side of the house and had to come out for some air."

"I think it'll pass," I told her.

"Don't let the baby look up," she warned, and turned away from talking to me, as if the open use of her voice exposed her more fatally to the rays.

Superstition, I thought, walking back through my yard, clutching my child's hand as tightly as a good-luck token. There was no question in her touch. Day, night, twilight, noon were all wonders to her, unscheduled, free from all bondage of prediction. The sun was being restored to itself and soon would radiate influence as brazenly as ever—and in this sense my daughter's blind trust was vindicated. Nevertheless, I was glad that the eclipse had passed, as it were, over her head; for in my own life I felt a certain assurance evaporate forever under the reality of the sun's disgrace.

Why is the eclipse so disturbing to the narrator? Why does the little girl seem unaffected by it? When have you had a similar experience, one in which some kind of eclipse seemed to dim your assurance and threaten your sense of stability?

Giorgio de Chirico, *Mystery and Melancholy of a Street,* 1914

These few lines from the Revelation of St. John the Divine (21:1–4) describe the reverse of an eclipse. They invite you to dream about the future, not in the nightmarish manner of Huxley and Orwell, but with whatever starry-eyed hope you can summon.

AND I saw a new heaven and a new earth: for the first heaven and the first earth were passed away; and there was no more sea. And I John saw the holy city, new Jerusalem, coming down from God out of heaven, prepared as a bride adorned for her husband. And I heard a great voice out of heaven, saying, "Behold, the tabernacle of God is with men, and he will dwell with them, and they shall be his people, and God himself shall be with them, and be their God. And God shall wipe away all tears from their eyes; and there shall be no more death, neither sorrow, nor crying, neither shall there be any more pain: for the former things are passed away."

Have you ever experienced some sort of revelation—a vision of what your future might be? Describe your concept of the new Jerusalem, your own utopia for some tomorrow.

These three photographs return you to today, but the manner in which you respond to them involves all your yesterdays and, by implication, all your tomorrows.

Cubic crystalline structure of etched tungsten (magnification 8,750 X) seen through an electron microscope.

Where are you in this picture? What does this picture tell you about yourself? How do you answer back?

Where are you in this picture? What does this picture tell you about yourself? How do you answer back?

Orion nebula, a galactic nebula approximately 1,000 light-years from earth.

Where are you in this picture? What does this picture tell you about yourself? How do you answer back?

Earth as seen by the Apollo 8 astronauts, 20,000 nautical miles away.

conclusion

In responding to all these readings and questions, you have had to take on different roles and use different voices. You have expressed yourself in different styles as you confronted the various situations this book set up. The following two essays discuss why you, or any speaker or writer, has to dramatize himself in different ways depending on the circumstances, why he has to adopt what is called a *persona*.

The first essay, "Meeting People in Daily Life and in Prose," attempts to show that we are all "actors" in our ordinary social behavior, and that we act our roles with body language as well as with words. In writing and reading we perform a similar dramatic act. If we are writing a story, we consciously adopt the verbal manner and character of the person telling the story, the narrator. If we are reading a story, we undergo a transformation into the "assumed reader" of that story.

The second essay, "Reading the First-Person-Singular," focuses more specifically on the choices that a writer has to make in order to produce a distinctive "I." These choices include decisions about vocabulary, sentence structure, and grammar.

meeting people in daily life and in prose

WALKER GIBSON

It may be helpful to begin a study of verbal style by reminding ourselves how much we experience, and how much we communicate with one another, in ways that are not verbal at all. Consider for example the familiar moment in the ordinary course of social or business life, when we are introduced to a new acquaintance. Like most of human experience, it is a moment susceptible to a more complex description than we usually grant it. Facing a new face, we make a series of judgments based on a large range of half-conscious, and nonverbal, sense impressions. The words uttered by our new acquaintance—how do you do?—may be banal enough, but the physical voice that utters them is rich in meaning, just as the physical appearance of the person we are confronting is open to immediate, and of course potentially faulty, interpretation. Is he friend or foe? One to be encouraged as an attractive addition to life, or a threat to our own dearly-beloved ego? Can I handle him or will he handle me? We begin answering such questions immediately at the point of confrontation, and even though we know the tentative quality of our answers, having learned our lesson about snap judgments, we make them anyway. For we are bombarded with impressions of such power and meaning that to ignore them we would have to be a clod, or an extremely well-disciplined and reserved sensibility.

Suppose we consider some of these impressions.

First there are matters of sheer physique. Is our new acquaintance taller than we are? Shorter? The same? What does this imply about our *standing* vis-à-vis one another? (Can anyone claim to be quite oblivious to this distinction, for all its savagery? When we *look up to* or *down on* someone else, we may do so metaphorically or we may do so literally, but often we do both.) Do we associate this person's bigness, furthermore, with the character of the bully, or with that easygoing good nature of the large mind in a large body? Or neither? If he is small, do we associate his smallness with some sort of anxious inferiority, or rather an attractive delicacy or refinement? Or something else? Our fleeting judgments here, and our consequent adjustments of our own behavior, are based in part, no doubt, on some dim past experience of tallness and smallness, but, more to the point, on a large number of other physical impressions that we quickly gather in at the moment. The manner of dress, the cut of the hair, the depth of the eyes, the grasp of the hand, the significant contortions of the mouth as it politely smiles (or as it doesn't)—all these and a dozen other physical impressions, with their inevitable associations, color our split-second response, to be filed away for corroboration or correction in the light of further evidence.

There follows an auditory impression—the four words (for instance), How do you do. There are ways of saying those four words, reinforced by appropriate facial expression and perhaps gesture, that express hostility, or boredom, or irrepressible self-satisfaction; just as there are other ways that express eagerness to be of service, gay amiability, or a readiness for a grand passion. The way a person says "How do you do," and the way he looks and behaves as he does so, are combined and interfused in practice, so that we hear a voice and feel a grip and see a facial expression all in one muddle of sensation. Sometimes we even smell things. And it is next to impossible to feel neutral about these matters, though we may try to *think* neutral. The most we can do is reserve our impressions with as much readiness for correction as possible. I dislike this fellow, but then some of my best friends have had these shaggy eyebrows and this unctuous manner. Or: I do find this person attractive, but then I remember all the smiles like this one that have turned out to be empty after all.

The familiar social moment I have been discussing can be looked at as well from our own point of view, as an *actor* in the situation. We too are eager to "make an impression," consciously or not. During that first moment of meeting a new individual, we adopt a posture more or less deliberately calculated to express a *self* with a relation (friendliness, reserve, hostility, boredom) toward the other person. The motives and impulses that prompt us to adopt this or that role and relation are mysterious in the extreme; they must lie somewhere in the very depths of personality. . . . What is obvious enough, though, in our practice of taking a role in a social situation, is the great variety of resources that we have at our disposal, to make our posture work. Even our preparations were elaborate, and significant. We dressed that morning in a certain way, presumably from personal choice to some extent, and our "choice" was a choice of an exterior face to confront the world with, a role to play. We parted our hair and tied a necktie—or we didn't. We have grown a beard, or a mustache, or we have not. For a woman, the term *make-up* well describes one part of her self-expression. We are all makers-up, with or without cosmetics. Once on the scene, the situation of how-do-you-do, we may use a wide variety of techniques for further dramatizing the self. The shrug of a shoulder, the lift of an eyebrow, the tilt of the head—all these are familiar, perhaps automatic, expressions of personality. Then there are people who stolidly refrain from such activity—they just stand there—and this too is literally *self*-explanatory. Our way of managing our voice is of course enormously important, quite aside from any verbal message and quite aside from the inherent virtues of our voice-box itself. We may be naturally endowed with a voice of richness and beauty, or with a quavering falsetto, but these gifts are less important than our immediate meaningful control of voice on the scene of action. Visual maneuvering of our lips can also impress, and between the sneer of disdain and the smile of invitation there are a hundred subtle elaborations. What we do with our eyes, beyond simply meeting another's eyes, says much. It is, in sum, a considerable battery of weapons we have at our command, and beside it the actual words we may stammer forth look pale indeed. How do you do? Yes, isn't it a pleasant day.

Life is not always lived, fortunately, at this rather brutally physical level. Eventually, often, people do say things to one another, and the things they say matter. Words do count. Yet even in our most successful

Illustration by Frank Gauna reproduced by special permission of *Playboy* Magazine; copyright © 1971 by Playboy.

and reasonable conversations, our words are footnoted, supported, even contradicted by our bodies and our dumb feelings, by a whole complex of details in the situation. No doubt these distractions (if that is what they are) diminish with longer acquaintance. Still, when someone tells us something, no matter how well we may know him, how adjusted to his appearance we may be, our understanding of his meaning is almost certainly more than verbal, involving a sense of the *him* that is talking, at the moment, in the flesh, before us.

    A simple experiment has been tried with a tape recorder, to suggest some of these influences in communication. A recording is made of an ordinary social conversation among several friends. Then a written version is transcribed from the recording, and distributed to people not present at the occasion. To them the typescript is likely to seem not only dull and lifeless, but in places actually mysterious, incomprehensible. The tape recording is then played, and the conversation begins to take on color and interest, while ambiguities are often cleared up by inflection and tone of voice. Personalities emerge, conflicts become apparent that a reading of the words on paper could not identify. But of course it is still a very pale expression of the experience. What would be needed to render the conversation with some verisimilitude would be several television cameras in color, a highly skilled director, and a video tape reproducing gesture, facial expression, clothing, and physique. But even then . . . .

Communication, whatever it is, is more than a matter of words, and in some familiar situations it is a great deal more than words. When in ordinary social and business life we identify ourselves before others (or indeed before ourselves), when we convey attitudes and information, when we take in the intentions of our fellow creatures, we use several of our senses at once, and we use them in complicated ways. We are *present,* clothed and combed, three-dimensional, taking up space and filling the air with our peculiar personal accents. We present ourselves by being present. The fact that we do this, as often as not, with nonchalant ease should not obscure the variety and richness of our communicating.

The distinction I am working toward should be obvious enough. *The writer is not physically present to his reader.* He is all words. The writer has no resources at all for dramatizing himself and his message to his reader except those scratches on paper—he has no bulk, no audible voice on the airwaves, no way of introducing himself beyond what he can make his reader "see" by means of abstract written words in various arrangements. To these words the reader responds much as he responds in a social situation—that is, he infers a personality—but he has only words to go on. Therefore the writer's particular choices of words as he makes his introduction in prose have an absolute kind of importance and finality. His reader is by no means so ready to reserve judgment, to wait and see, as a new social acquaintance. A reader can shut the book at any moment, at the slightest displeasure. Measured against the ordinary social life of meeting and speaking, the writer's handicaps seem enormous. Measured against almost any other medium of communication we can think of, the written language suffers by comparison, in respect to flexibility and directness and power of expression. Compared with an obviously limited device like the telephone, for instance, the written document has several advantages—such as portability, easy duplication, a wider vocabulary, and the possibility of careful preparation—but the dramatizing of a self may be easier on the phone, for all one's physical removal from the listener. The exact degree of reluctance that any native speaker of English can put into his enunciation of the syllable "we-e-ell" over a telephone wire is exceedingly difficult for the writer to duplicate without a great many words and a great deal of skill. A businessman deciding whether to pursue a particular operation by phone or by letter may choose the letter as more suited to his immediate situation. It can be revised before mailing, and filed after. But if it is direct personal force that he wants to employ, the power of a dramatized personality with the ability to adjust immediately to the other's response, then he will certainly choose the phone. Or better still, he will ask his man to lunch.

Yet surely I am not defending the telephone or the lunch table over the written word. Surely there is something wrong-headed in what I have been saying. It may be, as many modern linguists have been saying, and to much good effect, that the written language is merely a "dialect" of the spoken language, and an overrated one at that. But if those black marks on paper suffer great handicaps—as they do—without lips or eyes or voiceboxes, without gesture or the presence of a physical speaker, how is it that some of the finest characters we know come from books? And by "characters" here I do not mean people like Hamlet or Mr. Micawber, admirable though these are, but the *voices* that address us in written prose. Somehow or other, the writer is able to compensate for his handicaps, exploit his advantages, and *introduce* himself to us in a special role. That is part of his skill, part of his art. . . .

But before going further, we ought to ask, Who is being introduced in a piece of prose, and to whom? These are sticky critical problems of long standing. Is the writer himself saying how do you do? There is a sense in which he certainly is, but most statements about an author's self-revelation in his works (especially works of fiction) are naive. It is one of his selves at best, one of his possible voices, one of his roles, that he is introducing us to. The problem is posed most clearly when, in fiction, we are presented to a narrator who is "worlds apart" from his creator and from us. The speaker we are introduced to in *Huckleberry Finn* is obviously not Mark Twain, whoever he was, or Samuel L. Clemens, whoever *he* was. Nor is it Huck himself, exactly, for though we hear the voice of Huck talking to us, we are well aware that there is somebody else very much in the wings, somebody superior to Huck intellectually while sympathetic with him morally. It is as if we were exchanging glances over Huck's head with this somebody, who is "more like us," while Huck babbles on. This other person can be called "Mark Twain" in a loose sort of way, but as scholarship has shown, *and would show about anybody,* Mr. Clemens the Real Man had a bewildering number of voices, moods, grievances, problems, selves. It would be better to use a term like "the implied author" or "the author's second self" to suggest the restricted, artificial role that the real-life writer creates to stand behind his also-created first-person-narrator. In *Huck* this "second self" is a very genial fellow indeed, who can even refer comfortably to his "own" name, or can make his narrator do so:

> You don't know about me without you have read a book by the name of *The Adventures of Tom Sawyer*, but that ain't no matter. That book was made by Mr. Mark Twain and he told the truth mainly. There was things he stretched, but mainly he told the truth.

There is a story by Ring Lardner called "Haircut" which has won more notoriety for its radical narrative technique than for its worth as a story. Here the "other self" behind the narrator is superior both intellectually *and* morally to the barber who tells the story, and who condemns himself in our eyes by the things he says and the way he says them. But is this "other self" Lardner, this wiser intelligence who, with us, sees through the barber's crudities and cruelties? Possibly, in a way. Possibly, while he was writing the story. But anyone acquainted with authors knows that they are just as mysterious and changeable as the rest of us. When, for instance, a writer repudiates one of his early works, it is probable, not that he has lost sympathy with his narrator, but that he has lost sympathy with the "second self" controlling the narrator. Lardner might well have come to feel, in the case of his oft-cited story, that the second self in "Haircut" is a rather oversimple fellow. And he is. Narrators, after all, are relatively fixed;

they end when the story ends; authors can change their minds and grow up.

In any case it seems useful to recognize that in most first-person-singular accounts of events we are really dealing with two voices, one that of the narrator, the other that of the second self, the Assumed Author, the Creator-Identity, or what you will. Nor is this doubleness confined to fiction. A man writing an autobiography, or even a letter, has the same problem. He poses an "I" doing the talking, and implies another "I" wryly or comfortably or even tragically standing back of the narrator. Behind both of these, of course, stands the true-to-life Real-Life-Writer, who is a mass of chemistry, nerve-endings, and irrelevance. *His* intentions are mixed and mysterious—to make money, finish his difficult paragraph, have dinner, who knows?

. . .

The experience of reading, then, is a confrontation with a voice, or personality, clear or confused—a personality who by means of words on paper gets himself *introduced* to us. But what about *us,* the reader? It is not generally understood that the reader too, like the author, undergoes a transformation, that he too becomes a kind of ideal or second self as he exposes himself to the expectations of the language. Early in his career Henry James argued that an author has to "make his reader very much as he makes his characters," and this is quite literally true. As readers, we are made over every time we take up a piece of writing: we recognize that there are assumptions and expectations implied there and that as sympathetic listeners to the voice speaking to us, we must share these assumptions. Sophisticated readers are able to move in this manner in several directions, and to keep separate their true-life personalities from the roles that the language is temporarily asking them to play. Thus, to mention obvious examples, it is possible for nonbelievers to be successful readers of *Paradise Lost* or the poems of Hopkins; it is possible, with one of one's selves, to suffer the appropriate moral agonies posed by a Victorian novel, while at the same time recognizing that in one's true-life self, facing a similar situation in a true-life world, one would adopt another point of view. Much of the force of modern advertising comes from the writer's skill in defining a particular set of ideal characteristics with which the confused real reader may be expected to desire identification. . . .

In all our reading, however, it is vital for us to maintain clearly a distinction between ourselves as real people acting in a real world, on the one hand, and ourselves as that particular bundle of assumed values that any piece of language implies. This, in the case of advertising, is the way we keep our money in our pockets. In the case of polemical writing, it is the way we keep from changing our party with every word we read. In the case of fiction, it is the way we keep from imposing the values of art too crudely on the problems of life.

reading the first-person-singular

WALKER GIBSON

The Latin word *persona* means *mask*—the theatrical mask that Roman actors wore on the stage, as Greek actors did before them. Everyone knows the masks of comedy and tragedy still used for decorations on theatre curtains and proscenium arches. Actually, there were dozens of such masks in the classical drama, representing special types of characters; an actor wearing a particular grimace or furrowed brow or staring eye could assume that his audience would immediately recognize him as portraying a particular and familiar type of personality.

Today, in speaking of literary matters, we use the term *persona* or *mask* in a slightly different but related sense. Obviously, when an author writes a book he does not literally wear a mask. In fact, a central difficulty in the experience of writing is that it happens in isolation from the audience: there is no one else present to wear a mask *for*. We use the word, then, in a metaphorical sense—it is as if the author, as he "puts on his act" for a reader, wore a kind of disguise, taking on, for a particular purpose, a character who speaks to the reader. This persona may or may not bear considerable resemblance to the real author, sitting there at his typewriter; in any case, the created speaker is certainly less complex than his human inventor. He is inferred entirely out of the language; everything we know about him comes from the words before us on the page. In this respect he is a made man, he is artificial.

It is natural that we should be troubled by expressions like "putting on an act" or "taking on a character." Can't we simply speak and write as ourselves, honestly and candidly? Of course we can, as long as we realize that even our most "honest" acts are indeed acts, in at least two senses of that word. They are acts in the sense that they are forthright and affirmative actions, calculated to bring order into a situation. They are also acts in the sense of playacting, since the means of communication we choose, the roles we play, the language we use, are creative decisions we make, even though we usually make them quite unconsciously. When we call someone a phony or a hypocrite, we usually mean not that he is playing a role, but that he is playing (in our judgment) a wrong role, an inappropriate or misleading one. We make such judgments about people all the time, as we must and should. But we should do so with a vivid sense that in our own performances there is an inevitable element of playacting.

Often persona is used in just that critical sense of hypocrisy or deviousness. It is when we feel that the role being played is obviously affected, or too deliberately self-conscious, or calculated somehow to take us in, that we speak of "so-and-so's persona" almost as a term of abuse.

We spoke above about the inevitable element of playacting in all our performances. Sometimes the very words we use will suggest the double sense of our "acts" of communication: the sense, that is, of serious practical activity combined with role-playing. The word *per-*

formance is an example. We may say that William Rogers performed very creditably as Secretary of State, or we may say that Lauren Bacall performed very creditably in *Applause*. These are obviously quite different kinds of behavior, but the identical verb suggests that there is something dramatic about all behavior. When you recall that our words *person, personality,* are derived from a Latin word meaning *mask,* you may be given pause about the very identity of your own precious character. And as for *character* itself—we use the word interchangeably for a man's deepest moral qualities and for a role he may play on a stage.

Another term we often use for this "actor" speaking in a piece of literature is, naturally enough, *speaker,* and *the voice of the speaker* is a familiar phrase in literary analysis. But note that this too is metaphorical: there is no literal person speaking, and he has no voice. Nothing is literally heard. In reading and writing, there are none of those helpful accompaniments we count on in the actual practice of conversing, such as vocal intonation, facial expression, gesture. One of the writer's principal problems is to compensate for these losses, for most people are more convincing in person than on paper. That is why writing has to be learned. Somehow the writer has to evoke, out of mere ink marks on paper, a character whose language the reader will trust, enjoy, profit from.

Sometimes, especially in our own time, a writer performs his act by endeavoring to put on paper the words and rhythms of actual conversation, as realistically as he can. He tries, in other words, to break the barrier between spoken and written language; he tries to write like a talker. This is particularly true of some modern fiction. Many of you know J. D. Salinger's *The Catcher in the Rye*. It begins:

> If you really want to hear about it, the first thing you'll probably want to know is where I was born, and what my lousy childhood was like, and how my parents were occupied and all before they had me, and all that David Copperfield kind of crap, but I don't feel like going into it, if you want to know the truth. In the first place, that stuff bores me, and in the second place, my parents would have two hemorrhages apiece if I told anything pretty personal about them.

Mr. Salinger was of course no teenager when he wrote this novel, but for his particular purpose he took on a teenaged persona, naming him, you remember, Holden Caulfield. Here we have Holden beginning to tell the story of his recent adventures—and the word *tell* is appropriate. We are to share in the illusion that this story was not written at all—as if we were somehow overhearing someone talking to us. It is as if Holden had told the story to someone who had a tape recorder, and his talk was later printed up from the recording.

How do we decide, as readers, that the voice we are aware of here is more that of a teenager-*talker* than that of a *writer?* First, there is the simple matter of vocabulary: you notice words and phrases that are more familiar when listening to people talking than when reading what people write. "My lousy childhood," or "that kind of crap," or "that stuff bores me." Such expressions, in print, may be commonplace inside quotation marks, as parts of a conversation, but here the entire discourse seems part of a conversation. In the first sentence, Holden begins by referring to us, the listener. "If you really want to hear about it . . ." And what is this "it" he mentions? It is what happened to him, but we have to guess that, for Holden doesn't try to explain. When we talk to someone we take a lot for granted, as Holden does here. It is as if we knew him before we opened the book; as if a dialogue had already been going on, which the first page only continues—but from here on we hear only one side of this dialogue.

A careful reader will be conscious of other details in the language that are calculated to put before him the persona of a teenager talking. Holden uses contractions ("you'll," "don't") as one does in speech. His sentences meander in a loose sort of structure. And he exaggerates in what we recognize as a particularly youthful way—"two hemorrhages apiece."

We have stated that this practice of creating a conversational voice may be especially noticeable in the fiction of our own time, but actually Holden's voice has distinguished forbears. Here is an even more familiar author, of a hundred years ago, also adopting the role of a teenager, though the expression *teenager* would have seemed to him very strange.

> You don't know about me, without you have read a book by the name of *The Adventures of Tom Sawyer,* but that ain't no matter. That book was made by Mr. Mark Twain, and he told the truth mainly. There was things he stretched, but mainly he told the truth.

Again, the details that alert the reader to the presence of Huckleberry Finn are obvious enough. The word "without" in the first line will suffice for comment. Used for "unless," it is of course colloquial. It is also regional, not to be found everywhere in the United States, and perhaps hardly at all elsewhere in the English-speaking world. This usage is also dated, though still present in some communities. Even if we did not know when the book was written, or when the "telling" was supposed to be taking place, we could reasonably guess that it was some time ago simply on the basis of this archaic use of "without."

But, obviously, not all first-person-singular narrators beginning tales of their own lives project before us a loose-talking conversationalist of the Huck and Holden kind. In fact, Mark Twain and Salinger would not have written the way they did if it were not for the existence of a traditional way of telling one's own story that implies a voice of a very different kind. They both deliberately departed from a "norm," a "proper" style for such personal accounts. Suppose we look at a version of such a norm in the very work so deprecatingly alluded to by Holden Caulfield. Here is the way David Copperfield begins his story:

> Whether I shall turn out to be the hero of my own life, or whether that station will be held by anybody else, these pages must show. To begin my life with the beginning of my life, I record that I was born . . . .

What can you see in these words that you would be unlikely to hear someone say aloud to someone else? The vocabulary is not at all abstruse, though "that station" is probably an expression you would be unlikely to hear someone utter aloud with that meaning. More to the point is the way the whole first sentence is put together. It begins with two fairly lengthy subordinate clauses, balanced in what we call parallel structure. Very few people can talk this way. The sentence is so neatly organized that it looks as though someone had figured it out carefully beforehand. One can write this way; only rather literary people talk this way. This persona, then, is first a more literary kind of fellow. We should note, too, his sophisticated wittiness, as in the playing with the word "life" in the second sentence. How does that pun affect the way we respond to this fellow?

We can see, then, a general distinction as to the persona an author may choose. He can sound like a talker, or he can sound like a writer. A damaging characteristic of much amateur writing lies precisely here: the voice may sound like both talker and writer at the same time. The persona, that is, emerges as double, a split personality. Such a muddle can succeed in certain kinds of rather fancy literature, but only when the author is well aware of what he is doing.

We can try to clarify this distinction between talking-style and writing-style by revising the examples we have already looked at. Suppose we try to make Holden Caulfield sound like a writer rather than a talker. (We will absolutely ruin him, of course, in the process.) Here is the beginning of that first sentence again:

> If you really want to hear about it, the first thing you'll probably want to know is where I was born, and what my lousy childhood was like, and how my parents were occupied and all before they had me . . . .

It would not be difficult to take the general meaning of Holden's message and translate it into a style that would sound more traditionally bookish, more like a writer-persona. For instance, one could rewrite those *where, what,* and *how* clauses into phrases more closely parallel, more precisely balanced:

> The place of my birth, the nature of my childhood, the occupations of my parents—these are no doubt pieces of information you will want to be given.

In writing such a version, we change "you'll" to "you will," and "thing" to "pieces of information." A passive infinitive concludes the sentence. And the order of parts, the elaborate trio of noun phrases at the start, is simply not the sort of thing people find congenial or even possible in their ordinary talk.

The noun phrases themselves deserve further comment. When you change a clause with its independent verb ("where I was born") into a noun phrase ("the place of my birth"), you have changed your mask from talker to writer, or at least you are moving in that direction. It is by such choices that a persona is made. Indeed, most informal-colloquial voices will display a relatively high proportion of independent verbs, perhaps one for every seven or eight words. On the other hand, most formal-literary voices use far fewer such verbs, perhaps as few as one for every twenty or twenty-five words. Notice that in the revision of Holden's sentence the number of independent verbs has been reduced from six to two.

Suppose we try a similar transformation upon the character of Huck Finn, this time without reducing the proportion of verbs. Here is his first sentence again:

> You don't know about me, without you have read a book by the name of *The Adventures of Tom Sawyer*, but that ain't no matter.

We can make Huck a little older and more educated, a writer rather than a talker, by simple changes in the vocabulary and in the arrangement of parts. We begin with a subordinate clause.

> Unless you have perused the volume entitled *The Adventures of Tom Sawyer*, you can have little knowledge of me, but that is of small consequence.

A reverse process can be applied to the opening lines of *David Copperfield*, in which the traditional, formal-literary voice becomes a loose, idiomatic, contemporary talker:

> I don't know whether I'll be the hero of this story or not—maybe somebody else will.

Here one of our changes has to do again with subordination: the clause follows the main subject-verb pattern, rather than preceding it as in the original. Other details should be obvious: the substitution of "will" for "shall," the use of contractions, the higher proportion of verbs.

These alterations of persona will suggest that there are specific rhetorical "tricks" one can perform to change the character of one's stylistic mask. By and large this is true. But one must beware of making such tricks into too easy a formula. It is generally true that a subordinate clause placed *before* the main subject-verb, rather than after it, will tend to make the voice more literary and formal. But notice that Holden Caulfield's original first sentence actually begins with such a clause ("If you really want to know about it . . ."). In Holden's case, of course, the effect of this placement of the clause is more than compensated for by his other colloquial weapons.

These observations about style and grammar are intended to make explicit a simple but central fact about the writer's situation. This is the fact of his options, his choices in presenting himself to his reader and the world. Finally these choices come down to hard decisions he must make between one phrasing and another. His sensitivity in making these decisions is the measure of his performance as a writer.

If you still want to learn more about yourself and your world, read Sophocles' *Oedipus the King.* The voices in this play—whether that of the proud or of the blinded king, or of his mother-wife, or of the Chorus—are varied and dramatic. On the surface this ancient classical drama is a detective story: who murdered the king of Thebes? But it is also like a vast unexplored cave; you can penetrate it as deeply as you want. Among the questions the play raises are: How do you perceive yourself? To what extent are you what you actually do rather than what you intend to do? Is what happens to you dependent on your character, or is your character dependent on what happens to you? At the deepest level, Sophocles invites you to ask yourself, Who am I, and Is it worth the effort to find out?

Socrates, a contemporary of Sophocles, claimed that the unexamined life is not worth living. This book, in a decidedly unclassical manner, has attempted to ask Sophocles' question and reassert Socrates' claim. The picture on the next page suggests an alternative solution for

you.

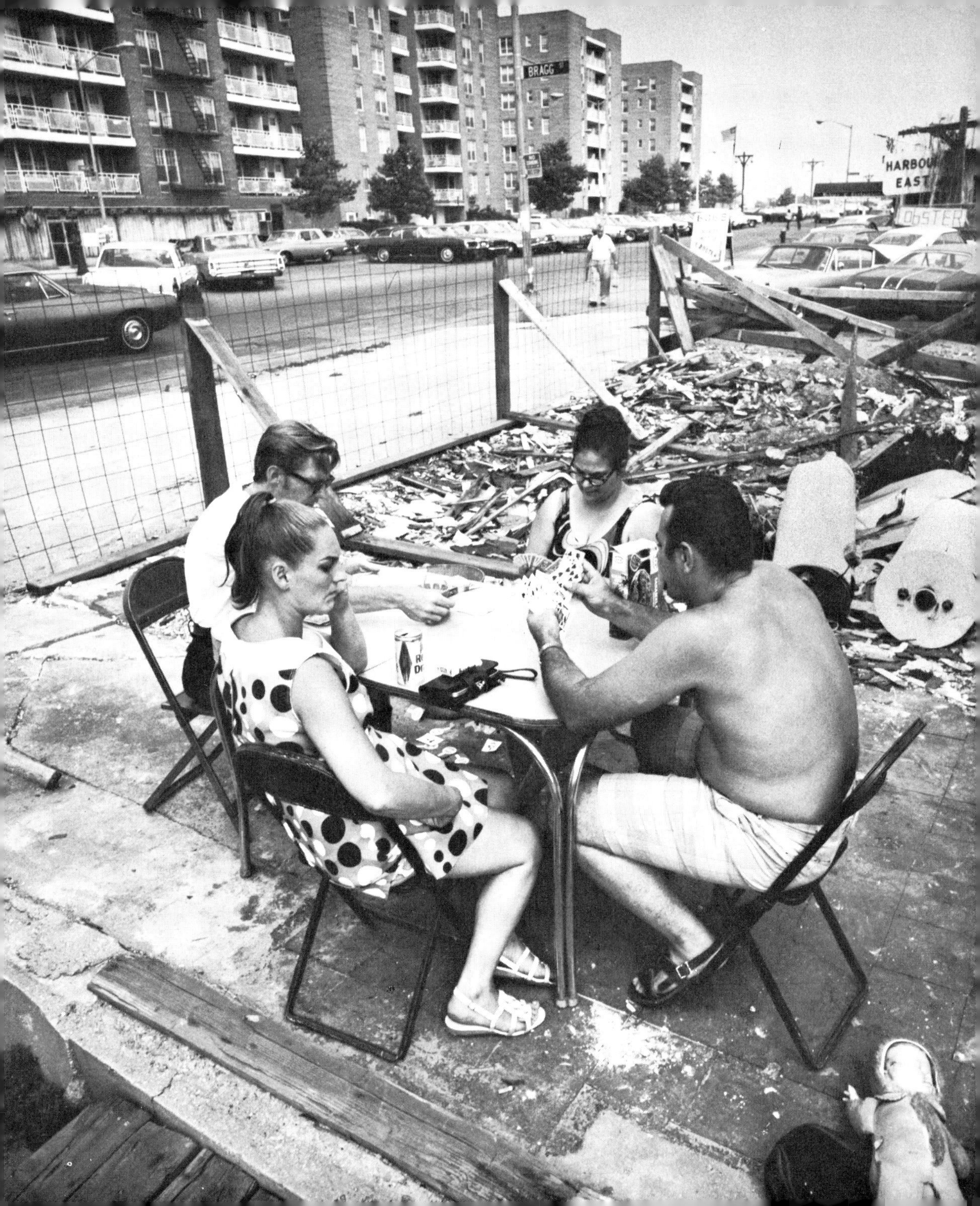
BRAGG
HARBOU
EAST
LObSTER

arrangement with The New American Library, Inc., New York, New York. JAMES FRAZER. From *The Golden Bough*. Copyright 1940 by James Frazer. Reprinted by permission of The Macmillan Company. HOW GRANDGOUSIER LEARNED OF GARGANTUA'S MARVELOUS MIND. Taken from *All the Extant Works of François Rabelais*, translated by Samuel Putnam. Copyright 1929 by Covici Fried, Inc. Used by permission of Crown Publishers, Inc. ALDOUS HUXLEY. From pp. 198–201 (hardbound edition) in *Brave New World* by Aldous Huxley. Copyright 1932, © 1960 by Aldous Huxley. Reprinted by permission of Harper & Row, Publishers, Inc., Mrs. Laura Huxley, and Chatto and Windus Ltd. GENE YOUNGBLOOD. From the book *Expanded Cinema* by Gene Youngblood. Copyright © 1970 by Gene Youngblood. Published by E. P. Dutton & Co., Inc., and used with their permission. RICHARD HUGHES. From *A Moment of Time* by permission of Richard Hughes and Chatto and Windus Ltd. CARLOS CASTAÑEDA. From *The Teachings of Don Juan: A Yaqui Way of Knowledge*. Originally published by the University of California Press; reprinted by permission of The Regents of the University of California. SIGMUND FREUD. Reprinted from Volume 2 of *The Life and Work of Sigmund Freud* by Ernest Jones, M.D. Copyright © 1955 by Ernest Jones. By permission of Basic Books, Inc., Publishers, New York, and The Hogarth Press. FERN HILL. Dylan Thomas, *Collected Poems*. Copyright 1946 by New Directions Publishing Corporation. Reprinted by permission of New Directions Publishing Corporation, J. M. Dent & Sons Ltd., and the Trustees for the copyrights of the late Dylan Thomas. ROBERTO. From *The Children of Sanchez* by Oscar Lewis. Copyright © 1961 by Oscar Lewis. Reprinted by permission of Random House, Inc. GEORGE ORWELL. From *1984* by George Orwell. Copyright 1949 by Harcourt Brace Jovanovich, Inc. Reprinted by permission of Brandt & Brandt. THE UNKNOWN CITIZEN. Copyright 1940 and renewed 1968 by W. H. Auden. Reprinted from *Collected Shorter Poems 1927–1957*, by W. H. Auden, by permission of Random House, Inc., and Faber and Faber Ltd. N. SCOTT MOMADAY. From *The Way to Rainy Mountain*, by permission of The University of New Mexico Press. TOWARDS A WALK IN THE SUN. Copyright © 1968 by William Kgositsile. Reprinted from *Black Fire: An Anthology of Afro-American Writing*, edited by LeRoi Jones and Larry Neal, William Morrow & Co., New York. Used with permission of the author and the Ronald Hobbs Literary Agency. PROLOGUE. From *Invisible Man* by Ralph Ellison. Copyright 1952 by Ralph Ellison. Reprinted by permission of Random House, Inc. DOVISCH IN THE WILDERNESS. From *Dovisch in the Wilderness and Other Stories*. Copyright © 1968 by Herbert Wilner. Reprinted by permission of the publisher, The Bobbs-Merrill Company, Inc. THE LOTTERY. Reprinted with the permission of Farrar, Straus & Giroux, Inc., from *The Lottery* by Shirley Jackson. Copyright 1948, 1949 by Shirley Jackson. Originally appeared in *The New Yorker*. HAN'S CRIME. By Naoya Shiga. Copyright © Naoya Shiga. Reprinted by permission of Orion Press. MAN AND ANIMAL. By Susanne K. Langer. Originally appeared in *The Antioch Review*. NIGHT-SEA JOURNEY. From *Lost in the Funhouse* by John Barth. Copyright © 1966 by John Barth. Reprinted by permission of Doubleday & Company, Inc. THE MYTH OF SISYPHUS. From *The Myth of Sisyphus and Other Essays* by Albert Camus, translated by Justin O'Brien. Copyright © 1955 by Alfred A. Knopf, Inc. Reprinted by permission of the publisher. ECLIPSE. Copyright © 1963 by John Updike. Reprinted from *Assorted Prose*, by John Updike, by permission of Alfred A. Knopf, Inc. MEETING PEOPLE IN DAILY LIFE AND IN PROSE. From *Tough, Sweet & Stuffy* by Walker Gibson, Copyright © 1966 by Indiana University Press. Reprinted by permission of the publisher. READING THE FIRST-PERSON-SINGULAR. Adapted from *Persona: A Style Study for Readers and Writers* by Walker Gibson. Copyright © 1969 by Random House, Inc. Reprinted by permission of the publisher.

ILLUSTRATIONS

4–6 Courtesy, Janus Films by arrangement with Grove Press, Inc. **8, 12** From *Cognitive Psychology* by Ulrich Neisser. © 1967 by Meredith Publishing Company. By permission of Appleton-

Century-Crofts, Educational Division, Meredith Corporation. **9–10** From *The Intelligent Eye* by R. L. Gregory, London, Weidenfeld & Nicolson, Ltd. 1970. **11** Editions Denise René, Paris/New York. **19** Geri Davis. **21 (top)** From *The Science of Language* by John Hughes, Random House, Inc., New York. **21 (bottom right)** Amenities sign designed by Lance Wyman for 1968 Olympic Games in Mexico. From **Graphis** No. 140, 1968, p. 517. **22 (top)** Drawing by Romona Matos, Courtesy Henry Street Settlement House, New York. **22 (bottom)** Hap Stewart. **23** Dr. Victor Glasser. **24–25** Dick Hyman. **26 (top)** Diana Henry, EPA/College Newsphoto Alliance. **26 (bottom)** N. R. Farbman, *Life* Magazine © Time Inc. **27 (left)** "Circus" by Bruce Davidson, © 1966 Mangum Photos, Inc. **27 (right)** Frank Herrman. **28** Geri Davis. **30** Philadelphia Museum of Art, Louise and Walter Arensberg Collection. **31** Linda Lindroth. **32** Computer-processed picture by L. D. Harmon and K. C. Knowlton, Bell Telephone Laboratories, Inc. **33** Marilyn Cooper. **36–37** From James Agee and Walker Evans, *Let Us Now Praise Famous Men*, Boston, Houghton Mifflin Company, 1960. **39** Photo: Harold Becker. Courtesy, Dick Carroll, Young & Rubicam, Inc. Detroit. **44** Geri Davis. **51** Harbrace Photo. **53 (top)** Linda Lindroth. **53 (bottom)** Marilyn Cooper. **54** Advertisement prepared by Rumrill-Hoyt Inc. for Pharmcraft, Division of Pennwalt Corporation. **59** Marilyn Cooper. **64** George Ratkai. Courtesy, McCall's Magazine, August 1971. **65** Hap Stewart. **66** Bruce Davidson, © 1964 Magnum Photos, Inc. **67** Arthur Tress. **68** Constantine Manos, © 1969 Magnum Photos, Inc. **69** Inge Morath, © 1966 Magnum Photos, Inc. **77** Collection, The Museum of Modern Art, New York. **81** Advertisement created by Smith-Greenland Company, New York City. **82** Prepared by Grey Advertising, Inc., for Revlon, Inc. **90–91** Ferdinand Boesch. **100** Geri Davis. **101** Mrs. Arlene Sklar-Weinstein. **114** Fogg Art Museum, Harvard University. Gift, Paul J. Sachs. **143** Al Momaday. Courtesy, University of New Mexico Press. **149** Ken Heyman. **211** Ambrotype Positive/negative, ca. 1885 by unknown photographer. Gernsheim Collection, Humanities Research Center, The University of Texas at Austin. **233** "Electronic City" by Roger Canessa. **255** A Private Collector. Harbrace Photo. **257** From *Micro-Art: Art Images in a Hidden World*, by Lewis R. Wolberg, M.D. New York, Harry N. Abrams, Inc., 1971. Photo: Clark D. Smith. **258** Lick Observatory, California Institute of Technology. **259** NASA. **279** Arthur Tress.

281

```
A  2
B  3
C  4
D  5
E  6
F  7
G  8
H  9
I  0
J  1
```